RESEARCHING GEOGRAPHY

This book is a one-stop comprehensive guide to geographical inquiry. The volume:

- traces the step-by-step account of the whys and the hows of research methodology;
- introduces complexities of the geographical perspective, selection of research topic, choice of supervisor and formulation of research proposal;
- fine-tunes the sequence of data collection, analysis, representation and interpretation, and spells out the skill of writing research with geographic flavour; and
- reinforces concepts and ideas with examples so as not to leave any scope for ambiguity.

The **second edition** updates on the variety of emerging perspectives in geographic research, use of spatial technologies in practice, sampling at different spatial levels and insightful interpretation of data.

Lucid, engaging and accessible, this book will be an essential companion for researchers and students of geography, social sciences and South Asian studies.

Gopal Krishan is Professor Emeritus in the Department of Geography at Panjab University, Chandigarh, and National Fellow of the Indian Council of Social Science Research (ICSSR), New Delhi, India.

Nina Singh is Professor of Geography and Dean of the Faculty of Social Sciences at Maharshi Dayanand University, Rohtak, Haryana, India.

RESEARCHING GEOGRAPHY

The Indian Context

Second Edition

Gopal Krishan and Nina Singh

LONDON AND NEW YORK

Second edition published 2020
by Routledge
2 Park Square, Milton Park, Abingdon, Oxon, OX14 4RN

and by Routledge
52 Vanderbilt Avenue, New York, NY 10017

Routledge is an imprint of the Taylor & Francis Group, an informa business

© 2020 Gopal Krishan and Nina Singh

The right of Gopal Krishan and Nina Singh to be identified as authors of this work has been asserted by them in accordance with sections 77 and 78 of the Copyright, Designs and Patents Act 1988.

All rights reserved. No part of this book may be reprinted or reproduced or utilised in any form or by any electronic, mechanical, or other means, now known or hereafter invented, including photocopying and recording, or in any information storage or retrieval system, without permission in writing from the publishers.

Trademark notice: Product or corporate names may be trademarks or registered trademarks, and are used only for identification and explanation without intent to infringe.

First edition published by Routledge 2017

British Library Cataloguing-in-Publication Data
A catalogue record for this book is available from the British Library

Library of Congress Cataloging-in-Publication Data
A catalog record for this book has been requested

ISBN: 978-0-367-20794-6 (hbk)
ISBN: 978-0-367-20796-0 (pbk)
ISBN: 978-0-429-26356-9 (ebk)

Typeset in Bembo
by Apex CoVantage, LLC

CONTENTS

List of figures	*vii*
List of tables	*viii*
Preface	*ix*
Rationale for the second edition	*xii*

PART I
Laying the foundation

1

1 What is geographic perspective?

3

2 Essential features of quality of a thesis in geography

20

PART II
Prefatory phase: the prelims

27

3 Issues pertinent to a thesis in geography

29

4 Research proposal: issues and formulation

44

5 Literature search and review

48

PART III
Traversing the path: data management

57

6 Typology of data

59

vi Contents

7	Data collection	65
8	Data analysis	112
9	Data representation	181
10	Data interpretation	206

PART IV
Catching up with the destination: the finale   **215**

11	Research writing	217
12	The viva voce	236

Annexures   *242*
Index   *245*

FIGURES

5.1	Some questions addressed by literature search and review	49
8.1	Basic types of graphs	130
8.2	India: regional backwardness: factor_1 housing and amenities, 2011	164
8.3	India: regional backwardness: factor_2 demographics, 2011	165
8.4	India: clusters based on composite index of quality of living space, 2011	167
9.1	Map elements	188
9.2	Urbanisation level: 2011	189
11.1	Typology of development models	224
11.2	Major environment problems	225

TABLES

3.1	A tentative time chart for a PhD student	41
6.1	Salient features of qualitative and quantitative methodologies: a comparative view	61
8.1	Correlation coefficient of regional backwardness variables	159
8.2	Total variance	160
8.3	Loadings of different variables on the two components	161
8.4	Communalities of individual variables	163
9.1	India: literacy by states/union territories, 2011	183
10.1	Wolcott's ways to interpretation	207
11.1	Apposite use of verb tenses in different research documents	222
11.2	Salient features of thesis/dissertation and technical report	230

PREFACE

The genesis of this book is rooted in a growing realisation that lack of training in pertinent methodology is the weakest link in the process of research in Indian geography. Its effect is visible in poor delivery mechanisms. Such a sensitisation emerged from a perusal of dozens of doctoral theses and MPhil dissertations received for evaluation from different universities in India. These exercises were generally found as lacking in conceptualisation on the theme adopted for research and detailing of methodology to address it. The capacity to draw inferences from given facts and the ability to offer an effective message from the research product are also inadequate in general. As a consequence, most of the theses tend to be merely descriptive, statement of the obvious with scarce element of surprise and hardly anything fresh to excite. The book reaches out to those research student entrants who may frequently get lost in heavily loaded references difficult to comprehend. Thus partly it is a beginners' guide.

Time and again serious concerns have been expressed on the status of research in India. Geographic studies suffer from certain obvious deficiencies and imbalances (Dayal 1994); the further you explore the question, the more disgusting the exercise becomes (Ahmad 1997). Two extreme situations occur: on the one hand there is evidence of weak links in geographic training in Indian universities (Gosal 1980); on the other there are symptoms of adolescence in its waywardness and rash zeal for concepts and techniques anew (Arunachalam 1980). Geography in India has dimensions and characteristics of a dinosaur: a huge body, a long tail and a tiny little head (Raza 1981). The ailments of Indian geography are embedded in 'missing methodology', 'sterile stereotypes', 'feeble fieldwork', and 'intellectual neocolonisation' (Mukerji 1991). The evolved scene of Indian geography resembles a polycyclic landscape – the best and the rest go together (Krishan 2000). Mountains of geographic research in the country produce only a proverbial rat.

More recently a group of eminent geographers expressed concern at the substandard quality of teaching, research and action in Indian geography. The

x Preface

proceedings of this event under the title National Workshop on Philosophy and Research Methodology of Geography held at the Centre for Earth Science Studies, Thiruvananthapuram, on 7–8 December 2011 were published as a special issue of the *Transactions, Institute of Indian Geographers* in 2012. Earlier an elaborate and research-based discourse on the pathetic state of research in Indian geography was provided in her book *Indian Geography: Voice of Concern* by Kapur (2002). Our book is in fact a concern for such a voice.

Research as a subject is taught at various levels. It is our belief that a sound knowledge of research methodology is essential for undertaking any study based on research. Besides, several geographers get an opportunity to work in research institutes where they are expected to prepare 'research reports' for sponsoring authorities, such as the Government of India, the European Union or the World Bank. Here again many of them find it hard not only to prepare the research proposal but also to ensure the finalisation of a quality product. Some of them may not be adept in framing a table or mentioning references in a standardised form. They may learn all this in the process of preparing the report, but then it becomes a long-time affair and certainly not effective to the desired degree.

Moreover, there are situations when a student is applying for admission to a foreign university, which may ask for submission of a 'brief note' on the proposed course of study or research. The candidate may not know how to go about this. A shoddy effort does not prove effective enough in realisation of his or her goal.

It is in all such contexts that we were compelled to write this book. We were guided by an additional consideration. There may be several books on research methodology, but very few focus on research as it is practised in the discipline of geography specifically. A number of books that line the library shelves dwell on social research methods. There is hardly any book with a geographic thrust. Of course, from time to time some books have appeared on quantitative methods in geography, but hardly a few deal with research methodology in the discipline in a comprehensive manner. The idea germane to this book emerged from such a situation. A need was felt to bring out a research methodology book that was entirely in geographic spirit and flavour and would produce good researchers in the discipline. Since the focus is on research in practice, an effort was made to capture the needs of a research student at different stages while pursuing the assignment and responding to them as effectively as possible.

Agreed that tenets of research in various disciplines may be common to a great degree, but at the same time each discipline may have its own spirit and purpose. Knowledge production is not a neutral and perspective-free pursuit. It is rather embedded in the practices and ideologies of its creators and the contexts within which they operate. In geography too, the questions for research are to be specific to the nature and style of the discipline.

Most issues of the world can be subjected to geographical research. These may range from physical or environmentally determined to political, economic or cultural constructs. Given the breadth of geographical inquiry, the subject is similarly broad with respect to the conceptualisation it adopts and methods it employs to address them. This book aims to acquaint students with and train them in the craft of carrying out geographical research.

Geography has professional obligation in the world of learning. It has to perform this in the light of its own specific theory and practice. Any academic discipline is constantly developing and changing in conjunction with emerging ideas in the field of knowledge and emergent issues seeking solution. Geographers are obliged to be aware of all this and to place the tools of research at the disposal of humanity. It may also adapt theories developed in other disciplines, such as sociology, economics or political science. A purposeful 'borrowing' of ideas from other disciplines serves to make the strange familiar and helps geographers to conceive of the world in new ways (Culler 1997). In any case, a research effort in geography has to remain anchored on the core of the discipline.

Thus, the present book *Researching Geography* stems from a desire to address specific nuances of research in geography. Discussions on how a hypothesis is constructed with a spatial twist, data are managed with geographic tools and writing is ensured a spatial complexion are the hallmarks of this book. The insights for writing it have been gained through our personal experiences in teaching and also conducting and supervising research over several decades.

This book has no claim to profound scholarship. If at all, it has ensured simplicity, clarity and brevity in conveying any message. The effort has been towards being intelligible. It does have a claim to be making a geographic difference. Every observation is tagged with an example from India, by and large. The main objective is to make it as palatable to a research student as possible. It visualises and traces a student's journey through research and maps out a desired path. Hence its four sections have been entitled as: Laying the foundation; Prefatory phase: the prelims; Traversing the path: data management; and Catching up with the destination: the finale.

References

Ahmad, A. 1997. "Fifty Years of Geography in India and Abroad." *Presidential Address*, 20th Indian Geography Congress, Thiruvananthapuram.

Arunachalam, B. 1980. "Neglected Frontiers of Indian Geography." Presidential Address, 3rd Indian Geography Congress, Bombay.

Culler, D. Jonathan. 1997. *Literary Theory: A Very Short Introduction*. Oxford: Oxford University Press.

Dayal, P. 1994. "The Agenda for Indian Geography." *Presidential Address*, 17th Indian Geography Congress, Hyderabad.

Gosal, G.S. 1980. "Frontiers of Geographic Research and Teaching in India." *Presidential Address*, 1st Indian Geography Congress, Chandigarh.

Kapur, Anu. 2002. *Indian Geography: Voice of Concern*. New Delhi: Concept Publishing House.

Krishan, Gopal. 2000. "Indian Geography: Tasks Ahead." *Annals of the National Association of Geographers, India* 20 (1 & 2): 131–141.

Mukerji, A.B. 1991. "What Ails Indian Geography?" In *Emerging Trends in Indian Geography*, edited by Jaymala Diddee, 135–155. Pune: Institute of Indian Geographers.

Raza, Moonis. 1981. (Untitled). *Presidential Address*, 4th Indian Geography Congress, New Delhi.

RATIONALE FOR THE SECOND EDITION

When Routledge informed us that all the copies of the first edition of our book *Researching Geography*, published in 2017, were already sold, we felt overwhelmed. The feeling was that our love's labour in the interest of research students stood rewarded. As the next step, the publisher was kind in offering us two alternatives: to reprint the same version of the book or to come out with its second edition. We opted for the latter. This we reckoned was an opportunity to enrich further the quality of our book that had already received wide acclaim.

With that purpose in mind, the text of the book was revisited most carefully. We realised that in the first chapter, 'What is geographic perspective?', an extended discourse on a variety of shifting perspectives, such as positivist, radical, humanist, critical and others would add value to the book. This will enable any research student to be aware of the specific perspective in which the assignment was being pursued by her or him. In the same vein, it was deemed necessary to distinguish between spatial thinking and geographic thinking. The two are often taken as synonyms, while they are not. To the same effect, the section titled 'Reading the Literature' was fortified with examples from review articles published in the *Annals of the American Association of Geographers and Population and Development Review*.

Personal feedback from research students reinforced our belief that in any geographic research based on a collection of primary data, the identification of an appropriate sampling technique is the most critical issue. This calls for an awareness about all the sampling techniques geared towards different spatial scales of a country, a region, or a locality. Hence in the chapter titled 'Data Collection', the entire section on sampling was given a fresh appeal. Three illustrations of sampling for large-scale surveys at the national level also find a place in the revised version of the book. Survey as a way of data or information collection was also spruced up. A special focus was placed on the latest spatial technologies, such as GPS, smartphones and drones, in use for surveying today.

Similarly, in the chapter titled 'Data Analysis', a further extended treatment of geospatial technologies, such as Remote Sensing and Geographic Information Systems, was deemed worthy. These tools of data analysis had already found a place in the original book but called for the incorporation of a practical exercise and a more detailed discussion. This was done. The 'data analysis', thus, could be hooked more firmly to new quantitative geography.

It was also realised that a restructuring of the chapter on 'Data Interpretation' would render it a greater coherence and clarity. The issue of interpretation is skipped in most of the books on research methodology, and research students are not sure of the manifestation of this concept in practice. We did the needful by elaborating on the conceptual and technical dimensions of this input in any research writing.

Despite insertion of all these changes, around 90 per cent of the book remains the same. It had already been crafted with the utmost care. The new additions are embellishments by way of strengthening some crucial chapters, incorporating some state-of-the-art techniques in geographic research and streamlining some otherwise complex concepts. Certainly, the objective of the second edition remained the same as that of the first one: to inculcate the spirit, style, and substance of geography in any research undertaken under the banner of this discipline.

For making this possible, we express our gratitude to Routledge for creating an ecology for us to be more of ourselves.

25 April 2019
Gopal Krishan
Nina Singh

PART I
Laying the foundation

1

WHAT IS GEOGRAPHIC PERSPECTIVE?

Books on philosophy and methodology of geography invariably contain full-length chapter or discussion on 'what is geography'. Besides, books continue to be written with focus on 'what geography is about', 'what geographers do', 'how geographers think', 'why geographers think that way', 'doing geography', 'new theories, new geographies' and so on. The last quarter of a century has seen several contributions such as *The Geographer's Art* (Haggett 1990), *Geography's Inner Worlds* (Abler, Marcus, and Olson 1992), *The Challenge for Geography – A Changing World: A Changing Discipline* (Johnston 1993), *Thinking Geographically* (Hubbard *et al.* 2002), *What Is Geography?* (Bonnett 2008), to name a few.

Rightly so, ever since the Greek word 'geo-graphy', or 'earth description', was first used by scholars about 300 BC, the field has been evolving, and its focus, content and discourse are continually getting reinvented.

Geographers engage in area studies, or with what Hartshorne (1959, 21) terms the areal differentiation of the earth's surface as the home of man. They lay great stress on the interaction between humanity and natural environment on the earth's surface (Ackerman 1963, 435). Some tend to explore spatial organisation as expressed in dynamic arrangement of phenomena in a region (Taaffe 1970, 1). For many the basic purpose of the discipline is simply 'to account for spatial variation' (Amadeo and Golledge 1975). Thus, there are many geographies, some new, some old. All have slightly different philosophical basis with varying emphasis, and some are more widely practised than others. For example, Hartshorne (1959) saw geography as an idiographic science with its primary focus on systematic description of the specific, whereas Yeates (1968) saw geography as a nomothetic science with its thrust on theory building. Others lay in the grey zone between the two.

4 Laying the foundation

Nature of geography

These plentiful works remind us that geography has meant different things in changing contexts of time, place and intellectual climate. It has always employed both qualitative and quantitative methods of research, looked at the particular and also the general and engaged with scales of study at global, regional and local levels. Observations by Livingstone (1993), Godlewska and Smith (1994), Godlewska (1999a, b), Livingstone and Withers (1999), Driver (2001), Martin (2005), and Withers and Livingstone (2005) are evidence of this. Refinement and redefinition have been a continuing process in geography. For that reason a variety of definitions of the discipline exist, with no clear consensus as to what geography is, what geographers do or how they should study the world (Unwin 1992).

The problem is more deep-rooted than appears on the surface. Geography has all through gone over an identity crisis. It is often asked what distinctive thing this discipline does that others do not do. A misunderstanding is evident from a perception that it simply gathers material from other disciplines.

The identity crisis stems from geography's confounding position within the organised structure of knowledge. It is a science with natural and social constituents. By this virtue it is neither a pure natural science nor a pure social science. Its intellectual origins as a distinctive field date back to classical Greece when humanity was considered an integral part of nature. Geography included descriptions of both animate and inanimate things. Individual scholars continued to produce geographical works that were cosmographic in nature. Geographical societies had flourished during the nineteenth century, and by 1885 there were nearly 100 geographical societies spread across the world (Freeman 1961, 52–53). Their activities were, however, distinct from academic geography, which became a university specialism at the turn of the twentieth century. By this time the intellectual world had already divided knowledge into natural or physical sciences, humanities and social sciences. Geography, with its natural and social constituents, had to be fitted into an already established order of organised knowledge, which has proved uncomfortable and has caused a search for an identity (Haggett 1990).

Geography is pluralistic in nature. It follows both regional and systematic approaches. The former approach builds knowledge by regions; the latter examines regional variations in individual or group of phenomena. Across the wide canvass of geography, scholars learn and deliberate upon a vast variety of specific topics besides being continually engaged in refining and developing new geographic information and methodology. In addition, geographers apply linguistic, mathematical and cartographic methods in varied combinations.

Given its pluralistic nature and broad subject matter, geography has evolved as an amazingly multidisciplinary field with an international outlook and openness to interdisciplinary collaboration. Physical geography intersects with the natural, earth and life sciences, such as geology, meteorology, oceanography, hydrology, astronomy and biology. Human geography interacts with a large number of the social and behavioural sciences, particularly economics, political science, sociology, social anthropology, psychology and history. A part of human geography also blends with humanities, especially philosophy, ethics, languages, literature and cultural studies. Methodological specialities within geography overlap with statistics and mathematics (Quantitative Geography) and computer science and information technology (GIS and Remote Sensing). There are still other areas of geography that lay emphasis on the communication of 'geographic craft'. The closing years of the last century have seen the emergence of a new 'geography of virtuality' (Crampton 1999) or 'cybergeographies'. These are quasi-geographical spaces with their own flows, interactions and spatial relations (core and periphery). Geographers are debating as to what extent virtual geographies replicate or differ from physical geographies. Integration of the physical, human and technical aspects in the study of the earth as the home of humanity is one of the profound challenges facing us today (Montello and Sutton 2006, 12).

Geography is about space and the content of space, both physical and cultural. It has pervasive presence in our everyday affairs. An understanding of our hometown, neighbourhood or university campus is essentially geographic in nature. It is based on our awareness of where things are, of their relationships and of the varying nature of places we frequent. Thus, geography is a spatial science, focused on the spatial behaviour of people, spatial relationships that are observed between places and the spatial processes informing those relationships.

Perspectives in geographic research

A researcher often muses about how to reflect and research on a particular idea, phenomenon or area. The guiding light is the prevailing world view. Geographer's continual engagement with different philosophical traditions made it necessary for any research in geography to contend with a variety of competing perspectives and paradigms. A perspective is a way of viewing, thinking or interpreting something. A paradigm, according to Kuhn (1970), refers to the dominant concepts and practices of a scientific discipline at a given time. A scientific revolution takes place with a shift of a paradigm. This causes a change in the standpoint of knowledge itself. Geography has undergone a variety of changes of this kind over time.

Hence it is essential to not only keep the geographic spirit at the core of research being pursued but also to be conscious of the perspective in which it is being constructed or the paradigm it is following. Often, a new researcher takes the current paradigm as worthy of pursuit and may not be aware of other alternatives. Here an effort will be made to provide a brief note on different perspectives that are relevant to geographic research.

Geography in its early formative years as a discipline during the nineteenth century and the first half of the twentieth century existed as an empirical and descriptive science. The emphasis was on empirical questions for which data could be collected. How *are* the available food resources distributed among inhabitants of the different parts of the world? This is an empirical question. Such a position is based on the philosophy of empiricism. Empiricists consider facts to be those things

6 Laying the foundation

which can be experienced by the senses, speak for themselves and require little theoretical explanation. These represent the ontology, or reality or fact, of empiricists approach existence. The sense experience helps us gain knowledge. This is its epistemology, or method of gaining knowledge (Bird 1993, 45).

The traditional regional school of geography that dominated for much of the middle twentieth century was empiricist. The emphasis was on the field collection of data and its synthesis through maps, leading to generalisations. This involved defining regions by classifying areas of the earth's surface with distinct assemblages of phenomena. To Hartshorne, 'the ultimate purpose of geography, the study of areal differentiation of the world, is most clearly expressed in regional geography' (1939, 468).

Positivism in geography

Representing the nature of modern geography, this perspective adheres to the application of principles and methods of science to understanding reality. A piece of research is positivistic in nature if it follows the underlying principles of objectivity and formal logic. Positivism insists on facts which can be sensed, described, measured and modelled that are important in the construction of knowledge. Its defining features include systematic procedures of inquiry; formulation of generalisations, theories and laws; and verification or falsification in each case.

Researchers in natural sciences affirm that all reality can be explained with the help of scientific laws. Hawking and Mlodinow (2010) have something fascinating to offer in this regard. In their book *The Grand Design*, they assert that the theories of quantum mechanics and relativity are capable enough to explain the origin of the universe. We do not need God as its creator.

The adoption of spatial science approach in human geography is premised on the philosophy of positivism. It puts greater emphasis on the unity of science, on hypothetic-deductive methods and on the use of 'hard' data. A number of theories fall in its domain, such as Christaller's central place theory, Von Thünen's model of land use, Weber's industrial location theory, Edward Ullman's spatial interaction theory and Ravenstein's gravity model of migration, among others. Johnston (1986, 33) maintains that Harvey's book *Explanation in Geography* (1969), which represented the philosophy and methodology of the spatial science school, had a strong overtone of logical positivism.

Positivists, just like empiricists, reject the normative concerns of 'ought to be' and metaphysical questions of 'esoteric nature' which are 'independent of our senses' and cannot be measured scientifically. Positivism and empiricism are to be distinguished from each other. While the former follows a systematic scientific approach to verification in its research investigation, the latter leans on the description or just simply the presentation of a fact.

In the late 1960s and early 1970s, there was a drift away from positivism, but the purer forms of physical geography and parts of human geography remained positivistic. Most 'isms' that inform geography are contained in human geography. Such a tendency with its non-quantitative focus has tended to distance the two essential components of geography: physical and human.

New human geography

The new perspectives in human geography were first linked to 'diversity of viewpoints' consistent with the emergence of a variety of philosophical avenues and research strategies within which spatial organisation remained important (Harvey and Holly 1981, 37). Second, the adoption of new technologies came as a great booster for the discipline. The most influential of all has been the advent of Geographic Information Systems (GIS). This has been a 'fundamentally facilitating and applications-led technology, which transparently assesses the importance of space, and as such is central to our geographical understanding of the world' (Longley 2000, 157). Finally, the new perspectives were needed to explain the subjective dimension of reality beyond the objective one.

Behavioural geography began with a disillusion with 'location theories' and the concept of 'economic man'. Decision makers were not simply 'rational' but rather 'satisficers' noted for incomplete knowledge and cultural biases. Behaviouralists recognise that human action is not without its spatial manifestation. The power of place is evident in shaping our emotions, thoughts and behaviours. An individual is no longer the same when in a place of worship, or a cinema hall or a nursing home. Behavioural geography, occupying the space between positivist and humanist geographies, maintained generally a positivist framework and overall commitment to scientific methods. 'Hazard perception', 'mental maps' and 'behaviour in location' have been the most popular themes. The objective is to seek a holistic view of interrelation between environmental experience and behaviour in places.

Welfare geography, meanwhile, emerged as a strong reaction to distortions in social conditions and sought to make contemporary human geography more relevant. It was meant to investigate geographies of inequality, map spatial variations in the quality of life and provide input to planning practices. Welfare geography, however, remained accommodated within a positivistic liberal framework. Liberalism is defined here as combining 'a belief in democratic capitalism with a strong commitment to executive and legislative action in order to alleviate social ills' (Bullock 1977, 347).

Unlike behavioural and welfare geographies, which were in flow with the prevailing economic and social systems, radical geography was political in nature and called for a revolution in theory and practice.

Radical – Marxist geography was a group of fresh approaches that took shape in the late 1960s. Radicalism provided the empirical base, and Marxism rendered the underlying theoretical support (Peet 1977, 21). In the 1980s, these were placed under the umbrella of 'critical geography'. In between was the emergence of humanist geography during the 1970s.

Radical geography, in the form of Marxist geography later, emerged as a reaction against the growth of spatial science in the framework of positivism, which was seen

8 Laying the foundation

as being guided by the tenets of capitalism in the formation of social and economic space. It was pointed out that the positivistic methods analysed 'how things *seemed* to be rather than considering how they *might* be under a different political dispensation'.

Harvey (1973, 129–130) observed that positivism 'simply seeks to understand the world whereas Marxism seeks to change it'. In that sense, the different versions of Marxism all share a *critical approach* to modern society with its aim not only to study but also to change it. In focus were a variety of crises emanating from capitalism. The way inequality, poverty and exploitation often are the product of capitalist interventions in resource exploitation began to be explored. In spatial terms, the disparity in access to public services, discrimination in development investment, locational marginalisation of the poor and exploitation of the periphery by the core emerged as issues of special research interest. It was contended that all research must carry social relevance. On the whole, radical geography/Marxist geography did not question the spirit and style of geography but called for action-oriented research.

Marxism continued to inspire and influence the research and policy in a significant manner. Geographers' adoption of Marxism and the influence of other radical currents, such as anti-racism, feminism and post-colonialism, caused an enduring and heterodox radical presence in geography. Critical geography has come to signify all this as an umbrella term.

Critical geography began to take shape towards the end of the 1980s. It had its roots in Marxism as its theoretical foundation and was in the nature of a political project. While sympathetic to Marxist ideology, it focused on questions of culture, identity and inclusiveness, beyond class-based analysis. It is different from the more homogeneous radical geography by its very nature of being a conglomerate of 'a plethora of Marxist, antiracist, disabled, feminist, green, post-modern, post-colonial, and queer geographies' (Castree 2000, 956). Hubbard *et al.* (2002, 62) observe that critical geography is diverse in its ontology, epistemology and methodology, and lacks a 'distinctive theoretical identity', unlike Marxist geography.

McDowell and Sharp (1999, 44) place critical geography as 'a broad catch-all category' for the diverse theoretical arguments.

Critical geography aims to produce knowledge, not for its own sake but to meaningfully change the world. Activism is its forte. The goal is to produce spatial patterns that are socially just. The socialist city, with residential flats for everyone in place of a variety of houses, is one such example.

Thus, the first item on the agenda of critical geography is to highlight the role of the spatial organisation as a factor in social inequality and oppression (Blomley 2006). It also believes that only a reformed spatial organisation can serve as a tool for ensuring social justice. Critical geography generates knowledge which challenges the spatial dimensions of discrimination, oppression and alienation.

Humanistic geography was the most profound critique of and reaction against the positivist approach to knowledge. Marking a departure from the 'objectivity' focused method of natural sciences and aiming at capturing the subjectivity defined experience of place, space, environment, landscape and regions, it came into prominence in the 1970s. Such an experience finds expression in an individual's

What is geographic perspective? **9**

identity with a place; a multiple sense of territoriality at the local, regional, and national levels; and nostalgia for landscapes of fond memories. An inquiry into the kind of landscapes, which are perceived as generative of fear or else booster of energy will be a research exercise in humanistic geography. Likewise in a study of poverty in India, we may first try to find out, in the spirit of humanistic geography, how poverty is perceived differently in various parts of the country.

Tuan (1976, 266) defines humanistic geography as the study of peoples' relations with nature, their geographical behaviour and their feelings and ideas in regard to space and place. His book *Topophilia: A Study of Environmental Perception, Attitudes, and Values* deals with 'the affective bond between people and place or setting' (1974, 4). *Topophilia* is 'love of place'. This is often reflected in the yearning of migrants for their native lands. The members of the diaspora always carry tender reminiscences of the natural setting, music and cuisine of their geographical roots.

Geographers turned to new sources of information such as letters written by members of the diaspora back home, works of art and fictional writing for their insights into landscapes. Works of fiction, such as John Steinbeck's *The Grapes of Wrath* and Thomas Hardy's *Tess of the D'Urbervilles: A Pure Woman*, were used as sources to throw light on contemporary landscapes and society. A 'subjective' tendency typified the new cultural geography. The humanistic approach cultivated a subjective interpretation of the world (Gosal 2015, 315–316).

Feminist geography appeared in *Antipode* (Burnett 1973; Hayford 1974) around the early 1970s. It has followed a trajectory from early empirical work (first wave of documenting women's spaces), to radical feminist geography (second wave) and further to all such perspectives in their post–modernist and post-structuralist forms (third wave feminism).

Feminist geography seeks to explore how gender relations differ throughout the world and influence or have important bearing on the social structure and geography of different areas. Feminists view human society as patriarchal, where women have been relegated to the 'private' sphere and where their labour is undervalued and ignored. They often infer the exploitation of women based on the way space is organised in a given context.

Effort here is made to highlight the discrimination which women face in appropriation and possession of space, place and environment. This is often illustrated through the low percentage of land registered in the name of women, or their low representation in national or state legislatures or restrictions on their space mobility. In the initial phase, it was pointed out that women themselves were grossly underrepresented in research and teaching at the university level. This led to a distortion of having missed the feminist perspective in the body of geographical knowledge.

Feminist approaches have to a large extent ushered in a 'new theoretical sensitivity' in geography. New themes, such as female perceptions of the local environment, lived experiences of women in particular places and spatial strategies of women to keep themselves in safe situations are the new items on the menu of geographic research.

Post–colonial geographic research is the outcome of political critique to 'unveil geographical complexity in colonial domination over space' (Chrush 1994,

10 Laying the foundation

336). Post-colonialism builds on the anti-imperialism discourse of radicals. This approach focuses on the impact of the colonial phase in the history of now independent countries on their existing spatial patterns and processes, and the way the colonial legacy is being reacted to or reconstructed at present. The world regional geography cannot be easily explained and interpreted without taking into account the impact and imprint of the former colonial powers, such as the British, French, Spanish, Portuguese and Dutch, on the spatial systems of their former colonies. The spatial contours of their development in various spheres represent a significant influence of the colonial power which ruled over them.

Geographic studies in a post-colonial mode display primarily a threefold interest: (i) imprint of the colonial rule on the landscape of the country, (ii) continuation or transformation of such a situation in the post-colonial period and (iii) efforts at erasing the spatial symbols of colonial rule after independence.

What were the spatial contours of the development map of India during the colonial period? How are these represented in the development map of today? In which way was the colonial organisation of space for administration a factor in the emergence of regionalism in India after independence? Such questions seek geographical answers. A study of changes in the names of places, localities and roads as inherited from the colonial times also makes an interesting topic for research.

Post-modern and post-structural geography

Human geography, in particular, has been embracing still newer perspectives since the 1980s when it opened up fresh spaces for thinking, understanding and representing the world as practised in the social sciences and humanities. Geography became pluralistic with a new trend of citing the subject of geography as 'geographies in the making' for some time now, as is evident in the recent issues of *Progress in Human Geography*. The world was seen as much more complex, fragmented and multiple, which could not be explained by using modern assumptions of coherence and causality entirely (Peet 1998, 195).

All of this was the outcome of marked changes in several areas that the world experienced in recent decades. These included globalisation, transition to post-industrial society and emergence of a rising middle class, wherein an increasing number of people are engaged in tertiary and quaternary services in comparison to agriculture and manufacturing. Globalisation, in particular, was seen as the birthing of a new world order. The different parts of the world have now become much more interactive, interdependent and, above all, visible. A kind of geographic renaissance is being experienced, and geography has become one's destiny (Krishan 2018, 6).

At the political level, there was the fragmentation of the Soviet Union into Russia and independence for a number of East European and Central Asian countries. Also, massive digitisation in association with the Internet contributed its bit. A lot of metadata, such as a variety of data about all the towns in the world over time, became available. All such developments stimulated geographers' research appetites

What is geographic perspective? **11**

for new themes and made the discipline fall in the new world view of the mainstream in the form of post-modernism and post-structuralism.

Post-modernism and post-structuralism are concepts of the post-industrial era. Post-industrialism means a modern society in which a majority of the workforce, as already stated, is employed in tertiary and quaternary services. Marxist class analysis, in such a situation, is rendered feeble because production is globalised, financial resources move worldwide and the conflict between the local capitalist and worker loses its teeth. Foucault (1986) pointed out that 'the present epoch will perhaps be above all the epoch of space'. A variety of geographies were taking shape to expound on heterogeneity, particularity and uniqueness (Gregory 1989, 70). Soja (1999, 2000) made the argument that space had long been neglected in social theory; post-modernism provided an opportunity to place it back at the centre of debates.

In order to gain deeper insight into the spatial practice of post-modernism, we can turn to the case of a post-modern city. Cities have come to acquire some notable post-modern characteristics. Examples abound – New York, Tokyo, London, Hong Kong, Paris, Sydney, Los Angeles. A restructuring of the cities is in place from their former industrial base with massive working forces to sites and scapes of high technology, big finance and white-collar jobs. A prominent feature of post-modern cities is their imposing diversity. This becomes manifest in their complex topography of ethnicity, hetero-architecture and dominance of high-tech structures. Such a diverse social mosaic, for some, brings in differences to be celebrated, and to others, it projects 'new forms of inequality and geographically uneven development' (Soja 1995, 133).

Post-structuralism is a philosophy of science which emerged as a critique of modern knowledge and is sceptical of any form of structuralist explanation, capitalist or Marxist. It holds the view that there are no deep structures that can explain everything. Action is based on mutual relations of people, and it is geographically, culturally, socially and historically situated.

Post-structuralism is spatial, as it attends to the 'difference that space makes' or operates as a factor. A 'bottom-up' approach to our understanding of geographic reality is emphasised. The argument made is that the relationship between society and space, as intervened culturally, is best reflected in the people's language. The way we live our lives within society, the constraints that operate and the empowerment that is exercised all get subsumed in language. All knowledge is embedded in nuances of the vocabulary which people use.

Deconstruction and discourse analysis are post-structural tools of research. Deconstruction is a technique for teasing out the incoherencies, limits and unintentioned effects of a text, and discourse is an elaboration of this. Truth for a post-structuralist is within the discourse (Cresswell 2013, 211).

Themes in geographical studies that have benefitted considerably from post-structuralism are power relations among geographical spaces, man–land relations and public policy. Who controls the geographical space and who falls under domination, who owns the land and who actually labours on it and in which way do the poor, minorities, and women get affected by any public policy decision? Such are the questions at the core of post-modern geography.

12 Laying the foundation

Hence in terms of perspectives in geography, two broad epochs can be distinguished: the one modern, that is before World War II and until 1960, when positivism held sway, and the second post-modern, when several new perspectives emerged along with the continuation of the positivist perspective. The fresh perspectives were either ideological in nature, such as radical geography; or were reactive to positivism, as in the case of humanistic geography; or were extensions of positivism, as represented by behavioural geography. Positivist geography stood for objectivity, humanistic geography for subjectivity and radical geography for ideology. Today, critical geography, which offers a critique of any spatial organisation as an instrument of social inequality and oppression, has gained popularity. Meanwhile, post-structuralism, with its focus on the difference that space makes, is enriching geography further. Common to all these varying strands in our discipline have been space and place.

It is evident that geography straddling across nature and culture has adopted a wide spectrum of theoretical choices with add-ons of new technical developments of GIS and satellite mapping. The binary of physical and human is fading as research projects cutting across this division have become favourites, such as the clearance of rainforests in the Amazon, desertification processes in the Sahel, desiccation of the Aral Sea and living conditions in global cities. All of these are representatives of 'creeping environmental problems induced by human action' (Matthews and Herbert 2008, 123). This has led to the prominence of the environment as the third major dimension of geography. The discipline now has three well-defined domains, physical, human and environment, in place of the two earlier, physical and human.

In this light, it has been rightly suggested that existing scholarship cannot conform to the ideals of any particular philosophical school. It should reinvent itself. In place of locating research in any particular 'ism', the need is to cultivate an integrated visualisation. We need to 'explore the possibility of engaging across, rather than having to choose between ontological, epistemological and methodological difference' (Sheppard 2015, 5). The days' of 'boxed isms' seem to be over.

On geographic perspective

Research reports, dissertations, theses and articles in India are generally seen to carry inadequate appreciation of the geographic perspective. What Indian geography currently requires is detailing of fundamental geographic concepts and skills essential for the production and communication of geographic knowledge. This has its own implications for the quality of research output.

Geographical research must be guided by spatial perspective. What is distinctive about any research in geography? In which light is a geographer obliged to observe the world? What is the nature of spatial thinking, reasoning and presentation style? Geographic knowledge is built upon some primitives. These are place specific and, as mentioned above, involve the parameters of areal differentiation, spatial interaction, spatial diffusion, spatial organisation and spatial planning (Krishan 2013a). Earlier Berry (1964, 2–3) had acknowledged three principles that defined the discipline of geography: (i) emphasis on synthesising concepts and not the phenomena of study; (ii) spatial point of view; and (iii) the geographic concepts related to spatial distribution, arrangements, interaction, integration, organisation and spatial processes.

Indeed location, both absolute and relative, is an essential element in all geographic inquiry. The phenomena may be symbolised by dots, lines, surfaces or three-dimensional models (Cole and King 1968). A geographer is expected to exercise particular attention to the arrangement of phenomena on landscape as a part or whole of the earth. A direct attention is to be given to their causal connections and relationships rather than coincidence and mere juxtaposition (Chapman 1966). The ultimate goal is to identify spatial patterns and processes.

In that light it would be instructive to take a note of the recommendations of the National Council for Geographic Education constituted by the Association of American Geographers on what should go in for geography teaching. It listed five basic concepts and topics that are essential elements in any geographic inquiry at all levels of instruction. These are as follows:

* The significance of absolute and relative **location**
* The distinctive physical and human characteristics of **place**
* Human–environmental **relationships** within places
* **Movements** expressing pattern and change in human–spatial interaction
* Formation of **regions** and change therein

Here some additional comments will be in order. First regional synthesis, wherein the spatial and ecological approaches are fused, is basically a geographer's major obligation. Suitable spatial segments of the earth, usually termed regions, are identified. The intent is to comprehend their internal morphology, ecological linkages and external relations. It is only in relation to culture that parts of the earth receive specific meaning. Cultural regions, therefore, provide a better framework for geographical understanding than natural regions.

Second, the scale of investigation makes a great difference in any generalisation that can be drawn from the observations made. The study of world agricultural patterns, for example, may focus upon global climatic regimes, eating habits, development levels, renting of spaces for agriculture and trade patterns. The issues and concerns change when we have to study cropping patterns at local level where topography, soil conditions, water availability, farm size, ownership, easy access to capital, marketing facility, remunerative prices, procurement policy or even personal management preferences may be of greater explanatory significance.

Even at the individual level, scale matters. A person from Jaipur is a *Jaipuri* in Rajasthan, a *Rajasthani* in India and an *Indian* in the United States.

Third, places go through a variety of changes as manifest in evolution and revolution, cycle and fluctuation, stagnation and progress, tradition and innovation, and retrospect and prospect. A geographer has to reckon with such dynamics of places or regions.

14 Laying the foundation

Above all, a geographer has to be aware of the contrasting philosophical and methodological viewpoints as these took shape in the course of the history of the discipline. Many of the conflicting ideas have been already settled. Dichotomy of regional and systematic studies has resolved itself in the larger concept of regional approach. Site and situation are seen as complementary aspects of place and space. Function and form supplement each other. And so do quantitative and qualitative data. Likewise, diverse views regarding the nature and scope of geography are to be seen as providing a holistic complexion to the discipline. Together, they serve the end purpose of geography, which is not merely to understand the earth as the home of man but also to be conscious of man's experience in space (Lukermann 1964).

On spatial and geographic thinking

Spatial thinking is essentially a distinct cognitive or knowing ability (Metoyer and Bednarz 2016, 1). It is a style with its own concepts, tools and usage. It involves 'thinking in space', or taking into account the role of space in daily life; 'thinking about space', or relying on maps to highlight spatial concepts of differentiation, interaction and diffusion; and 'thinking with space', or transforming 'non-spatial' ideas into spatial characterisation, like sense of belonging (Anthamatten 2010, 170). In terms of its influence and prevalence, spatial thinking is on par with mathematical or verbal thinking. This enables geographers to observe and analyse the identified patterns and processes spatially.

P. Gersmehl and C. Gersmehl (2006, 2007) identified thirteen modes of spatial thinking. These are location (absolute and relative), condition (described through the geographic concept of site), spatial connection (traced through situation), influence (inferred via spatial aura), delineating a region, drawing spatial comparison, spatial hierarchy (situating a place into a spatial hierarchy), tracing a spatial transition, identifying a spatial analogue, analysing a spatial association, determining spatial patterns, constructing and using a spatial model and mapping spatial exceptions. When we think and work with these parameters, we indulge in spatial thinking. This requires a spatial orientation of mind, defined as spatial visualisation, perception and cognition. Tools, such as geospatial technologies (GST), for example, virtual globes and GIS, facilitate the acquisition of spatial thinking (National Research Council 2006).

It is through spatial thinking that the base of geographic knowledge gets generated. If we intend to identify the geographic pattern of settlements in an area, this will call for spatial thinking. If we are in the process of locating additional high schools in a district, this will again depend on our power of spatial thinking. If we feel interested in discerning the seating preferences of students in a class, this will require spatial thinking for an answer. All such queries are to be reflected in terms of 'what, where, how and why'.

One has to distinguish between spatial thinking and geographic thinking. While spatial thinking is a way of observing phenomena around at present or over time, geographic thinking is concerned with their intrinsic content. Geographic thinking

What is geographic perspective? **15**

goes beyond spatial thinking to include the recognition and usage of spatial concepts, the knowledge derived through these concepts and the formal construction of generalisations and theories.

Geographic thinking is an inimitably powerful way of seeing the diverse and differentiated world. It aims at making connections between scales, from the global to the local (Jackson 2006). Its value as an academic device depends on the extent to which it can clarify the spatial relations among local, regional and global processes, and contribute to our understanding that might explain the features of an area or place (Holt-Jensen 2018, 19).

Geographic questions

Geography deals in diverse topics, but geographers share a commonality in the similar questions they ask and the universal set of basic concepts they make use of to frame their answers. Like any other discipline, it is defined by the questions it asks (Lukermann 1964). The basic queries common to various topics in geography are: How is each phenomenon arranged on the earth's surface? Does it make a difference where things are located? How different phenomena are spatially interconnected? What is the sum total of them in a given area (region)? By asking different questions, but within the geography's terms of reference, we can get nearer to matters of vital concern to man.

Geographic study of a language, for example, requires that we try to answer questions about how and why that very language shows varying characteristics in different locations and how the present distribution of its speakers came about. Going further, we could investigate as to how language is associated with other attributes of the area. As geographers, our interest is in understanding how things are interrelated in different regions and to give proof of the existence of 'spatial systems' (Fellmann, A. Getis, and J. Getis 2005, 4).

Geographers use the word *spatial* to frame their questions and form their concepts. The word *spatial* is derived from *space*. For geographers it always carries the idea of the manner of distribution of things and phenomena, occurrence of movements and the operation of processes over the whole or part of the earth's surface. To them space is a segment or whole of the earth's surface area, inhabited or available to be occupied by humans.

The starting point of a geographic study is the nature of places. The questions relate to: How places are alike or different from one another? How are these interrelated? Some of the attributes of places may be listed as follows:

- Places have location, distance and direction with respect to each other. All these can be viewed in absolute and relative sense. They bear a size, large or small, in terms of area, population or any other measure. Hence the issue of scale is important.
- Places have both physical structure and cultural content: natural landscape and cultural landscape. These develop and change over time. This gives an idea of their evolution.

16 Laying the foundation

- Places interact with each other involving questions of accessibility and connectivity. The process of spatial diffusion, signifying spread of something from one place to another, is ever present. One of the expressions of interconnectivity and diffusion is globalisation which integrates the economy, culture and ecology of different parts of the world with each other.
- Places have their internal arrangement of things in some meaningful pattern. This takes the form of spatial organisation. Such spatial organisations may be in all variety, depending upon purpose, such as for administration, defence, planning and so on.
- Places are amenable to generalisation. These may be generalised into regions of similarities and differences. Regions are defined as earth spaces or areas that exhibit internal uniformity of significant elements and external variation or difference from surrounding territory. Or they may be functionally integrated within despite internal variety. These are not 'given' in nature. They are devised in the nature of spatial summaries intended to bring order to the boundless diversity of the earth's surface. Going a step further these may also be reorganised. Names assigned to regions convey a complex set of interrelated attributes.

What constitutes the basis of geographic knowledge? This leads us to the task of identifying the parameters of geographic perspective. The perspective indicates the approach we are to follow in any investigation or study.

Three illustrations

Here we illustrate some research questions in population geography, urban geography and development geography framed in a geographic spirit.

If you have a general interest in population geography, you need to decide which particular question you find as most fascinating for exploration. Questions could be several. How do various parts of India differ from each other in terms of quality of living space, as inferred from demographic data of the Census of India? Is India homogenising demographically? What is the association between economic and social parameters of its population in spatial terms? Of special interest could be an unearthing of demographic anomalies on the population map of India. An anomaly refers to a scenario opposite to what is expected. How a remotely located state like Mizoram has higher concentration of population in urban places and a relatively high-income state like Himachal Pradesh is poorly urbanised? There is much more to go into such regional anomalies (Krishan 2013b).

Vimal (1994) carried out a critique of the success of Chandigarh as a planned city at different scales. This is evident from the research questions she raised for that purpose:

i   Has Chandigarh been successful in functioning as a growth pole for its surrounding region?
ii To what extent does the internal layout of the city conform to the original plan and which have been locational and spatial departures in the process?

iii Does a typical Chandigarh sector meet the expectations of the plan in emerging as a self-sufficient neighbourhood unit in terms of daily needs and social life of its residents?

Singh (1998) made an attempt to examine the implications of restructuring of administrative organisation of space on the development process. Haryana was the case adopted for this study. The questions raised in geographic spirit were:

i How did the reorganisation of old Punjab and carving Haryana out of it influence the development process in the new state? Which aspects of economic, social and political space were influenced to a greater degree? Which areas benefited or suffered more?

ii Was there spatial convergence or divergence of the development process? What were the contours of regional disparities at different points in time? Did the various dimensions of development – economic, social and political – behave alike or otherwise in spatial terms?

iii Can we put forward a geographic theory of the impact of administrative reorganisation of space on the development process?

References

Abler, Ronald F., Melvin G. Marcus, and Judy M. Olson, eds. 1992. *Geography's Inner Worlds: Pervasive Themes in Contemporary American Geography*. New Brunswick, NJ: Rutgers University Press.

Ackerman, E.A. 1963. "Where Is the Research Frontier?" *Annals of the Association of American Geographers* 53 (4): 429–440.

Amadeo, D., and R.G. Golledge. 1975. *An Introduction to Scientific Reasoning in Geography*. New York: John Wiley & Sons.

Anthamatten, Peter. 2010. "Spatial Thinking Concepts in Early Grade Level Geography Standards." *Journal of Geography* 109 (5): 169–180.

Berry, B.J.L. 1964. "Approaches to Regional Analysis: A Synthesis." *Annals of the Association of American Geographers* 54 (1): 2–11.

Bird, James H. 1993. *The Changing Worlds of Geography: A Critical Guide to Concepts and Methods*. 2nd ed. Oxford: The Clarendon Press.

Blomley, Nicholas. 2006. "Uncritical Critical Geography?" *Progress in Human Geography* 30 (1): 87–94.

Bonnett, Alastair. 2008. *What Is Geography?* London: Sage.

Bullock, A. 1977. "Liberalism." In *The Fontana Dictionary of Modern Thought*, edited by Alan Bullock and Oliver Stallybrass, 347. London: William Collins.

Burnett, K.P. 1973. "Social Change, the Status of Women and Models of City Form and Development." *Antipode: A Radical Journal of Geography* 5 (3): 57–62.

Castree, N. 2000. "Professionalisation, Activism, and the University: Whither 'Critical Geography'?" *Environment and Planning A* 32: 955–970.

Chapman, J.D. 1966. "The Status of Geography." *The Canadian Geographer* 10 (3): 133–144.

Chrush, J. 1994. "Postcolonialism, Decolonialization and Geography." In *Geography and Empire*, edited by A. Godlewska and N. Smith, 336–337. Oxford: Blackwell.

Cole, J.P., and C.A.M. King. 1968. *Quantitative Geography: Techniques and Theories in Geography*. London: John Wiley & Sons.

18 Laying the foundation

Crampton, J.W. 1999. "Virtual Geographies: The Ethics of the Internet." In *Ethics in Geography, Journeys in a Moral Terrain*, edited by J. Proctor and D.M. Smith, 72–91. New York: Routledge.

Cresswell, T. 2013. *Geographic Thought: A Critical Introduction*. Chichester, UK: Wiley Blackwell.

Driver, F. 2001. *Geography Militant: Cultures of Exploration and Empire*. Malden, MA: Blackwell.

Fellmann, Jerome D., Arthur Getis, and Judith Getis. 2005. *Human Geography: Landscapes of Human Activities*. 8th ed. New York: McGraw-Hill.

Foucault, M., and Jay Miskowiec. 1986. "Of Other Spaces." *Diacritics* 16 (1): 22–27. The Johns Hopkins University Press.

Freeman, T.W. 1961. *A Hundred Years of Geography*. London: Duckworth.

Gersmehl, P., and C. Gersmehl. 2006. "Wanted: A Concise List of Neurologically Defensible and Assessable Spatial Thinking Skills." *Research in Geographic Education* 8 (1): 5–38.

———. 2007. "Spatial Thinking by Young Children: Neurologic Evidence for Early Development and 'Educatability'." *Journal of Geography* 106 (5): 181–191.

Godlewska, A.M.C. 1999a. "From Enlightenment Vision to Modern Science? Humboldt's Visual Thinking." In *Geography and Enlightenment*, edited by D.N. Livingstone and C.W.J. Withers, 236–275. Chicago: University of Chicago Press.

———. 1999b. *Geography Unbound: French Geographic Science from Cassini to Humboldt*. Chicago: University of Chicago Press.

Godlewska, A.M.C., and N. Smith. 1994. *Geography and Empire*. Oxford: Blackwell.

Gosal, G.S. 2015. *History of Geographic Thought*. Chandigarh, India: Panjab University.

Gregory, D. 1989. "Areal Differentiation and Post-Modern Human Geography." In *Horizons in Human Geography: Horizons in Geography*, edited by D. Gregory and R. Walford, 67–96. London: Palgrave.

Haggett, P. 1990. *The Geographer's Art*. Oxford: Blackwell.

Hartshorne, R. 1939. *The Nature of Geography: A Critical Survey of Current Thought in the Light of the Past*. Washington, DC: Association of American Geographers.

———. 1959. *Perspective on the Nature of Geography*. Association of American Geographers Monograph Series (No.1). Chicago: Rand McNally.

Harvey, D. 1973. *Social Justice and the City*. Arnold: London.

———. 1969. *Explanation in Geography*. Oxford, UK: Blackwell.

Harvey, M.E., and B.P. Holly. 1981. "Paradigm, Philosophy and Geographic Thought." In *Themes in Geographic Thought*, edited by M.E. Harvey and B.P. Holly, 11–37. London: Croom Helm.

Hawking, S., and Leonard Mlodinow. 2010. *The Grand Design*. New York: Bantom Books.

Hayford, A.M. 1974. "The Geography of Women: An Historical Introduction." *Antipode: A Radical Journal of Geography* 6 (2): 1–19.

Holt-Jensen, Arild. 2018. *Geography: History and Concepts*. 5th ed. London: Sage Publications Ltd.

Hubbard, Phil, Brendan Bartley, Duncan Fuller, and Rob Kitchin. 2002. *Thinking Geographically: Space, Theory and Contemporary Human Geography*. London: Continuum.

Jackson, P. 2006. "Thinking Geographically." *Geography* 91 (3): 199–204.

Johnston, R.J. 1986. *Philosophy and Human Geography*. 2nd ed. London: Arnold.

———. 1993. *The Challenge for Geography – A Changing World: A Changing Discipline*. The Institute of British Geographers. Oxford, UK: Blackwell.

Krishan, Gopal. 2013a. "Challenges and Concerns of Geography." *Punjab Geographer* 9: 1–6.

———. 2013b. "In the Quest of Question for Geographic Research." *Transactions of the Institute of Indian Geographers* 35 (1): 1–11.

———. 2018. "Globalization, World Order, and Geography." *Transactions Institute of Indian Geographers* 40 (1): 1–8.

Kuhn, T.S. 1970. *The Structure of Scientific Revolutions*. Chicago: University of Chicago Press.

Livingstone, D.N. 1993. *The Geographical Tradition: Episodes in the History of a Contested Enterprise*. Cambridge, MA: Blackwell.

Livingstone, D.N., and C.W.J. Withers, eds. 1999. *Geography and Enlightenment*. Chicago: University of Chicago Press.

Longley, Paul. 2000. "Spatial Analysis in the New Millennium." *Annals of the Association of American Geographers* 90 (1): 157–165.

Lukermann, F. 1964. "Geography as a Formal Intellectual Discipline, and the Way It Contributes to Human Knowledge." *The Canadian Geographer* 8 (4): 167–172.

Martin, G. 2005. *All Possible Worlds: A History of Geographical Ideas*. 4th ed. New York: Oxford University Press.

Matthews, J.A., and Herbert, D.T. 2008. *Geography: A Very Short Introduction*. Oxford: Oxford University Press.

McDowell, L., and J. Sharp, eds. 1999. *A Feminist Glossary of Human Geography*. New York: Arnold.

Metoyer, Sandra, and Robert Bednarz. 2016. "Spatial Thinking Assists Geographic Thinking: Evidence from a Study Exploring the Effects of Geospatial Technology." *Journal of Geography* 116 (1): 1–14.

Montello, Daniel R., and Paul C. Sutton. 2006. *An Introduction to Scientific Research Methods in Geography*. Thousand Oaks, CA: Sage.

National Research Council. 2006. *Learning to Think Spatially: GIS as a Support System in the K – 12 Curriculum*. Washington, DC: National Research Council and National Academies Press.

Peet, R. 1977. "The Development of Radical Geography in the United States." *Progress in Human Geography* 1 (2): 240–263.

———. 1998. *Modern Geographical Thought*. Oxford: Blackwell Publishers Ltd.

Sheppard, E. 2015. "Thinking Geographically: Globalizing Capitalism and Beyond." *Annals of the Association of American Geographers* 105 (6): 1113–1134.

Singh, Nina. 1998. *Administration and Development of Indian States*. New Delhi: Anmol Publications.

Soja, E.W. 1995. "Postmodern Urbanization: The Six Restructurings of Los Angeles." In *Postmodern Cities and Spaces*, edited by S. Watson and K. Gibson, 125–137. Blackwell: Oxford.

———. 1999. "Thirdspace: Expanding the Scope of the Geographical Imagination." In *Human Geography Today*, edited by D. Massey, J. Allen, and P. Sarre, 260–278. Cambridge: Polity Press.

———. 2000. *Postmetropolis: Critical Studies of Cities and Regions*. Oxford: Blackwell.

Taaffe, E.J., ed. 1970. *Geography*. Englewood Cliffs, NJ: Prentice Hall.

Tuan, Y-F. 1974. *Topophilia: A Study of Environmental Perception, Attitudes and Values*. Englewood Cliffs, NJ: Prentice-Hall.

———. 1976. "Humanistic Geography." *Annals of the Association of American Geographers* 66 (2): 266–276.

Unwin, T. 1992. *The Place of Geography*. Harlow: Longman.

Vimal, Bindia. 1994. *The Planned City of Chandigarh: A Geographical Analysis*. Unpublished PhD Thesis, Department of Geography, Panjab University, Chandigarh.

Withers, C.W.J., and D.N. Livingstone. 2005. "Introduction: Geography and Revolution." In *Geography and Revolution*, edited by D.N. Livingstone and C.W.J. Withers, 1–21. Chicago: University of Chicago Press.

Yeates, M.H. 1968. *An Introduction to Quantitative Analysis in Economic Geography*. New York: McGraw-Hill.

2

ESSENTIAL FEATURES OF QUALITY OF A THESIS IN GEOGRAPHY

A thesis in geography must have a geographic flavour, phraseology and thrust, and should make an effective use of illustrative material, such as maps, diagrams and tables of data as a supportive device. This sums up what is expected from a quality doctoral thesis in geography. The statement is brief, hence requiring an elaboration point-by-point.

Style of geography

How to ensure a geographic flavour? This is done by doing things and writing in ways that reflect 'thinking with space and transforming non-spatial ideas into spatial representations'. It is fairly recognised that various disciplines approach the same subject from varying perspectives. So while there are similarities of theme, there can be differences in perspectives. Geography's unique contribution rests on recognising the salience of space, place and human–nature relations, factors often 'forgotten' or neglected by other disciplines. Geographic approach remains unique in its insistence on unfolding the role that geographic factors like location, distance, direction, interaction and arrangement make in giving shape to things on the earth's surface.

Equally critical is the use of geographic phraseology in any writing on the subject. Each discipline tends to evolve its own vocabulary and idiom. Consider, for example, the following statements sifted randomly from the available geography literature:

- Your entire life is determined by the **address** in which you are born.
- All physical processes, human decisions and individual actions **take place**.
- What exists anywhere or is done by anyone is the consequence of a **locational decision**.
- All planning is simply the desired **future geography** of any region.
- One has to believe in a geographic being who is always concerned with proper use of **territory**.

Essential features of quality of a thesis **21**

The basic purpose of any discipline is to share the fruits of its intellectual activity. This involves communication, which comprises language as a tool to conceptualise, communicate, elaborate and ultimately collaborate. The language of geography is what relates to any aspect of space – location, areal differentiation, spatial interaction and region, for example. Moreover, advancements in the discipline give birth to fresh expressions. At one time, it was enough to talk about distributional pattern of various crops, at another of agricultural regions, subsequently of agricultural systems and now of food security. Disciplines evolve and so do their concepts, terms and vocabulary in usage. We have to be conscious of new language tools and be in tandem with the evolving geographic idiom and terminology.

Then there is the question of maintaining geographic thrust in writing the treatise. Geographical inquiry involves description, explanation, prediction and evaluation. Each of these steps seeks to answer a definite set of 'key questions'. Description is focused on seeking answers to questions of 'what' and 'where'. 'What' refers to the specificities of the phenomena being studied, be it physical, biotic or cultural, and 'where' refers to the nature of their location, spatial distribution, patterns these make and associations these have with other phenomena, ultimately defining the character of the area under study. Explanation requires answers to the questions 'how? and why?' To understand how and why is to look for causal factors as embedded in the nature of areas. The processes that are operating to change the spatial locations, distributions, patterns, structures and systems are also to be looked into. Prediction is meant to project the current trends into future and to visualise the scenario of geographic landscape that is likely to emerge. Evaluation is pertinent to questions like: What are the likely alternative solutions to current problematic situations? How space ought to be organised for that purpose? In what ways should environment be managed so as to optimise the spatial outcome?

Salient geographic parameters

Each of the above set of key questions is related to some concepts and directive principles. Answer to the question 'what' is related to the ideas of natural and cultural environment, while search for answer to the 'where' question leads to the concepts of location, distributional pattern and areal association. The question 'how' is linked to the concepts of spatial organisation, spatial systems and region. The processual question 'why' finds answer in the concepts of spatial interaction, people–environment relationship, environmental perception and spatial behaviour. The question 'what will' is referred to the past as key to the future. The issue of 'what ought' or evaluation lies in the domain of sustainable development, spatial justice and harmony between natural and human resource base. Above all, a theme of persistent interest to a geographer is the degree of convergence and divergence in the character of different areas, especially in terms of regional disparities, lifestyle and demographics.

A geographic thrust in a research effort calls for a clarity on the concepts enunciated in the foregoing paragraphs. The fact is that the entire thesis beginning with title, review of literature, methodology and chapter sequence should have a geographic bearing. Likewise, the review of literature in geography is organised best in

22 Laying the foundation

spatial framework. Often the books and research papers gone through are reviewed in their chronological order. At times, these are structured by themes or subthemes related to the topic. For a geographer, the first-order grouping of literature surveyed should be in terms of territorial hierarchy of studies carried out at the international level, followed by those at the national level, and further down at the subnational and local levels. Under each category, the studies can be further classified by theme and chronology, as appropriate.

The overall discussion in the text is to be soaked in geographical spirit. This means that the patterns of areal differentiation, spatial interaction and spatial diffusion should be clearly brought out. Equally critical is to build a picture of spatial organisation of whatever is under research scrutiny. Christaller's central place theory is the best example to illustrate this point. The researcher is expected to have cultivated an ability to identify a spatial pattern of whatever is under examination and also be in a position to trace the spatial processes by which a spatial pattern took form. It is not enough to identify the distributional pattern of population in a given area; it is equally essential to find out the way this pattern took shape in the space over time. Both spatial pattern and process are to be taken care of.

One essential commitment of geography is ecological analysis. In this, the focus is on identifying man–environment linkages (vertical bonds) within a geographical region (horizontal bonds). For much of the history of the discipline, 'environment' largely meant physical space (the tangible natural world). Over time with an increasing emphasis on the human aspect, the term 'environment' began to expand and take on many new forms – built environment (the material additions that people had made to the physical world), behavioural environment (comprising human interactions and movements), sociocultural environment (the unseen and veiled structure of customs, beliefs and values that determine human relations), the economic environment (the nature of economic activity, regionalism), the political environment (the defined boundaries and legal and political structures governing human actions) and the cognitive environment (the inner geography of the world in our consciousness).

Since the Second World War, the geographic knowledge of each of these environments has become really complex. These were instrumental in giving birth to a variety of perspectives and 'isms' in the discipline. As a consequence, we witnessed the emergence of several new perspectives in geography, such as humanistic, radical and feminist. Each has developed its own specific theoretical construct or adapted acceptable ones from other disciplines, questions raised, data requirements and methodology (Golledge 2002, 2).

And finally, regional synthesis, an outcome of fusion of spatial and ecological approaches, is the prerogative of geography. Appropriate spatial segments of the earth's surface, usually termed 'regions', are identified and examined at different spatial scales, ranging from macro- (global) through meso- (national and subnational) to micro- (locality) levels. Broad observations and generalisations are to be made at the macro-level, followed by deeper ones at the meso-level and specific ones at the local level.

GIS, mapping and fieldwork

Geographic Information System (GIS) has transpired into the language of geography. In that nature, it is evolving and expanding in response to the ever-changing nature of demand and technology. Its beauty lies in its capacity to connect things, communicate and collaborate – the very stuff the world needs. It has advanced frontiers of new knowledge for all the sciences that focus on spatial location.

Geography since the turn of the millennium is at the centre stage again. The World Development Report (2009) focused on the identification and understanding of the interrelationship between geography, economic activities and living standards and depicted the consequence of these for public policy. The report charted the changes that go with development in three spatial dimensions: rising 'density', falling 'distance' and persisting 'division'. The importance of geography is strikingly made out in Robert D. Kaplan's (2012) book *The Revenge of Geography*. Raymond Aron's notion of 'probabilistic determinism' (Draus 1985) and the English historian Norman Davies's (2005, viii) view that causality is composed 'from a combination of determinist, individualist, or random elements' hold that geography matters.

Jack Dangermond, founder and president of ESRI (Environmental Systems Research Institute), while holding the view that geography influences and connects cultures and societies, observed that GIS could help chart a better future. Geography provides a structure for understanding patterns, relationships and processes at differing spatial scales – global to local. GIS is a support for thinking about things, modelling future, visualising, integrating and referencing what we know. It has diverse uses ranging from its typical geographic application for modelling groundwater aquifers to its use by researchers at the Burn Center, a part of the US Health System. This centre provides a complete, nationally recognised programme of care for patients suffering from burn injuries, based on a study of the ontology of the brain.

GIS administers and makes use of five major concepts of geography – maps and globes, data models, geodata sets, methodological flow models and metadata. Naturally, the parameters of spatial language would include location, areal differentiation, interaction and diffusion; spatial systems and subsystems; regionalisation at macro- through meso- to micro-scales; measurement of distance, direction, area and shape; and quantitative expressions in terms of trend surface, network analysis and spatial modelling. This encompasses virtually all that a geographer needs as illustrative material not only to serve as a base but also to represent the entire gamut of research undertaken.

A map is central to geographical practice. It breaks the barriers to languages and is the essence of geography. Geographers need maps constantly in the lecture room, in the study, in the field. Maps are so important in geographic work that these can form a touchstone for determining whether a work is in fact geographical. To Hartshorne (1939, 249), the test of the geographic quality of any study a researcher is mapping is 'if the problem cannot be studied fundamentally by maps – usually by a comparison of several maps – then it is questionable whether or not it is within

24 Laying the foundation

the field of geography'. On similar lines, Sauer (1956, 289) observes that the most primitive and persistent trait of a mind bent towards geography is liking maps and thinking by means of them. Haggett (1990, 6) puts the same idea most succinctly: 'Geography is the art of mappable'.

The fact is that map plays a distinctly more pronounced role in geography although it is important to a civil engineer, a *patwari*, a historian or a geologist. Geographers include courses such as map making, map designing, map reading and map projection in their core curriculum. Non-geographers realise the centrality of maps in any geographical writing and look to geographers for the production, analysis and interpretation of maps. It is relevant to recall that the term 'Geographic Information System' was coined by computer scientists to describe the software they had invented to link and map areal data. All this reinforces a significant though not exclusive harmony between geography and mapping.

Harvey (1969, 1972) likens theory to a map. It provides a picture of a landscape and reveals and communicates basic patterns and relationships between features in a landscape. Theory too performs similar functions, detailing knowledge about the world, revealing relationships between data and communicating such knowledge. Both use specific 'languages' to construct, store and communicate knowledge. In all cases of map and theory, a consistent set of rules is used in their creation; the effort is to create internal consistency and control any misrepresentation.

Geographers use maps to convey spatial information visually in a number of ways, each designed to simplify and clarify the infinite complexity of spatial content. These are scientific in nature because of the implied precision of their lines, scales, colour and symbol placement. Mapping software is now being increasingly employed in map production. In computer-assisted cartography, the content of standard maps – locational and thematic – is digitised and stored in computers. GIS extends the use of digitised data and computer manipulation to investigate and display information through an integrated software package meant for handling, processing, analysing geographical data and answering queries, whether relating to social structure of cities or the movement of avalanches. GIS offers a major change in the technology of mapping and the manipulation of map data. It has stimulated new geographical thinking and the development of new forms of analysis.

Mapping, through methodological tools of GIS and cartography, would not be as effective a support to research if not combined with fieldwork. Geographical study cannot be restricted entirely to libraries and laboratories; it is about getting out into the world to explore. Exploration is a search for the new. It is said that the 'age of discovery may be over but the process of geographic discovery is unending'. Here we are brought to appreciate the criticality of fieldwork in any geographic study. The concept of 'fieldwork' originated in geomorphology and land surveying. Over time, it extended over virtually all branches of our discipline. It is getting linked with tourism in a big way. Eco-tourism, heritage tourism, religious tourism and so on are now buzz words. Current trends suggest that fieldwork is central to an expanding market of popular geography. It is undergoing a new phase of mass participation and becoming democratic (Bonnett 2008).

References

Bonnett, Alastair. 2008. *What Is Geography?* London: Sage.

Davies, Norman. 2005 (1981). *God's Playground: A History of Poland, Volume I: The Origins to 1975.* New York: Columbia University Press.

Draus, Franciszek, ed. 1985. *History, Truth and Liberty: Selected Writings of Aron Raymond.* Chicago: University of Chicago Press.

Golledge, Reginald G. 2002. "The Nature of Geographic Knowledge." *Annals of the Association of American Geographers* 92 (1): 1–14.

Haggett, Peter. 1990. *The Geographer's Art.* Oxford: Basil Blackwell.

Hartshorne, R. 1939. *The Nature of Geography: A Critical Survey of the Current Thought in the Light of the Past.* Chicago: Rand McNally.

Harvey, D. 1969. *Explanation in Geography.* Oxford: Blackwell.

———. 1972. "What Is Theory?" In *New Movements in the Study and Teaching of Geography,* edited by N. Graves, 236–275. London: Maurice Temple Smith.

Kaplan, Robert D. 2012. *The Revenge of Geography.* New York: Random House.

Sauer, Carl O'. 1956. "The Education of a Geographer." *Annals of Association of American Geographers* 46 (3): 287–299.

World Development Report. 2009. *Reshaping Economic Geography.* Washington, DC: The World Bank.

PART II

Prefatory phase

The prelims

3

ISSUES PERTINENT TO A THESIS IN GEOGRAPHY

Any research is meant to add a new piece of knowledge to the existing base. This contribution may be by way of a fresh idea or technique or interpretation arising from research. In a formal sense, it can be a thesis at the PhD level or a dissertation at the MPhil level. A thesis is meant to make a mark in the field of research, while a dissertation is intended primarily to acquire competency in pursuing research.

There are different entry points to PhD programme in India. A fresh postgraduate or a student having qualified the National Eligibility Test of the University Grants Commission has to undergo a bridge course, known as a pre-PhD course. This is meant to strengthen the base of the candidate in the philosophy and research methodology of the discipline. In addition, students with MPhil degree and teacher fellows in general constitute the pool of aspirants for doctoral programme. The reason for joining the research programme varies. Mostly it is to earn the requisite degree for being eligible to apply for a job in a college or university. Teacher fellows are prompted by the consideration of getting a promotion. There remain a few candidates who join research for the sake of research.

The prefatory phase involves decision making on the part of the research student on several issues. Every decision is to be well rehearsed and finalised after a careful thought. The major issues that seek resolution with a vision may be listed as follows:

- Selection of the broad area of research
- Choice of the supervisor
- Formulation of the research question
- Statement of the topic
- Writing of the research proposal
- Formal enrolment and registration

Selection of the broad area of research

The first issue in the research process relates to the selection of the broad area of research within the discipline. With 'no idea' to 'vague idea' regarding this, the research student begins to fish for a supervisor. In many cases, the 'ease of earning the degree' outweighs all other considerations. 'Soft' supervisors are sought after. Amidst all this, one begins to contemplate on the issue of identification of the broad area of research.

Given the fact that everything has a geographic context, one can draw focus from practically any aspect of reality. The choice has to be judicious for a well-executed, worthwhile and interesting research. This could be guided by a number of considerations. First, it aligns with an emerging field of research, has practical relevance to the prevailing situation and needs of society and has a tenor of freshness. Second, it offers an opportunity to acquire competence in a new methodology. Finally, it is multidisciplinary in nature, being in the nature of development studies, environmental studies and area studies, and will bring the researcher in interface with a variety of scholars.

In any case, the broad area of research should be of personal interest to the student and compatible with approval of the supervisor. The whole idea is not just to arrive at a research area but a good one – novel, exciting, relevant and feasible. Sometimes, a theme contemplated may look like non-geographic, such as Corruption in Indian Governance. This is not a point of worry since any enquiry can be carried out by applying geographical approach and concepts. In this case, for example, one could work on the incidence of corruption as varying from one state to another. Which are the sites of corruption mints? Which are the places where corruption money is spent? How is corruption a part of the overall character of an area and with what effect? and so on.

McGuire (1973) has proposed some approaches that may help generate research ideas. These in all variety range from observation to discovering the unique to search for anomalies and so on. A modified version of McGuire's ideas is as follows:

i   *Intensive reflection and observation*: Recall the way Newton arrived at the idea of gravitation by observing and reflecting on an apple falling from the tree, and Stevenson thought of steam engine by looking at the behaviour of a boiling kettle. Look closely at a particular marsh, including its shape, size and depth; its water temperature, clarity and chemical makeup; and its flora and fauna. This could lead to research on the functioning of an aquatic ecosystem.

ii   *Paradoxical situations*: Notice that families often return to hazardous areas after a disaster, such as flood or fire. Why people have fixation to certain sites even if prone to risk? This could lead to further research on the variables that influence response to disaster events.

iii   *Daily life experience*: Identify an analogy between people's tendency to shop at closer stores over more distant ones. Why distance matters? This could lead to research on the 'gravity model' of spatial interaction.

iv **Preference modes**: Recall places that have been auspicious for you. Which are problematic? What explains such coincidences in life? This could lead to research on areal differences in place preferences.

v **Contrasting patterns**: Naga villages are located higher on the ridge, while in Himachal Pradesh these are located mostly along river valleys. Why this difference? This could lead to research on the factors that influence siting of settlements.

vi **Reducing complexity to simplicity**: Break down a person's daily mobility patterns related to activities like work, shopping, recreation and so on. Do such journeys vary by modes of transport and why? Answers to such questions could lead to a model of how commuters organise their travel to different destinations.

vii **Identification of exceptions to general findings**: Try to locate anomalies in any distribution, that is things existing at places where not expected or not existing where expected. Christaller posed to himself why certain cities existed where these were not expected, and were also absent where expected. In the long run, he could come out with his Central Place Theory which assumed an isotropic surface to begin with. An isotropic surface is the one where travel time to cover a given distance is the same in any part of the area.

Going beyond all this is a prime need to go through the themes of the best of recent theses, the most stimulating papers in world-class journals and latest books on philosophy of geography by reputed scholars. You may also scan the quality magazines to figure out what is in popular interest. Such readings can sensitise you to what is worth researching in the light of evolving scenario.

Once the broad area of research has been identified, it becomes easy to fine-tune the focus on a specific subject. If one finds population geography of prime interest, it can be narrowed down to a particular aspect of population, such as migration, religious composition or family dynamics. Identification of the broad area of research makes easier the selection of supervisor.

Choice of the supervisor

Most critical in the Indian situation is the choice of the supervisor. The quality of a thesis depends more upon the quality of supervision than upon a candidate's own ability in the Indian context. It is the supervisor who brings out the best in the student and is looked upon as a mentor rather than simply the one who is meant to guide the thesis.

Phillips and Pugh (2000, Chapters 8 and 11) describe what a research student expects from the supervisor and what in return the supervisor wants from the student. A research student expects the supervisor to be actively involved in his or her work, provide both quantity and quality of time and be constructively critical and encouraging. The supervisor is expected to be well versed in the research area, empathetic and supportive and possibly be helpful in getting a job after the

32 Prefatory phase: the prelims

award of degree. On the other hand, the supervisor expects the research student to be proactive, regular in contact and honest in reporting the progress of work. The student should respond to any supervision with maturity of judgement and put forward his or her viewpoint fearlessly. The student has to remain excited about the research undertaken and produce a quality thesis within the specified time frame.

In our view, a research student should be most judicious in the choice of supervisor. The supreme decisive considerations should be the eminence of the supervisor in the field of specialisation, high degree of competency in research methodology and inspiring management of research supervision. A note may be taken of the supervisor's style in terms of easy accessibility to the research student, being responsive to the student's viewpoint and proficient in harnessing the potential of the student. Above all, the supervisor should be a person of integrity and a model of research ethics.

A supervisor has some additional obligations too. Realising the criticality of the supervisor's role in the promotion of quality research, he or she must be equipped with intellectual, emotional and moral fibre to the best advantage of the research student's morale and performance. The supervisor may have to develop a style by which he is encouraging in the beginning, a hard task master in the middle phase and supportive towards the end.

The irony is that most of the research students look for a 'soft' supervisor who is friendly, tolerant even of a substandard work and helps in an early submission of the work. One cannot expect right kind of research training under such a supervisor. This is a sure route to perpetuation of poor quality of research. Rather, what is expected on the part of the student is commitment to research, production of exceptional quality and strict adherence to research ethics. Much depends upon the capacity of the research student to fish an appropriate question for investigation.

Formulation of the research question

Every research piece should have a focus. About 20 per cent of the time ultimately invested in research may be used for discovering the research question and finalising the topic. This is the most vital aspect of any research. It requires a lot of reading, thinking, fieldwork and discussion.

For example, if you have a general interest in development geography, you need to decide which pertinent research questions you would like to address in this context. You may be interested in discerning the development experience of newly formed states, such as Uttarakhand, Jharkhand and Chhattisgarh. In a study of this kind, Singh (1998, 2) observes that formation of Haryana as a consequence of reorganisation of Punjab in 1966 rendered this territory homogeneous culturally, integrated spatially and strong administratively. The regional aspirations of the people in Haryana got addressed and provided the needed stimulus to its development impulses. In spatial terms, the eastern half of the state continued progressing faster than its western counterpart despite regular political patronage to the latter. It seems that the role of the private sector investment is more critical than public sector support, which is always limited, in the development of any area.

Naxalism-affected districts of north-eastern peninsula in India are often labelled as 'red corridor'. These areas are congruent with rugged relief, forest land, tribal population, mining activity, feeble transport links and virtually a non-functional government. A map of insurgency would blend when overlain over a map depicting these conditions. Almost similar conditions of topography, vegetative cover, tribal people, mineral wealth and connectivity exist in southern Rajasthan and its environs. Mercifully, this region is safe from any extremist movement. What explains such a regional differentiation? Are there lessons to learn from the Rajasthan experience for analysing such other parts of India (Krishan 2013)?

A geographer could very well be interested in the study of special economic zones of India. Which was the venue of the first special economic zone in the country and why? What is the present spatial pattern of special economic zones and which factors explain regional disparity in it? What is the internal morphology of a special economic zone and the nature of its external linkages? How have special economic zones impacted upon the geographic character of different areas? Answers to such questions may give a clue to a solution to issues relating to such implantations of geographic nature.

Likewise, if you have a general interest in retail geography, you need to frame questions of special interest to the research you intend to undertake. The emergence of shopping malls in a city may fascinate you and generate several questions for research. Why is the mall located where it is? What is its impact on urban geography of the existing city in terms of shopping patterns, traffic flow and land values? Is the internal morphology of the mall well laid out? Such questions can help the research student in constructing the title of the topic for research. The fact is there is basically no research topic; there is always a research question. All research should be geared to finding an answer to a question.

In the case of North-East region, there is a suggestion from some quarters to deterritorialise the spatial framework of its constituent states. How? For example, all Naga-inhabited areas could be brought under the ambit of one administration. The same holds good for other major tribal groups. What can be the geographer's contribution to such a proposition? The response should be an outcome of a rigorous research. Geographers are obliged to suggest alternative spatial organisation for administration. It should promote development, be protective of ecology and be a facilitator of societal harmony (Krishan 2000, 139).

To discover a question is a part of research training. It requires a lot of purposeful reading, discussion with the experts and thinking on one's own part. Help can be taken from a perusal of already approved theses and dissertations of high quality, articles in the latest issues of the disciplinary journals and research-based books and book reviews. Even a purposeful focus on particular magazines, newspapers and television debates can also lead to a question worthy of research. Equally fruitful will be a discussion with the potential users of your research, especially in the domain of governance.

34 Prefatory phase: the prelims

While going through your information sources you have to meaningfully cull out ideas that serve your purpose. You have to find out the variety of research questions that were raised for enquiry, the methodology that was followed towards that end, the conclusions that were arrived at and the questions for future research that were listed. A familiarity with the writings of other researchers is essential to place your own work in a wider context. You can avoid duplication of any research already done and justify the need of pursuing what you intend to do. Above all, this process helps in identifying gaps in current research and in framing questions to which you would like to know the answers. This will not only distinguish your study from others but also impart some degree of originality to your research.

Statement of the topic

The specific research question may be spelt out and transformed into a topic. While doing so, address the basic questions of the aspects of feasibility, value, symmetry and innovativeness of the topic. These are detailed as follows:

- Is research feasible on this topic? The feasibility is to be referred to matters like availability and access to data and information, requisite competence and technical skill, financial support, time at disposal and freedom from any risk, such as new data that may emerge through the 2011 census for a person who started his research work in 2009 on the basis of 2001 census data.
- Does it have sufficient value? The value can be judged from whether it is important to society at large or sufficient to sustain the interest of the researcher. This can also be referred to as some special contribution it can make to the discipline.
- Is it symmetrical or in accordance with the current paradigm of the discipline? Research symmetry is to be viewed in terms of its compatibility with the current thinking and practice in the discipline. For instance, a theme like pricing of water supply is not much symmetrical in geography, and hence could be avoided for serious geographic research.
- Is it innovative by way of carrying a fresh theme or is it already over-researched? Picking a topic for the sake of convenience or because it appears easy or seems 'trendy' or is a safe bet will almost lead to a poorly executed and unexciting study. A doctoral thesis executed under the title 'Urban Geography of Patna' or 'Agricultural Geography of Aligarh District' or 'Population Geography of Kerala' is not likely to arouse much interest. Research should combine originality (surprise) with contemporary relevance (value) and not be a stereotype. The topic must excite the reader outright.

Once you have selected a topic, the next step in any research exercise is to give expression to a concrete research proposal. This is meant to provide a comprehensive statement on the proposed plan of work. It is meant to spell out general scope of the research exercise, the basic research questions to be addressed, research methodology to be followed and the overall significance of the study. In short, the proposal explains what one intends to investigate, why and how.

Writing of the research proposal

We have already made a brief reference to the research proposal in the preceding discussion. Here we detail upon the process of preparing the research proposal. In doing so, we shall take up its various elements as these follow one another. These may be listed as follows:

i   Title of the proposed work
ii   Introductory statement
iii Review of literature for identifying the research question, formulating the hypothesis and specifying the objectives of the study
iv   Research design
v   A tentative chapter scheme and a statement on limitations of the study
vi   References/Bibliography

Title of the research proposal: The title is the face of the thesis. It must carry a geographic message. Hence all care should be taken in its construction. Some select illustrations of good titles of already accomplished doctoral works are listed below:

* The Development Process in a Newly Organised Indian State: A Case Study of Haryana
* Administrative Organisation of Space in an Indian State: A Case of Punjab
* Spatial Organisation of Service Centres in Outer Himalayas
* Trends in Regional Disparities in India since Independence: A Geographical Analysis
* Regional Variations in the Quality of Living Space in India
* Chandigarh Periphery Zone: 2020 (A Study in Futuristic Geography)

Introductory statement: This is meant to provide sufficient background for readers to understand where your study is coming from. The introductory part of the research proposal is meant to create a space for research. This is done by contextualising the theme of proposed study, highlighting the key issues involved, specifying the significance of the research undertaken, enunciating the specific research problem and providing definition of the key terms used. A brief note on each of these elements follows.

Contextualising the background of your research is to begin the introduction at the outset with reflections on the larger issue you intend to address. It is something that is widely believed. This should soon be followed by some meaningful reference to research already done on the issue. Special care should be taken of the recent works. Create a niche by indicating a gap in the research carried so far. Alternately, you may extend the previous knowledge in some way. The ultimate goal is to

36 Prefatory phase: the prelims

point out what was missed in the previous investigations. You need to establish a strong case for the research you propose to do. Once you have established a general ground, disrupt it with a statement of an issue. Make an observation that focuses on the research you propose to undertake.

Some proposals can begin directly with a statement of the research problem. Such a statement should highlight a situation of incomplete knowledge, consequences of that condition and a significant gap in research that needs to be filled. For example, the objective of research could be to trace the schemes of regionalisation of India, identify the criteria and indicators used in each case and infer their underlying conceptualisations.

A *conceptual* problem often arises in academic research. This happens when we do not understand something about the world as clearly as we would like. Through a well laid out procedure we solve this *conceptual* problem by answering a question that helps us to understand it better (Booth, Colomb, and Williams 2008, 53–55).

The word *problem* at times confuses beginners, something that we tend to avoid in our everyday life. However, it has a specific connotation in the world of research. In academic research, a problem is something we search for, explore, formulate, create or conceive. It is done to add something new or extend the frontiers of knowledge.

Here you may indicate the general scope of your work, but do not go far into much detail: put forward concisely, the rationale, significance or need for the study. Ponder over the existing factors, such as scanty research on your topic. State precisely what your work will contribute to your chosen field. Focus on the future implications. Highlight that it would open up possibilities for further research. All this is done to demonstrate the rationale of your project.

The research problem should be specific, have a sharp focus and define all terms carefully. In the process, you may move from the general to the specific. A perusal of the relevant literature will facilitate you to generate an issue for investigation, learn how to zero in to a specific and manageable area and build up an understanding of how others have tried to solve the same issue. Sometimes this understanding takes place in the course of actually collecting and analysing data. In such a situation, a peculiarity in the data may suggest a research question for investigation.

Kane (1990, 20) suggests some useful steps for developing a clearly specified research problem. First, choose your topic and decide what aspect of it you wish to study. Systematically engage your best critical thinking to raise questions in geographic perspective. Availability of requisite data is to be kept in view. Second, once you have identified a question ask yourself what will be missed if you don't answer the question. How not answering the question keeps us away from understanding the issue better than what we do know. Finally, remember that your work will be judged by its significance not only to you but also to others in the field.

This significance could be in terms of discovery of some new fact, explanation or idea. It may refer to a new technique devised for analysis or mapping. The significance may lie in the domain of planning and development, and hence be of practical value. Some research proposals require a separate section on the significance of the study. Finally, after highlighting the significance of your question from the readers' point of view, frame the research problem. It is expected to reflect conceptual thinking on your part. It is not enough to say that you intend to investigate how literacy rate differs from one part of India to another but pose the question in such form as 'how regionally varying patterns of literacy represent the differences in necessity, facility and propensity to get literate'.

On similar lines, Creswell (1994, 41) had identified four salient components for introductions: (i) frame a research problem, (ii) pitch the problem within the larger scholarly literature, (iii) deliberate on the deficiency in the existing literature about the problem and (iv) highlight the worth of this problem for the audience.

In qualitative research, based on literature rather than on quantitative data, the geographic perspective underlying the research should be clearly brought out. Take the case of research relating to 'Communalism in India'. Here the proposal must clarify how this study will be carried out in spatial perspective rather than in the spirit of political sociology. The research questions must focus on spatial parameters of this feature of Indian society, such as which type of areas are marked by higher incidence of communal disturbances or which kind of localities in a city are more prone to communal riots.

The introductory part of the research proposal should be explicit, engaging and exciting. Moving from general to more specific issues, it should introduce your topic through a statement, put forth research questions, and thus set the stage for what follows. There are other logical structures possible, but the one already stated often works out well. A brilliant design of an introduction, with edited comments, has been given by Creswell (1994, 45–48), Locke *et al.* (1993, 185–296) and Gilpatrick (1989, 57–60).

There are some other aspects of the introductory part of the research proposal. One pertains to linking of the research problem to a theory. For example, a study of the 'Service Centres in the Outer Himalayas' intended to verify the validity of Christaller's theory in a mountainous region of India (Chandna 1980). It was discovered that, given some specific conditions, several parameters of the theory, which essentially is based on an assumption of an isotropic surface, are met even in a hilly topography. A theory provides a framework for testing a hypothesis and helps in enunciating the objectives of a study, its procedure and data collection.

Another task involves a clarification on the technical terms. Take the case of the expression 'Sons of the Soil' (Weiner 1978). The need is to explain what it precisely means in your study. The intention here is to dwell on the theme of nativism or regionalism. At times, a research depends on an operational rather than holistic definition of a term. In her study of Haryana, Singh (1998) adopted definition of development as the 'quality of a regional system in terms of economic growth, social advancement, political maturity and ecological balance' and looked for indicators in each case for quantitative analysis. This is not to deny the possibility of defining development in several other modes. Operational

38 Prefatory phase: the prelims

definitions are constructed to address the issue of constraints of data in meeting the demands of a more comprehensive definition of the same concept.

Terms that are in current usage in professional and scholarly writing may also be examined. Several possibilities exist regarding their usage in your research writing. One option is to cite and use the definitions. The other variant is to review the already existing definitions, critique them in the provisos of their suitability to the proposed research and end up with proposing your own definition. Of course, the new definition has to be discernibly better suited to your study.

This initiates us into the phase of a systematic and purposeful review of literature. This is an extensive task and deserves a treatment in elaboration. A chapter further on is devoted to this essential aspect of research.

Research design: It is essentially the plan or strategy for sculpting the research. The action part of the research proposal is embedded over here. The specific questions may include: What is the study about? Which region or place will it cover? What time period will it span? Which data are required? How will that be collected? Which techniques will be used as analytical tools? In which manner will the findings be presented? Research design is intended to facilitate smooth sailing of the various research operations, in succession to each other.

Research methodology is the core element of a research design. It is a full plan for carrying out a research exercise. This is meant to spell out step-by-step progression of actions for conducting an enquiry. It also points out how the pertinent information is to be used to reach conclusions about the correctness of a hypothesis, or the right answer to a question put forth (Eisner and Peshkin 1990; Leedy and Ormrod 2001; Miller and Salkind 2002).

We may need to have an understanding of some terms relevant to research. The following is based on ideas of Löfgren (1996, as cited in Holt-Jensen 2009, 146–147).

i   **Ontology** is the basic philosophical foundation upon which the structure of any research rests. It is a description of what exists vis-à-vis what does not. For instance, social ontology in geography is concerned with spatial structure of a society, its elements and basic mechanisms that link these. Although we might have a basic idea of the social spatial structure, most of it is unknown to us. So we need a theory about how to get knowledge about the world, that is an epistemology.

ii **Epistemology** may be understood as 'construction of knowledge'. It concerns how knowledge is acquired or attained: premises or conjectures about how we can know the world (Hubbard *et al.* 2002, 6). Epistemology guides the formulation of research problem, the evaluation of theory, the choice of appropriate techniques for empirical investigation and the interpretation of results. It tells how to look for knowledge. To be applicable to research, an epistemology must be cast in a concrete form by way of models or programmes, that is methodology. The hypothetic–deductive approach is one such method.

iii **Methodology** is the process of conducting research through its various stages and phases – strategy, plan of action, and the process followed. It provides both the strategy and grounding for the conduct of a study, for example scientific method, ethnography or action research. Within each different methodology, there is a host of different concrete methods we can apply.

iv **Method** refers to the actual techniques or procedures used to collect and analyse data (Crotty 2003, 3). Interviewing, surveying and observation are some examples of data collection, while methods of analysis comprise quantitative or statistical treatment and qualitative or thematic exploration. A method is built up from techniques. It, thus, includes rules and recommendations on tools, or ways of collecting data, work up, techniques for analysing data or information and present data in relation to a given problem (Harding 1987, 2).

v **Techniques** focus on how to carry it out. For instance, collecting observation-based data can employ various techniques, such as straight observation or participant observation and so on.

vi **Tools** are the devices used in the collection of data for executing research. These include questionnaires, observation checklists and interview schedules (O'Leary 2010, 88–89).

Finally, any method or technique used is to be adapted to the specific research problem and its context being investigated. The approach to a particular research exercise will often need a combination of different methods.

Geographical research by its sheer variety and vast range of inquiry demands perhaps more thought than any of the other social and natural science disciplines. Regardless of its philosophical stance, all research in geography just like in other disciplines involves thinking and reasoning about the association or connection between methods, analysis and interpretation. Research design fills this important role. It has to carry an explicit statement. Clifford and Valentine (2003, 6–12) list six key points that one needs to keep in mind while formulating a credible research design:

Research questions to ask: Think about the topic and seek help from the relevant theoretical and empirical literature and consult the experts for framing a viable research question. A geographer, while examining any physical or cultural phenomenon, will raise a series of questions on the following lines: What is it and where is it? How did it come to be what and where? Where is it in relation to other things that affect it or are affected by it? How is it a part of a spatial system? How does its location affect people's lives and the character of the area in which it is found? For a physical geographer, these might include the morphology of a selected set of landforms, the geomorphic processes affecting them and the rate at which the landforms are changing. These questions are spatial in focus and analytical in approach (Fellmann *et al.* 2005, 7).

Appropriate methods: The questions raised and the sort of information required will guide the selection of appropriate method(s). A range of methods, including

40 Prefatory phase: the prelims

fieldwork or use of remote sensing and GIS or conventional cartography, are available to a geographer. Researchers may use a mix of quantitative and qualitative methods or different sources of information to maximise the outcome of the research question.

Management of data: Reflect on how you propose to analyse and interpret the data, both quantitative and qualitative, you have amassed. Think about the appropriate techniques you will employ to treat it. The objective is to ensure richness, depth and quality to the analysis.

Honouring time limits: Fix the parameters of your project by keeping in view the time limit and resources available to conduct the study. One should not over-commit or be over-ambitious in defining the scope of the research effort. The completion of a doctoral thesis is expected within three to five years.

Ethical issues to consider: The most common ethical dilemmas in human geography concern the matters of consent and confidentiality while seeking personal information (see Alderson 1995; Valentine 1999). In physical geography the question of consent (such as entry to field sites on private land) and also the potential impact of the research techniques (say pollution) on the environment are matters of ethical concern. Ethical musings do shape the questions we ask, whom we talk to and where we conduct the fieldwork. Questions bearing gender or ethnic or other biases have to be avoided. These choices in turn may have implications for what kind of material we gather, how to use and analyse it and what to do with it when the project is nearing its end.

Style of presentation: The entire research process is intended to result in a written document. This raises the question of presentation style. Here a geographer is obliged to project the specificity of the discipline.

A research design is, therefore, a blueprint or comprehensive plan for how to conduct a research plan. It covers operationalising variables for measurement including sample selection for collection of data to be used for hypotheses testing and analysing the results (Thyer 1993, 94). It is concerned with transforming a research question, a hypothesis or even an intuition or hunch or idea into a manageable project. The A to Z of the design process includes the initial formulation of the research question; kind of data to be collected; how the data are to be collected (methodology and methods); contemplating on sample and sampling, if required; decision on the analysis of the proposed data; consideration on presentation and dissemination of research (Hammond and Wellington 2013, 131). It may also be added that some scholars use it to cover the whole process of conducting a research project, while others use it rather narrowly to cover the process of designing only the data collection and subsequent operations.

Just as the research proposal states what is to be done, research design specifies how it is to be done. It is furtherance of the component of research proposal that specifies actual line of action. It forms the conceptual structure according to which a research exercise is carried out. It is analogous to the blueprint for construction of a building. Once done, the ease of various research operations is facilitated. The path to research is by no means a smooth, straight road but a bumpy, jerky and winding one.

At the same time, we must remember that there is no definite way or any magic or all pervasive formula to conduct research. Imagination and creativity are its two most critical elements.

Chapter scheme: The research proposal is expected to carry a comprehensive statement on the organisational structure of its text. This is meant to detail the sequence of chapters as these will follow each other. Normally research students have a tendency to simply list the title of the chapters. It is highly inadequate. There are two things that need to be addressed effectively in this regard. First, the logic behind the ordering of the chapters must be made clear and justified. Second, the contents of what is going to be discussed in each chapter need to be made explicit. This will call for a rigorous thinking on the part of research students right in the beginning. If the number of chapters is large, it is appropriate to group those under three to five sections. This will automatically classify the research work into sub-themes. Needless to add that the text of the thesis has to start with an introductory chapter and close with synthesis of conclusions arrived at in different chapters.

A research proposal enunciates not only what it would study but also what it would not. It is meant to not merely delimit the scope of the exercise but also to specify its limitations. While examining the impact of the Indo–Pakistan international border on the development process in border regions, we may have to delimit the study to the Indian side and express the limitation of not being in a position to cover the Pakistani side due to lack of access to information. It is best to express such a situation in the research proposal itself. Delimitation and expression of limitations are part of the research proposal. These set the parameters of the research work, tell the reader what will be included and also what will be left out and why.

Time schedule: It is always desirable to provide a statement on the time schedule you are going to follow in accomplishment of your PhD thesis. This shows your tendency towards self-discipline in taking a serious view of your research work. It indicates the relative importance you are going to give to different components and successive phases of research. A time watch on the progress of work is also set. A tentative time chart for a PhD student is given in Table 3.1.

TABLE 3.1 A tentative time chart for a PhD student

Activity	*Time in months*
Survey of literature	Three months
Identification of research question, topic and supervisor	Three months
Formulation of research proposal	Three months
Fieldwork and data collection	Six months
Data processing and mapping	Six months
Data analysis	Three months
Report writing	One year
Total	36 months or three years

References and bibliography

Here one may understand the distinction between references and bibliography. References are the readings that have been quoted in the text of the thesis, while bibliography covers not only the references but also other readings that have been gone through for general awareness but did not find a place in the text. Normally, bibliographies are listed by author names in alphabetical order. The best course would be to classify the various entries by some criterion, such as the nature of outlet in terms of books, reports, research articles, government publications etc., or by subthemes of the main theme. For a geographer, it will be pertinent to group these entries by their spatial scale of the international, national, subnational and local levels and to subgroup these further by the nature of outlet or subtheme. In any case, the logic behind the way the bibliography has been arranged must be made clear. It is also imperative to follow one style consistently, preferably Chicago or Harvard, in listing each entry.

Annexure

Some research proposals may carry an annexure that provides information of secondary importance not included in the text. A geographic study focused on creation of a new state in India may refer to Article 3 of the Indian Constitution (Government of India 2007), which is pertinent to this process but finds the details too lengthy to go in the main text. In such a case, it can go as an annexure.

Formal enrolment and registration: The procedure for registration to PhD is not uniform in all universities. In some enrolment has to precede registration, whereas in others it is direct registration without enrolment. Enrolment is simply an expression of intention to pursue research, while registration covers finalisation of the topic, choice of supervisor and submission of research proposal. For registration, in any case, preparation of synopsis under guided supervision is essential. A basic requirement is filling up the application form. The prospective candidate is advised to carefully read the ordinance and instructions in the application form. They should fulfil all the mandatory requirements before submitting the requisite documents.

References

Alderson, P. 1995. *Listening to Children: Children, Ethics and Social Research.* Ilford, UK: Barnardos.

Booth, Wayne C., Gregory G. Colomb, and Joseph M. Williams. 2008. *The Craft of Research.* 3rd ed. Chicago: University of Chicago Press.

Chandna, M.M. 1980. *The Spatial Organisation of Service Centres in the Outer Himalayas.* Unpublished PhD Thesis, Department of Geography, Panjab University, Chandigarh.

Clifford, Nicholas J., and Gill Valentine. 2003. "Getting Started in Geographical Research: How This Book Can Help." In *Key Methods in Geography*, edited by Nicholas J. Clifford and Gill Valentine, 1–16. London: Sage.

Creswell, J.W. 1994. *Research Design: Qualitative and Quantitative Approaches*. Thousand Oaks, CA: Sage.

Crotty, M. 2003. *The Foundations of Social Research: Meaning and Perspectives in the Research Process*. 3rd ed. London: Sage.

Eisner, Elliot W., and Alan Peshkin, eds. 1990. *Qualitative Inquiry in Education: The Continuing Debate*. New York: Teachers College Press.

Fellmann, Jerome D., Arthur Getis, Judith Getis, and Jon C. Malinowski. 2005. *Human Geography: Landscapes of Human Activities*. 8th ed. New York: McGraw-Hill.

Gilpatrick, E. 1989. *Grants for Nonprofit Organizations: A Guide to Funding and Grant Writing*. New York: Praeger.

Government of India. 2007. *The Constitution of India* (As Modified up to the 1st December 2007). New Delhi: Ministry of Law and Justice.

Hammond, Michael, and Jerry Wellington. 2013. *Research Methods: The Key Concept*. Oxon: Routledge.

Harding, Sandra. 1987. "Introduction: Is There a Feminist Method." In *Feminism and Methodology: Social Science Issues*, edited by Sandra Harding, 1–14. Bloomington: Indiana University Press.

Holt-Jensen, Arild. 2009. *Geography: History and Concepts: A Student's Guide*. 4th ed. London: Sage.

Hubbard, Phil, Brendan Bartley, Duncan Fuller, and Rob Kitchin. 2002. *Thinking Geographically: Space, Theory and Contemporary Human Geography*. London: Continuum.

Kane, E. 1990. *Doing Your Own Research: Basic Descriptive Research in the Social Sciences and Humanities*. London: Boyars.

Krishan, Gopal. 2000. "Indian Geography: Tasks Ahead." *Annals of the Association of Geographers, India* 20 (1 & 2): 131–141.

———. 2013. "In the Quest of Questions in Geography." *Transactions, Institute of Indian Geographers* 35 (1): 1–11.

Leedy, Paul D., and Jeanne E. Ormrod. 2001. *Practical Research: Planning and Design*. 7th ed. Upper Saddle River, NJ: Merrill Prentice Hall.

Locke, L.F., W.W. Spirduso, and S.J. Silverman. 1993. *Proposals That Work*. 3rd ed. Newbury Park, CA: Sage.

McGuire, W.J. 1973. "The Yin and Yang of Progress in Social Psychology: Seven Koan." *Journal of Personality and Social Psychology* 26 (3): 446–456.

Miller, Delbert C., and Neil J. Salkind. 2002. *Handbook of Research Design and Social Measurement*. 6th ed. London: Sage.

O'Leary, Zina. 2010. *The Essential Guide to Doing Your Research Project*. South Asia ed. New Delhi: Sage.

Phillips, E.M., and D. Pugh. 2000. *How to Get a PhD: A Handbook for Students and Their Supervisors*. 3rd ed. Buckingham: Open University Press.

Singh, Nina. 1998. *Administration and Development of Indian States*. New Delhi: Anmol Publications.

Thyer, Bruce A. 1993. "Single-Systems Research Design." In *Social Work, Research and Evaluation*, edited by R.M. Grinnell, 94–117. 4th ed. Itasca, IL: F.E. Peacock Publishers.

Valentine, G. 1999. "Being Seen and Heard? The Ethical Complexities of Working with Children and Young People at Home and at School." *Ethics, Place and Environment: A Journal of Philosophy and Geography* 2 (2): 141–155.

Weiner, Myron. 1978. *Sons of the Soil: Migration and Ethnic Conflict in India*. Princeton, NJ: Princeton University Press.

4

RESEARCH PROPOSAL
Issues and formulation

All researchers, be they intending doctoral students seeking formal registration or applying for research grant or accessing funding from any organisation, are required to present their research idea as a convincing case in the form of a research proposal. At the university level, the research proposal requires formal approval at different levels. The other situation is where approval is needed for research grant or funding circumstance. Here the issue is to make a success in a competitive research world.

The fact is that a research proposal is an elemental feature of any research work. It is a 'document which deals with what the proposed research is about; what it is trying to find out or achieve; how it will go about doing that; what we will learn from it and why that is worth learning' (Punch 2006, 9). It is expected to carry a self-explanatory message. In the same vein, Krathwohl (1998, 65) has his take on the definition of research proposal. He believes that it has to demonstrate how the research to be undertaken fills a need. It is a carefully prepared, enthusiastic, interestingly written, skilled presentation. The implication is that research proposal itself is a creation of meticulous planning and designing, involving considerable research. In a proverbial sense, a letter-perfect research proposal is in the nature of 'well begun is half done'.

A research proposal is judged on the two touchstones of its viability and the capability or capacity of the student to carry it out. Viability is referred as the possibility of its completion, worthiness as a research exercise and capacity of the candidate to see it through. For judging the ability of the candidate to make a success the best indicator is the quality of research proposal itself. It reflects his or her overall awareness of the theme chosen for study, skill in making a convincing case for research on a select topic and capacity to write with clarity in a comprehensive and coherent manner. The proposal is an instrument through which the faculty judges the candidate for his competence to pursue any research work (Locke, Spirduso, and Silverman 1993, xii).

In effect a proposal is a kind of stand-alone document, easily intelligible to a reader, even non-expert. It should be drafted and crafted in a manner that makes intelligent sense without the student interpreting it or clarifying to those who may not have discussed the work with them.

Even though the first draft of the proposal could be informal, the research student must ensure an acquaintance with the guidelines laid down by the institution as essential requirements of a thesis. These specifications spell out the expected nature and quality of the thesis, the duration within which it is to be completed, the literary style it has to follow and production matters it has to adhere to. Therefore, it is a good idea to work on the proposal in regular consultation with the supervisor. It can also be subjected to a review process by peers.

Before framing the research proposal, the research student must take care of certain imperatives. Most essential is an exciting enunciation of the title of the proposed work in the spirit of the discipline. Identification of a gap in current research through literature survey should be its basis. It is to be ensured that it promises an exploration into an undiscovered arena. The wider context of knowledge within which it is to be placed must also be ascertained. Immensely critical is also to look into the question of availability of necessary data for the purpose of proposed research. The research question to be pursued and hypothesis to be tested should be framed in the spirit and purpose of the concerned discipline. The area adopted for study should be justified and a brief description of it should be provided.

Likewise the time framework of the proposed study calls for justification. The relevance of the work should also be made explicit. Above all, the research student may take a vow to adhere to ethical principles, which include, for example, a truthful presentation of the results obtained, keeping a secular outlook and refraining from any kind of plagiarism. It emerges that the research proposal comprises the fundamental elements that are not very much different from those of any good piece of scientific writing.

A variety of situations define the requirements of a research proposal. The most frequent occasion is one when the research student is aiming an academic degree. One need may arise when a student is applying for a fellowship in a foreign country. Finally, the necessity is linked to seeking funding for research from a government or private agency.

Accordingly, we can classify the research proposals into the three following types:

   i   Research proposal for an academic degree
  ii   Research proposal for fellowship in a foreign country
 iii   Research proposal for an institutional funding or grant

Research proposal for an academic degree is a roadmap to be pursued while aiming at the destination of an MPhil or PhD degree. It should include a clear statement of the objective of the study, the specific research question to be addressed and the hypothesis to be tested. The reasons for choosing the said topic, its significance and approach to be followed in pursuing the whole work are to be clearly enunciated.

46 Prefatory phase: the prelims

The research question and the topic are, in fact, to be discovered through an identification of existing gap in research. That defines the topic for the study and its objective. In geographic research, it is equally important to justify the selection of the area adopted for study. The same applies to the time period to be covered by the study.

An elaborate section on the methodology to be followed is an essential part of the research proposal. It should be specific and not couched in general terms. Herein the data sources are to be mentioned and if primary data are to be the base of the study, the sampling procedure must be dealt in detail. The quantitative and cartographic techniques that are to be used for processing and mapping of data should be listed in a convincing manner.

Quite often, a researcher is not in a position to cover all aspects of the intended study. Such a situation can arise for reasons of paucity of time or non-availability of data. The research proposal is obliged to make a mention of its limitations or what it cannot or will not be in a position to pursue.

The research proposal is also to offer chapter scheme of the text of the thesis. This is not to be just a listing of chapters in a sequential order but a logical structuring of the entire exercise. Each chapter is to be justified in terms of its coverage and placement in order of various chapters. The whole thing ought to be presented as an integrated whole.

Research proposal intending to obtain a fellowship in a foreign university, such as the United States, the United Kingdom and the Netherlands, is in the nature of topic analysis. By its very definition it is to be brief, normally to be contained within two to three pages. It is a precise statement of the objective, methodology and significance of the study put together in a coherent manner. The nature and sources of data on which the study will be based are also to be mentioned. It must justify the conduct of the proposed research outside India. The topic suggested should be of interest to scholars abroad. One example is the Indian Diaspora in the United States. Suggest topics that align with the specialty of the department being approached for admission and fellowship. The thrust areas in which your own department is specialising may be avoided. It must emphasise the relevance of your training in a foreign university to your country/university/department back home. Indicate your desire to learn new technologies, such as GIS and remote sensing. Highlight that your training will have a diffusion effect. Also convince them that your stay for the purpose will be temporary. All this has to be a well-knit statement.

As a final piece, now we come to the issue of preparing a research proposal for institutional funding. Such a situation will arise when a government body, such as the *NITI Aayog* of India, or an international agency, such as the United Nations Habitat Center, or a private organisation, such as Sage Publications, is being approached for financial support. A proposal of this nature must take into account some factors additional to the general imperatives laid out above for an academic research proposal. A critical job here is to precisely define the terms of reference for the entire work. The proposal must be framed in a spirit and style that aligns with the objectives of the funding agency. The details of the budget, covering honorarium for the researcher, salary of the staff and financial implications of fieldwork, equipment, books and journals, computer assistance and production of the report must be detailed in a justifiable manner. It may be mentioned that the text of the report prepared will be preceded by an Executive Summary suggesting a line of action on the part of the sponsoring authority. Finally, a time frame for completion of the work should be fixed after mutually agreed terms. It has to be one that can be strictly adhered to, and honoured.

Evidently research proposals differ in terms of their purpose and destination and so do their messages and presentation style.

References

Krathwohl, D.R. 1998. *Methods of Educational and Social Science Research: An Integrated Approach.* New York: Longman.

Locke, L.F., W.W. Spirduso, and S.J. Silverman. 1993. *Proposals That Work.* 3rd ed. Newbury Park, CA: Sage.

Punch, Keith F. 2006. *Developing Effective Research Proposals.* 2nd ed. London: Sage.

5

LITERATURE SEARCH AND REVIEW

A review of the literature is required in preparation of a PhD thesis. It is meant to demonstrate one's knowledge and understanding of already conducted research on the same topic. The aim is to build the context in which one's own study is to be situated.

Literature review is a critical appraisal of all the main theories and findings relevant to your topic and deliberates on what other researchers have already found and concluded. Critical appraisal in academic reviewing means informed and considered evaluation, and is a part of one's scholastic or intellectual growth — 'of becoming an expert in the field' (Hart 1999, 1). Review articles are also written by synthesising the contents of available research, on a theme of special interest, such as 'Indian Cities'. In addition to all this, review reports are prepared for a specific purpose. A case in point is publication under the aegis of the International Geographical Union (IGU) of a status report every four years on the progress in Indian geography based on review of publications on various themes in the country.

A literature review is a very specific portion of argumentative writing, based largely on a purposeful critical perusal of pertinent journal papers, books and reports for creating a 'space' or niche for your own research. By reviewing the literature, you are showing the reader how your research is adding to the existing knowledge by placing it in a wider context. For this, you have to connect with the body of literature and also be able to capture, compare, contrast, synthesise and make arguments in ways that indicate a readiness to contribute further to the literature itself. At a more subtle level, writing the literature review enables the researcher to locate a study in the history of a particular field and key areas of debates and controversy. It is rather imperative to continually update the review through the project, particularly a long-term one, such as a doctoral research.

The thrust of review in the case of deductive or theory-based research may differ somewhat from that relating to inductive or empirical phenomena-based research. The former calls for a focus on evolution of the theory as it took shape over time and the latter takes into account the variety of thinking on the issue under consideration. Often an empirical study carries a component of theory too; hence review of literature in this case has to blend the two.

The varied sources of literature carry varying styles of referencing. Research students are advised to transcript all of these into a uniform pattern. Things will be facilitated if each reading, with the necessary notes, is listed on a separate index card. This will help in their classification as per purpose and also in standardising the referencing style. Normally Chicago System of Style or Harvard System of Referencing is recommended. There is a virtue in adopting a single system with consistency.

Why scan the literature?

All reading for research is investment in time. It must be done with a purpose, understanding and speed. It has to be highly focused. It must be used sensibly and meaningfully. Two things are involved in this process: looking for the writings available on the theme and reviewing them for locating research gaps. To begin with, it is a part of the process of topic selection to know the latest in the field, by identifying gaps in research on a given theme and reflecting on potential topics for research. It helps in learning as to how a question is raised, the ways it can possibly be answered and address prevailing controversies on a given topic. The earlier habit of proclaiming that 'nothing has been done on this theme' is to be shunned. Often not much effort has gone into locating the research that had already been accomplished. There is virtually no theme that has not been covered or being further explored. Hence, literature survey is a continuous process to remain in the know of the state of the art. How to get at the literature? How to read it? How to use it? These are the basic questions (Figure 5.1).

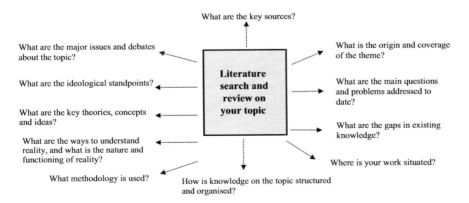

FIGURE 5.1 Some questions addressed by literature search and review

50 Prefatory phase: the prelims

Literature sources

These could be classified as primary, secondary, tertiary, quaternary and others. Research papers, research-based books, research reports, monographs, conference proceedings, government publications and above all the PhD theses constitute the primary sources. Secondary sources are represented by review articles, abstract bulletins, textbooks and encyclopaedia, which are based on primary sources. Next comes general bibliographies, subject bibliographies and annotated bibliographies, which are simply listing in nature and fall under the tertiary category. The internet, for obvious reasons of giving access to all compiled information and literature, is described as a quaternary source. Beyond these, there are some other sources of information, such as newspapers, magazines, panel discussions and television channels such as Discovery and National Geographic.

Undertaking a literature search

How to initiate and proceed with the process of literature search: in other words a survey that combines search with a system of well-defined purpose? The first step is to identify the diverse parameters of the topic you propose to undertake. This will help you in defining the key terms in each aspect of your study. In this case the *Dictionaries of Human Geography* (Gregory *et al.* 2009) and of *Physical Geography* (Thomas and Goudie 2000) are essential for a geography student to go through. High-quality encyclopaedia, all-purpose dictionaries and thesauruses will be of additional help for the purpose.

The second step is to prepare a tentative list of your readings. This involves search of literature through library catalogues, reviews and abstracts, citation indexes, bibliographies and websites. One has to develop a skill to navigate all this and fish out what is relevant to you. You may classify the inventory of your readings by chapter scheme of the research proposal. A more meaningful style of this recording may be by spatial scale of readings, which pertain to international, national, subnational and local levels.

The final step is to carry out the reading of the literature. It will be ideal if each reference is noted on a separate index card. Equally desired is a standardised style of taking notes on each reference, as will be discussed in detail later in this chapter. Now let us take a note of the first two steps mentioned above, followed by a note on reading of literature.

Reference tree in literature search

Under this model, an initial keyword is selected at the topic level and is used as a basis for searching. It leads to discovery of further keywords that will go under subheadings. For example, a study of regional disparities may begin by the keywords of development, region and indicators. Development may be further fabricated into economic, social, political and ecological; region into macro, meso and micro, and indicators into theory, concepts and techniques and so on. The whole process involves generation of successive keywords at different levels. A scope to pursue or abandon the search for keywords should be kept in view.

Accessing the sources

Library catalogues: Now these are available in two forms: conventional as index cards and as listing on the internet. In most libraries, geography books are scattered over different sections, such as earth sciences, social sciences, geography and travel. One has to be familiar with all this. At the same time, the integrative nature of geography demands that many books written by sociologists, economists, political scientists and others could also be relevant to his or her work. These are also to be skimmed appropriately. The same could be said about the research journals. One of the quickest ways to generate a list of references is to find the latest book or research paper covering your topic and look at its reference list.

Abstracts and reviews: One has to check recent issues of review journals, especially *Progress in Human Geography*, *Progress in Physical Geography* and *Subject Abstracts* for appropriate papers and updates on the literature in specific subfields. Most useful set of abstracts for geographers is *GeoBase*. Entries in this case are easy to sift from more important to less important. It covers earth sciences, human and physical geography, ecology, geology, environmental sciences, oceanography, pollution, waste management and nature conservation.

There are seven print abstract and indexing journals that are subsets of the *GeoBase* database, for example *Geographical Abstracts: Physical Geography* with ISSN 0954–0504 and start year 1989 and *Geographical Abstracts: Human Geography* with ISSN 0953–9611 and start year 1989. The tips for using GeoBase can be accessed on http://www.reading.ac.uk/web/FILES/library/tipsgeobase.pdf.

Citation indexes: These are a source for identifying journal papers, abstracts and reviews. ISI Web of Science is most notable for this purpose. It consists of three citation indexes covering the social sciences, arts and humanities and science.

Bibliographies: Specialised bibliographies are available. The most useful are the annotated ones. There are web-based geography bibliographies as well. Some examples include *Gender in Geography* (www.emporia.edu/socsci/fembib/index. htm), *GIS Bibliography* (campus.esri.com/library/), *Cold Regions Bibliography* and *Oxford Bibliography Geography*.

Websites: Websites are emerging as a popular source of surfing information. Easy access is their greatest virtue. But then these need to be evaluated critically for their origin, purpose, authenticity and credibility.

The purpose of the literature search is to locate the most appropriate references for your research project. For this you need to hone up your ingenuity to determine the relevance and credibility of a given resource. Play around with ideas, concepts and variables and try to build a solid literature base.

Reading the literature

How to read and how to write are said to be two basic strategies in academic research. Reading is essential for relating one's ideas to the wider literature on the topic. When you start searching for sources, you'll find ample literature on the topic – sometimes more than you can use. In that case, you must quickly evaluate

52 Prefatory phase: the prelims

the literature's usefulness, relevance and reliability. If your source is a book, browse its index for your keywords and then skim the pages on which those words occur; go through the prologue, introduction and concluding chapter, which may use a lot of your keywords. If the source is an edited book, quickly read the editor's introduction. Glance the bibliography for titles relevant to your topic.

If your source is a research paper, go through the abstract if it has one; scan the introduction, conclusion and section headings; read the paragraphs which seem most relevant; and check the references for titles relevant to your topic. If your source is online, follow the steps for a journal research paper. If it looks like a printed research paper, skim sections labelled 'introduction', 'overview' and 'summary'. If the site has a 'search' resource, type in your keywords. The source should be checked for a reliable publishing house, reputation of the author and authenticity of the sponsoring organisation. All material that appears online may not be in line.

Effective reading may take many different forms depending on your purpose — from skimming, through browsing, to in-depth text analysis and will rarely involve reading from beginning to the end (Kneale 1999).

Writing a literature review is not a ritual to be performed or a hurdle to be overcome. You will have to fathom which literature you are expected to include. These may include prior research; social significance of the problem; philosophical basis of inquiry, ramifications for policy, method and theory; and applications in practice.

Two articles published in the *Annals of the American Association of Geographers* under the titles 'People, Place and Region: 100 Years of Human Geography in the Annals' (Kobayashi 2010, 1095–1106) and 'A Century of Physical Geography Research in the Annals' (Aspinall 2010, 1049–1059) deserve a special reading by every research student. Herein the observations are primarily based on the presidential addresses, which are described as most inspiring in ideas and setters of new trends in geography. The journey of human geography during the twentieth century is described as successive phases of Darwinian environmentalism in the beginning to anti-determinist cultural geography at mid-century and the quantitative revolution in the decades following the post-World War II years. During the 1970s, humanism and Marxism held great sway as methodologies. The closing decades of the century were marked by the emergence of feminism and anti-racism as the popular trends, apart from a testing of economic and political theories. A spatial or regional approach has been a common feature of all this shifting emphasis in geography.

Likewise, physical geography has been in a regular evolving process in tandem with developments in earth and environmental sciences. Field-based observations and generalisations, aided by available tools, have been the traditional mode of methodology in physical geography. In the latter half of the twentieth century, the use of quantitative analysis, remote sensing and GIS also became common. Recently, physical geography has been leaning towards complexity science, which deals with dynamic, multi-dimensional and unpredictable systems. The focus is on human-environmental systems in an attempt towards raising a unified geography. This is quite a bit of progress from the study of elements and controls of physical phenomena, to efforts at their classification, and further to their process-based understanding.

The irony is that physical geography did not attract as much attention as human geography did. Of all the papers published in the *Annals* during the twentieth century, only about one-fifth belonged to this branch of the discipline. Until around the mid-1920s, physical geography functioned in an elementary form and provided a base for environmental determinism. During the next quarter century, physical geography suffered a decline due to a move away from environmentalism. It picked up pace again in the second half of the twentieth century. This re-emergence was linked to the development of spatial analysis, systems analysis and process thinking. Currently in focus are the themes of environmental variability or climate change, landscape dynamism and nature-human nexus.

Apart from such reviews in geography, research students working in the field of human geography are advised to render a regular reading of reviews published in *Population and Development Review*. This journal is brought out by the Population Council of the United Nations, New York, and deals with multiple aspects of population, social, economic and environmental change as related to the development process and policy formulation. Not only are the research papers published in it of outstanding quality but also the theme-based commentaries and book reviews are of a very special nature. The reviews are marked by a felicity of style, insightful observations and faithful representation of the basic message of books under review. Likewise, the book reviews published in the journal *Foreign Affairs*, published by the Council on Foreign Relations, Washington, DC, hold immense value for learning by any research student. Book reviews published in this journal are grouped by world regions, in addition to covering contemporary themes. These are great training resources for writing pithy and effective reviews in an intellectually stimulating style.

Reading is critical in helping to analyse and to situate a problem. The existing literature enables one to discover and highlight gaps in the existing knowledge. It helps in confirming the significance of what we are going to study.

Recording a research entry

Every reading should be recorded, as suggested earlier, as a separate reference. The basic points noted in each case should include the main question raised for investigation, any hypothesis stated and methodology followed. The spatial unit of analysis, such as state, district or individual settlement, sources of data, primary, secondary or both, and details of maps and diagrams should also be noted. The main findings and conclusions arrived at may be given special attention. A note may also be taken of the questions raised for future research. Finally, make a summary statement on the relevance of all this to your own assignment.

The scope of reading literature may be reduced by setting a date prior to which references may be followed only in special cases. This is because most authors refer to and summarise the work of their predecessors. Normally books and research papers published during the preceding 15 years should serve the purpose. This follows the idea of 15 years of cycle of knowledge getting a fresh lease after this duration. Some

54 Prefatory phase: the prelims

exceptions in respect of the classical literature can be made. Literature should be perused from the latest to backwards, in order of the year as 2019, 2018, 2017, 2016 and so on.

Managing of literature review

The process of literature review is like a spiral. It keeps coming back at various stages in your research. Keep a search diary, which includes the sources searched, the key words used and brief notes on the relevant references accessed. Make online searches and keep track of search engines and sources you have used.

If the number of references is large, focus on the most recent ones and the references most frequently cited. If you are finding too few relevant references, try some new search terms and consider broadening the topic or the geographical area. Reference managers or bibliographic management programs such as ProCite, Reference Manager, Endnote, Refworks, Zotero and Mendeley may be accessed to download the relevant literature, data and documents.

Extreme care should be taken in ensuring that you take full and correct details of every entry. These may differ in style by the authored or edited books, journal research papers and online sources. Try to reach the original source. The details of what needs to be noted are as follows.

For authored or edited books, record

- Author/s
- Year of publication
- Title (including subtitle, if any)
- Editor(s) and translator(s) (if any)
- Edition (if any)
- Volume (if any)
- Place published (the first if more than one is listed) publisher

For journals, record

- Author
- Date
- Title (including subtitle) of article
- Title of journal
- Volume and issue number
- Page numbers of article

For online sources, record

- URL (Uniform Resource Locator)
- Date of access

- Webmaster (if identified)
- Name of database (if any)

If you access a printed text online, cite reference from the original source as well as your source of online access. With the prolific cutting and pasting directly from the internet, it can be difficult to keep trail of the source of information. Hence paste the web link along with the information. There is a need to note down the exact time and date of accessing the site because of the transitory nature of internet content (Booth, Colomb, and Williams 2008, 85–86).

Structuring the literature review

Invariably a research student is confronted with the issue of organising literature review. Often this is done by way of listing the readings gone through chronologically, that is successive years of publication. The idea is to demonstrate the evolution of thinking on the concept you are tracing. Such a style becomes unimpressive if you are not successful in establishing the link between one stage and the next stage in development of that idea. Usually the research students lack the necessary ability to do the needful and hence the chronological approach ends up in simply listing of what has gone before in literature.

Another approach is to trace successive phases or trends in research on topic of your interest. A preliminary survey of literature will help in identifying the break points in evolution of the idea or in the use of methodology while dealing with that concept. In accordance, you can structure your review appropriately. Such an approach requires a necessary ability on the part of the research student to mark the critical break points in evolution of a theme. Often knowledge is polycyclic, that is several trends of thought coexisting at the same time. This makes the task rather difficult.

Still another way of organising the literature review is by subthemes of the main topic. This brings in a stronger element of theorisation in presenting the material. It demonstrates the skill of the research student in classifying any pile of literature. Such a procedure lays bare a bias on the part of scholars in overplaying or on the contrary ignoring research on certain aspects of the same theme. Thereby it facilitates identification of gaps in available research.

Finally, for a geographer the most meaningful way of classifying the research entries is by spatial scale on which they have been treated. Studies carried out on a theme at the international level are to be separated from those conducted at the national level and these in their turn are to be differentiated from those done at the regional or local levels. This is rarely done. Adopting this style will bring freshness in review of literature. It will also reveal as to how the studies differ in their focus at varying spatial scales.

One additional point of caution will be in order here. Often the research students simply list a research entry without digging out its specific message. A simple listing of an entry, without taking a note of its core idea or findings or methodology, hardly serves any purpose.

56 Prefatory phase: the prelims

Research writing of a thesis or dissertation is not a stand-alone document. It is imperative to establish its links with the work of others; may it be a piece of literature, or a statement of theory, or an elaboration of a research method that matches or supplements or is incremental to the specific research being pursued. We need to draw on the relevant work of others on a 'when and as needed' basis (Wolcott 2009, 65–90).

References

Aspinall, Richard. 2010. "A Century of Physical Geography Research in the Annals." *Annals of the Association of American Geographers* 100 (5): 1049–1059.

Booth, Wayne C., Gregory G. Colomb, and Joseph M. Williams. 2008. *The Craft of Research*. 3rd ed. Chicago: University of Chicago Press.

Gregory, Derek, Ron Johnston, Geraldine Pratt, Michael Watts, and Sarah Whatmore. 2009. *The Dictionary of Human Geography*. 5th ed. Oxford: Wiley-Blackwell.

Hart, C. 1999. *Doing a Literature Review: Releasing the Social Science Research Imagination*. London: Sage.

Kneale, P.E. 1999. *Study Skills for Geography Students: A Practical Guide*. London: Arnold.

Kobayashi, Audrey. "People, Place, and Region: 100 Years of Human Geography in the Annals." *Annals of the Association of American Geographers* 100 (5): 1095–1106.

Thomas, David S.G., and Andrew Goudie. 2000. *The Dictionary of Physical Geography*. 3rd ed. Oxford: Blackwell.

Wolcott, Harry F. 2009. *Writing Up Qualitative Research*. 3rd ed. Thousand Oaks, CA: Sage.

PART III

Traversing the path

Data management

6

TYPOLOGY OF DATA

The process by which the required data are collected, validated, analysed or processed, presented and interpreted to meet the requirements of research is termed data management. It is meant to optimise the information resources. The intention is to raise a strong base for the written text. The research gets ongoing with data management, followed by writing of the thesis/dissertation/report and defence of the thesis at the viva voce.

All data are to be managed. This process has to follow four successive steps as listed below:

- i Data collection
- ii Data analysis
- iii Data representation
- iv Data interpretation

Data are series of measurements, observations, information and messages. Based on their form these can be quantitative and qualitative. Quantitative data are to be understood in the conventional sense of being in the nature of statistics. Research students are already familiar with it. Qualitative data are, however, a fresh concept and call for elaboration.

Qualitative data

The very word *qualitative* suggests a thrust on the qualities of an object. In it, the phenomena, processes and meanings are not measured quantitatively but considered only in terms of their qualitative attributes. Inherent diversity apart, qualitative research comprises a set of interpretative, material practices. Following qualitative approach, the researcher is obliged to observe things in their 'natural habitat',

60 Traversing the path: data management

watching, listening, talking, recording etc. The phenomena are interpreted in the language and expressions of the people who bring meaning to them (Denzin and Lincoln 2011, 3).

A host of methods, such as field research, case study, grounded theory, ethnography, observation, participatory action research, interviews, focus group discussions, conversations, photographs, recordings and memos to self and archival research, are included in the category 'qualitative'. There is no distinct set of methods or practices in this context. The ensuing discussion elaborates on this.

Qualitative is an approach to knowledge that emphasises interpretation and understanding, particularly of daily life experiences. From its roots in the 1920s and 1930s in the Chicago School of Sociology and of Anthropology, the goal of qualitative research originally was to study the other beyond the known and quantifiable (Denzin and Lincoln 2000). There has been an increased use of qualitative methods in research since the 1980s as a result of 'qualitative turn' in human geography in association with radical, humanistic and feminist thrusts in the discipline.

The last few decades have witnessed several developments in favour of qualitative research in particular. The Association of American Geographers constituted a Qualitative Research Specialty Group on this theme. Expressly qualitative contributions as books, edited volumes and articles in journals of the discipline emerged (Hay 2010). *Progress in Human Geography* published reports on qualitative geography (Crang 2002, 2003, 2005). In geography, the book *Qualitative Methods in Human Geography*, authored by Eyles and Smith (1988), is the first one to explicitly focus on this topic.

Contemporary geographers employ diverse range of qualitative methods to capture the contextual or positioned nature of knowledge, values, feelings and practices. These methods of inquiry are meant to capture subjective spatial experiences in terms of their interpretations and underlying messages. Studies on topophilia 'or love for one's native place' is one such case. All this requires geographers to leave the laboratory and study people 'in situ' to the extent possible. This helps to validate our own perspectives and also the meanings which people attach to places of their interest. It amounts to actively engaging ourselves with the experiential world of our study.

In basic terms, qualitative data are usually unstructured, non-numerical. They comprise of words (in natural language), sounds and sensations. Such data are descriptive in nature, but their depth lends great insights into human mind. Since these record qualities rather than quantities, they are called qualitative data. This in no way means that they are more or less valuable than quantitative data.

Quantitative data

Quantitative data, on the contrary, are generally structured. These include quantifiable empirical facts amenable to analysis using numerical (statistical) techniques.

Typology of data **61**

Census figures (population), economic data (volume of international trade), climatic data (rainfall) and all such measurements are examples of quantitative data. These data must be understood and interpreted in relation to a particular subject matter and its specific context (Van Belle 2002, 4).

A distinction is often made between quantitative and qualitative data. The points of comparison are presented in the form of a chart shown in Table 6.1. Essentially, the approach to quantitative is scientific or objective; in qualitative it is subjective, naturalistic, humanistic and interpretative in nature.

The scientific method is based on positivist approach, and quantification is its central tenet. By comparison, the humanistic effort is based on the methods of

TABLE 6.1 Salient features of qualitative and quantitative methodologies: a comparative view

Qualitative	Quantitative
Humanistic, interpretative tradition	Scientific method
Subjective, multiple realities	Objective, objective reality
Ideographic	Nomothetic
Inductive	Deductive
Data are words or text, pictures and sounds	Data are numeric
Researcher as instrument skilled at observing, recording and coding	Data gathered by scientific equipment or questionnaires
Micro, small sample sizes	Macro, large sample sizes
Specificity	Generality
Research design emerges during study	Research designs are fixed before data collection
Incidence and frequency	Concepts and categories
Favours fieldwork, interviews, observations and documents	Favours the laboratory, standardised tests and instruments
Interpretative approach	Functionalist/statistical/positivistic
Idealistic	Realistic
Description of process through words, texts and observations	Exact measurements and data collection
Individuals	Populations
Extrapolation	Generalises from a sample to the population
Natural	Artificial
Conducts analysis along with data collection	Conducts analysis after data collection
Analysis seeks insight and metaphor	Analysis yields a significance level
Performs data analysis in a creative, iterative, nonlinear mode	Performs data analysis in a prescribed, standardised, linear fashion
Meaning and understanding from patterns	Explanation and prediction, tests hypotheses
Report writing uses revealing language and a personal voice	Report writing follows a standardised format

Source: Based and modified from Rob Kitchin, and Nicholas J. Tate. 2000. *Conducting Research into Human Geography: Theory, Methodology and Practice*. Harlow, England: Prentice Hall, p. 40.

62 Traversing the path: data management

humanities. Understanding meaning, value and human significance of life events (Buttimer 1979), as also attitudes, impressions and subjective relations of people to places, the 'sense of place' (Johnston and Sidaway 2004, 208), falls in the domain of humanistic geography. This is to bypass the positivistic approach. Following Bird (1993, 45) the humanistic approach may be characterised as follows:

- What exists is what people observe to exist (its ontological basis).
- Individuals create a world of meanings and knowledge that is subjectively obtained (its epistemological basis).
- Methodology will then be interpretative, with emphasis on individuals and subjectivity rather than replicability.

In addition we shall always need to use hermeneutic or interpretative methods in geography. Even map is not only a representation but also an interpretation of reality depending upon the purpose for which a map was prepared (Dorling and Fairbairn 1997). Initially developed for the exegesis (critical explanation or interpretation of biblical texts) the concept of hermeneutics was further extended by Dilthey (Rose 1980, 1981) to include all studies which involve scrutinising an author's intentions when evaluating a text. This involves, what Dilthey termed **verstehen** or interpretative understanding, putting oneself into another person's shoes and trying to discover human intentionality. **Verstehen**, a German word, stands for something between understanding and empathy (Dilthey and Jameson 1972).

A sharp difference between the quantitative and qualitative data is highlighted in terms of methods involved. In quantitative methods, a prior choice is made of concepts to study, variables to analyse and techniques to use for measuring values of those variables. Qualitative methods, in contrast, are open-ended and adopt less prior-structured techniques of data collection. The two methods, quantitative and qualitative, are not opposites of each other. They are complementary to each other in capturing the reality. While quantitative data measure the objective dimension of any object, qualitative data record the subjective dimension of its human element. This completes the whole picture.

Geographers today are rather increasingly using multiple methods, quantitative and qualitative, apart from cartographic. They draw data from a variety of sources and use scientific, multiple methods for analysis taking into account the context (Clifford and Valentine 2003). They appreciate the research value of both quantitative and qualitative methods and go for them individually or collectively as per requirements of a research exercise. The latter is also known as triangulation.

The term 'triangulation' derives from land surveying, where it refers to the use of a series of triangles to map out an area. Perhaps the most prevalent attempts to use triangulation have been reflected in efforts to combine fieldwork and survey methods. Another example is the use of two research methods together, such as a questionnaire and observation. In all such cases, the two methods individually constitute the two vertices of the triangle and their combination as the third vertex, to justify triangulation.

Typology of data **63**

Patton (2001, 247) advocates the use of triangulation: a combination of both quantitative and qualitative methods. Triangulation maps out, or explain more wholly, the complexity and richness of any research issue by studying it from more than one viewpoint. It serves twin purpose of review and verification of the reliability of a particular research tool and the validation of the data collected. Mixed methods had emerged in the social and behavioural sciences as another methodological component in the 1980s (Tashakkori and Teddlie 2010). Its central premise is that such a combined approach provides a better understanding of research problems than either approach alone.

Spatial data

Geographers have professional interest in facts relating to character of a place or the quantity or quality of some phenomenon that occupies a place at a given time. It transpires that any fact to be geographic has to have three components: the event or occurrence, its character or the quantity or quality; its location, the specification of its place of occurrence; and the time at which the event was observed (Thomas 1964). Thus geographical data by their very definition are spatial in nature. These comprise of 'place' data, such as population of various cities in India; 'route' data, for example the amount of flow of water along a river; and 'space' data, for instance per hectare yield of rice in different districts of India. Point data can also be exemplified by the distribution of airports in India, line data by the volume of traffic flow on the national highways and area data by state/union territory-wise per capita income of India. Area distributions can be discrete or discontinuous, for example area under vegetable cultivation, or continuous, for example distribution of temperature or contours of topography.

In fact, points, lines and areas are the three data primitives of spatial entities (Burrough and McDowell 1998; Star and Estes 1990). Data could also refer to surfaces or volumes in three-dimensional space. The continuous phenomenon in space gives a field view. It is generally measured on the basis of sampling discrete entities such as locations in space.

Alternatively stated, a point feature occupies a single location. A linear feature connects at least two points. An area or polygon is a feature contained in a boundary. A collection of similar areal units or polygonal features takes the form of a region. The spatial features are described using 'formal spatial languages in geography' (Harvey 1969, 212). A surface feature may be defined as the three-dimensional representation of a point, line or area. For example, the line of a river becomes a channel, and the city represented as a point contains an area.

It must be understood that in reality every data are area data since a place or a transport line or an administrative unit all cover area, but are distinguished as point, line and area distributions because of the form in which these appear on the map. It all depends on the spatial scale on which any data are being represented. Spatial data has two expressions including location data, simply referring to where anything is, and attribute data, describing the characteristics of the place being referred to.

Spatial data are analysed using descriptive, exploratory and modelling techniques.

64 Traversing the path: data management

References

Bird, James H. 1993. The Changing Worlds of Geography: A Critical Guide to Concepts and Methods. 2nd ed. Oxford: Clarendon Press.

Burrough, P.A., and R.A. McDowell. 1998. *Principles of Geographical Information Systems*. Oxford: Oxford University Press.

Buttimer, A. 1979. "Reason, Rationality and Human Creativity." *Geogrsfiska Annaler* 61B: 43–49.

Clifford, Nicholas J., and Gill Valentine. 2003. "Getting Started in Geographical Research: How This Book Can Help." In *Key Methods in Geography*, edited by Nicholas J. Clifford, and Gill Valentine, 1–16. London: Sage.

Crang, Mike. 2002. "Qualitative Methods: The New Orthodoxy?" *Progress in Human Geography* 26 (5): 647–655.

———. 2003. "Qualitative Methods: Touchy, Feely, Look-See?" *Progress in Human Geography* 27 (4): 494–504.

———. 2005. "Qualitative Methods: There Is Nothing Outside the Text?" *Progress in Human Geography* 29 (2): 225–233.

Denzin, N.K., and Y.S. Lincoln. 2000. "Introduction: The Discipline and Practice of Qualitative Research." In Handbook of *Qualitative Research*, edited by N.K. Norman and Y.S. Lincoln, 1–28. 2nd ed. Thousand Oaks, CA: Sage.

———. eds. 2011. *The Sage Handbook of Qualitative Research*. 4th ed. Thousand Oaks, CA: Sage.

Dilthey, Wilhelm, and Frederic Jameson. 1972. "The Rise of Hermeneutics." *New Literary History* 3 (2): 229–244.

Dorling, D., and D. Fairbairn. 1997. *Mapping: Ways of Representing the World*. Longman: Harlow.

Eyles, J., and D.M. Smith. 1988. *Qualitative Methods in Human Geography*. Cambridge: Polity.

Harvey, D. 1969. *Explanation in Geography*. London: Edward Arnold.

Hay, I. 2010. *Qualitative Research Methods in Human Geography*. 3rd ed. South Melbourne, Australia: Oxford University Press.

Johnston, R.J., and J.D. Sidaway. 2004. *Geography and Geographers: Anglo-American Human Geography since 1945*. 6th ed. London: Arnold.

Patton, Michael Quinn. 2001. *Qualitative Evaluation and Research Methods*. 3rd ed. Thousand Oaks, CA: Sage.

Rose, C. 1980. "Human Geography as Text Interpretation." In *The Human Experience of Space and Place*, edited by A. Buttimer and D. Seamon, 123–134. London: Croom-Helm.

———. 1981. "Wilhelm Dilthey's Philosophy of Human Understanding." In *Geography, Ideology and Social Concern*, edited by D.R. Stoddart, 99–133. Oxford: Basil Blackwell.

Star, E., and J.E. Estes. 1990. *Geographical Information Systems: An Introduction*. Englewood Cliffs, NJ: Prentice Hall.

Tashakkori, Abbas, and Charles Teddlie, eds. 2010. *Sage Handbook of Mixed Methods in Social & Behavioral Research*. 2nd ed. (English). Los Angeles: Sage.

Thomas, Edwin N. 1964. "Some Comments About a Structure of Geography with Particular Reference to Geographic Facts, Spatial Distribution and Areal Association." In *Selected Classroom Experiences: High School Geography Projects*, edited by C.F. Kohn, 44–60. Geographic Education Series No. 4. Illinois: National Council for Geographic Education.

Van Belle, G. 2002. *Statistical Rules of Thumb*. New York: John Wiley & Sons.

7

DATA COLLECTION

Data collection may be defined as the process of data generation (primary), gathering (secondary) and gleaning (tertiary) through observation, field survey, library visits, archives search, laboratory work, questionnaires, interviews, written source documents, internet access and so on. Data can be in the form of statistics, statements, photographs, text and sketches. The entire exercise has three components, as indicated below:

- Generation of primary data
- Gathering of secondary data
- Gleaning of tertiary data

One way to characterise the data is to base it on the source of data – primary, secondary and tertiary. The data are primary when it is collected personally for the purpose of a specific study. A geographer, who interviews people living in slums about the place of their origin and reason of migration, is an example of this kind. Secondary data are collected for some other purpose, by someone other than you. An example would be a geographer who uses data made available by organisations like Census of India and Centre for Monitoring Indian Economy. Tertiary data compiled from primary and/or secondary sources. *Bibliographic Guide to Population Geography* is one such example; *Geo Abstracts* is another.

The process of data collection is directly linked with the research objective, question and hypothesis. Research problem should guide what kind of data are required. It should not be the other way round, which normally is the case wherein research topic is guided by some readily available data. This is not to deny that at times data can throw up a research question.

66 Traversing the path: data management

Generation of primary data

Primary data generation is considered as of prime importance in authentic research. This is not to suggest that secondary data are of secondary importance. Both have their own respective value. One should undertake primary data generation where possible and supplement it with secondary data wherever relevant to strengthen the argument of research. Or primary data may be collected at the micro-level to confirm the validity of a generalisation based on analysis of secondary data at the macro-level.

Generation of primary data is more context dependent, meaning thereby it is directly linked to a research need. Besides one knows exactly how the data were produced. The main decision involves choice between producing qualitative or quantitative data, or a mix of the two.

For our purpose we will define primary data as the one that researcher collects by oneself. The measurements that one takes of stream velocity in the field, questionnaires that one administers to respondents on their place preference and measurements of soil samples that one picks up from different fields in a laboratory are all examples of primary data. Primary data in geography are generated through various methods such as fieldwork, laboratory work and surveys, to mention the more common ones.

Fieldwork

It occupies a significant place in academic and professional geography. A geographer's primary training should come, wherever possible, by doing fieldwork (Sauer 1956, 296). It leads to experiential learning. Several other scholars (Bunge 1979, 171; Chuan and Poh 2000; Harris 2001, 329; Hope 2009, 175; Kwan 2000; Ostuni 2000) have lent their support to this point of view.

Fieldwork is conducted to take physical measurements, scan the landscape through instruments or sketches and conduct interviews to generate statistical data. It is also used for collection of qualitative data such as making observations and taking field notes. It is something that connects physical and human geography (Stoddart and Adams 2004, 46). The field in fieldwork is all-encompassing. It is 'anywhere and everywhere, far and near, in material and virtual spaces, within places and also between them'.

Today fieldwork forms a combination of traditional style, skills and concepts with focused application of new technology that includes Global Positioning System (GPS) and GIS, visual and sound recording and communication technologies, such as Twitter. Hence field observations are taken not only in physical area but also in virtual area situations with the help of internet. There is an increasing tendency towards laptop geography, a new *avatar* of armchair geography. Taking the case of virtual space, Dodge and Kitchin (2006) describe 'fieldwork' on the internet as a two-way process. It serves as a means for accessing information and also as an object of inquiry in its own right. Here is an illustration. Focusing his research on geographically dispersed networks of Tibet nationals and activists on internet, Davies (2009) redefined 'the field' as a network of connected places rather than a single physical place.

Gold *et al.* (1991, 22–23) identify three traditions of approaches to fieldwork. These have overlapped and may not be mutually exclusive: (i) the exploration tradition, which exhibits the desire to go and see new places; (ii) the regional tradition, which examines the interrelationship of physical and human phenomena in areas; and (iii) observation and empiricism, which emphasises active learning through fieldwork. The current explosive popularity of geotechnologies, such as remote sensing and GIS, has ushered in a new mode of conducting fieldwork for verification of what has been identified with the help of remote sensing.

Observation, landscape reading, archival fieldwork, laboratory work and survey are different methods of conducting fieldwork (Phillips and Johns 2012). Both qualitative and quantitative data are generated in the process. A brief note to this effect follows.

Observation method: Geography has a rich tradition of observation as a data-generating tool. The purpose of using observational method is to take measurements in the field and to have a feel of the area. It is the only method available for description of the landscapes and for covering inadequacy of questionnaire or other methods. Scientific observation is something more than just looking. It is a technique involving systematically planned field measurements guided by a research design to address a specific set of research objectives. It could be checked for validity and reliability.

Observations can be *unstructured* by way of simply taking notes on the features in the area or *structured* where observations are carried out with the help of already drafted checklists. Help of cameras with laser technology is generally taken for making observations. The researcher has to be competent in the use of technology and a keen observer as well.

Observation method is more typical of research in physical geography in which case it includes field observations, physical experiments and field verification of works done in remote sensing and GIS environment. All this requires background knowledge about the specific use of technologies for generation of data about the phenomena under study. Physical geographers measure the phenomena in the field or take samples of the material, such as soil and water, from the field and analyse them back in their lab. The data collected typically focus on the form and function of earth's surface (geomorphology), biological organisms (ecology and biogeography), atmosphere (climatology) or hydrosphere (hydrology), as such (Rhoads and Wilson 2010, 35).

Human Geography also makes use of observation method. Herein the observations get influenced by the spatial–analytical perspective of the research student. A student hailing from the traditional school of positivistic thinking would take a sample of observations which fit the research purpose, for example, the photographs of buildings representing different phases of history or social groups. A radical geographer will be more interested in observations which expose spatial

68 Traversing the path: data management

patterns of injustice, for example the palatial buildings adjoining slums. A humanistic geographer will focus on features which are products of peoples' beliefs, attitudes and perceptions, such as places of worship, statues in public places and particular colours in coating of buildings. All such observations are taken with an insightful mind and quality technology.

Then we have a category of *participant observation*. As the name suggests, participant observation has two components: observing and participating. It refers to being a part of what is being observed. Laurier (2003, 133), a geographer who has used this technique in a study of café culture, explains that in order to understand people or communities, a participant observer has to spend time, being, living or working with them. Crang (1994) demonstrates another instance of participant observation by viewing how a waiter's work gets done. This was done by having a close eye on interaction between a waiter and clients at a café. Likewise a researcher may make a note of sites where families tend to relax at a picnic spot. Participant observation is a method that requires skill to negotiate access and manage relationships.

Participant observation is a mixing-in methodology in geography. Its style is to keep as close as possible spatially to the object under study. Hence it is quite different from methodologies that lay emphasis on distance and objectivity. This approach is not formal and structured. Rather it makes the researcher to go through all the stages that arise out of the setting and behaviour of the object under investigation. This technique can be applied to such apparently 'simple' spatial phenomena as people worshipping in a temple or shopping in a vegetable market or doing yoga in the open. In all such cases, the research is to provide a reading or explanation that describes them in revealing and appealing or exciting ways, in spatial terms.

Participatory action is still another type of observation. Under its umbrella, it covers a number of research forms explicitly oriented towards social transformation. It is a 'research "with" rather than "on" people' (Heron and Reason 2006, 144). Through this method, which is common in critical geography, we try to make research directly relevant to lives of ordinary people. A participatory action approach raises the questions of what geography is for, who benefits from it and in what ways, and what could, or should, be done by geographers to engage actively with local and global issues of social, economic and environmental justice – to 'effect meaningful change' (Heron and Reason 2006, 227). These are questions that all of us within the discipline of geography, whether we are teachers, researchers or students, would do well to consider. Here the focus is not simply on describing or analysing social realities but on changing it (Pratt 2000).

Kindon, Pain, and Kesby (2007) have taken a position that participatory action fieldwork is not just a method or toolkit, but an approach to centre stage those people who lie on the margins of society, economy and culture.

Young and Barrett (2001) used participatory action research methods to explore perceptions and experiences of street children in Kampala. For their research, they gave disposable cameras to the children and asked them to take pictures of the places that were important to them. The intention was to have a deeper understanding of a place, community or situation through the perspective of those who live in them. Put differently, this is an 'outsiders' endeavour to see the world from the angle of 'insiders'. This process may require hiding of identity on the part of the researcher. This is to avoid making the target group of study conscious of his or her presence so that they continue behaving in their normal way. This is not to deny that the researcher's observation may be more acute than an insider's less focused curiosity, dulled by routine observation and habitual experience (Burgess and Jackson 1992, 153).

Landscape reading: It involves describing and interpreting landscapes. This can be done by observing the landscape directly and also by collecting available documentary material of all sorts, including travel accounts, old photographs and newspaper reporting. The whole exercise takes place in stages. The first stage involves personal observations and collection of available documentary material. The next stage involves taking of photographs, making of sketches, drawing of paintings and recording of voices of birds, animals and people and so on. Final stage involves rendering a geographic orientation to all this material. The use of landscape paintings as a form of geographical data was pioneered by Cosgrove (1984). Subsequently, Daniels (1993) made use of geographical images in tracing the evolutionary progress of capitalism and nationalism in Europe and the United States. Such are the innovations in production of geographic knowledge through a variety of sources of primary data.

Archival visit: Fieldwork is not only related to visible, surviving landscape; it could also be archival. The documents, which may be statistical, cartographic, pictorial, letters, newspaper reports, written documents, diaries and so on, provide clue to human–environment relations, places and landscapes. Such archival material produces an ever more developing interaction between the scholar and the documents, and causes an ingenious, personal engagement with the past (Harris 2001, 333).

Laboratory work: Not all primary data need be collected in the field. For some projects the data collection can be done largely or wholly in a laboratory. In other instances, laboratory work will be combined with fieldwork as a part of data collection. A research student may have collected soil samples in the field but these require physical and chemical analysis in the laboratory. Take the example of a comparative study of deposits on two river terraces (Viles 2003, 225). If one is planning to do laboratory work on samples collected in the field, then one should consider the number, size and nature of samples required. In many areas of physical geography, it is common to see publications based on laboratory experiments (Dunkerley 2003; Harris, Davies, and Rea 2003). In GIS-based research, field verification is an essential input.

Experimentation is another type of laboratory work which can complement field studies. It is a very useful technique for process studies in physical geography. One can simulate the glacial processes in a laboratory and see how different landform features take shape under controlled conditions. This can lead to a better understanding of the genesis of such features in the actual world.

Surveys

A survey is a process of collecting data or information. Research students of geography, as of social sciences in general, are familiar with this mode of activity. It is to be carried out in a well-organised manner.

Surveys are powerful means for generating data. They are used for exploratory purposes, descriptive reporting and hypothesis testing. Large-scale surveys are carried out frequently by many public and private organisations or departments in various domains – be it surveys conducted by the Census of India, National Sample Survey Organisation or Operations Research Group. The Indian Naval Hydrographic Department assisted Hydrographic, Oceanographic and Coastal Zone Regulation Plan Surveys also deserve a mention.

Primary data, particularly in human geography, are generally generated by using survey tools, such as schedules, questionnaires and interviews. A schedule is a formalised way of listing information about a locality, community or household, among others. It is filled by the enumerator. The questionnaire is expected to be filled out by the respondent. A geographer's questionnaire would ensure that its queries are spatial in nature and appropriate to the place where it is to be circulated. An interview is a recording of what was discussed between the discussant and the respondent. Questionnaire data 'go wide', while interview data 'go deep' (Hammond and Wellington 2013, 141).

Traditionally the scientific instruments of surveying in geography have been the prismatic compass, plane table, theodolite, dumpy level, altimeter and others. Today, Global Positioning System (GPS) surveying holds a place of prominence. It is not bound by constraints such as line-of-sight visibility between survey stations. The stations can be deployed at greater distances from each other and can operate anywhere with a good view of the sky, rather than being confined to remote hilltops, as previously required. Being highly accurate, precise and cost-effective technology, GPS has eclipsed and will ultimately transcend the use of classical and conventional surveying instrumentation and techniques, such as triangulation, trilateration and traversing.

Land surveyors and mappers can carry GPS systems in backpacks or mount them on vehicles to allow rapid surveying. Some of these systems communicate wirelessly with reference receivers to deliver continuous, real-time, centimetre-level accuracy and unprecedented productivity gains. All of this is especially useful in surveying coasts and waterways where there are few land-based reference points.

Drone surveying and mapping is yet another spatial technology which is in increasing use. By its very nature, it is operationalised with the help of an unmanned aerial vehicle (UAV). This technology is particularly useful in research on large urban concentrations, disaster-affected localities and inaccessible areas. Sophisticated drones are equipped with cameras which provide geo-referenced photographs.

Nowadays, smartphones and computer tablets allow researchers to enter data, record field notes and document information using still images or video. New mobile devices equipped with applications for compasses and gyroscopes are used by students to conduct fieldwork. This is very much common in physical geography.

The new technologies are capable of capturing both the location and spatial context of a place. *Geotag, Twitter* and *Facebook* can also locate and map what is intended and within their reach. These are ubiquitous and in widespread popular usage.

When all is said and done, the traditional mode of surveying in interview-respondent style remains popular and universal. In geography, surveys have been used to capture the perceptions of people about the risk of natural hazards or the images of their mental maps of places. Surveys of source areas of migrants and reasons for movement to their destination place are typical in geography. Internal residential mobility or change of residence in cities has also been a subject of surveys. The list is unending.

The quality of a survey through a questionnaire depends on the merit of the questionnaire and the objectivity of the sampling design. A questionnaire is meant to generate data through a sample, which is representative of the population. The responses received are processed, and the results obtained are considered as applicable to the whole.

The process of conducting a survey through a questionnaire involves a resolution of a common set of issues: the questionnaire design, the mode of administering it and the sampling. Designing a viable questionnaire in terms of its content, question sequence and question wording is most critical. Then follows the decision about the mode of obtaining responses, such as a personal interview or by mail, by which the questionnaire will be administered. Finally, the issue of selecting the size and composition of the sample is to be resolved (McLafferty 2003, 88).

The questionnaire

A questionnaire is a meaningfully structured tool to obtain requisite information, not just an assemblage of a series of questions. It is to be differentiated from a *schedule*, which is an *inventory* of facts about something, for example Schedule 8 of the Constitution of India, which lists the official and regional languages of India; and a *form*, which is meant to elicit information for administrative purposes, for example an admission form. The purpose in each case is different.

An appropriate design of the questionnaire is critical since it generates data in tune with the goals of the research. Constituents of the questionnaire design are questionnaire format, its sequence, wording, length and response form. All these have to be well thought out to obtain a reliable and valid outcome apart from sustaining the interest of the respondent. Questions are to be framed in a manner that these draw genuine rather than superficial responses. These can be both descriptive and analytical in nature.

A basic requisite of the questionnaire format is that the sequence of the questions follows a logical order. This leads to a smooth flow from one topic to the next in order. Questions should be divided into appropriate sections. Each section should list related questions with a short heading describing its theme to puts things in perspective. This will make sure that respondents understand the purpose of the research. It is expected that they will give authentic answers to the questions of the survey.

72 Traversing the path: data management

Response format: A researcher must decide on the format of the question response. That is, whether to go for close-response questions or open-response questions. A discussion on the distinction between the two follows but here it suffices to add that close-response questions are frequently used in quantitative research while open-response questions are common in the case of qualitative research.

In close-response questions, a respondent is given a set of answers to a question and is expected to choose one of the listed alternatives. It may take different forms, such as multiple choice (the most appropriate one), scaling (on the scale of 1 to 10), semantic differential scaling (rating as very good, good, fair, bad, very bad), Likert scale (rating degree of agreement or disagreement, for instance strongly disagree, disagree, neither agree nor disagree, agree, strongly agree), ranking (1,2,3,4, . . .) and paired comparison ratings (number 2 and number 5 go with each other) and so on. For details on types of questionnaires using rating scales, you may read Kitchin and Tate (2000) and Montello and Sutton (2006).

Clear instructions should be given for answering close-response questions: for example, please circle one number; please tick one box per line. To reduce the effect of restricting the respondents to predefined answers, the options 'any other, please specify' 'no opinion' 'don't know' or 'not applicable' should be included where appropriate.

The responses to close-response questions are manageable to data entry, analysis and interpretation as they constitute a restricted set of categories. Equally true is the fact that such responses do not carry exact, precise and individual viewpoints that can be gleaned from open-response questions.

In the case of open-response questions, the respondent is not given a set of possible answers. Instead he or she is made to craft their own responses. Open-response questions allow adequate time and space for the respondent to share understanding, experience, opinion and interpretation as well as reaction to situations of geographical nature and socio-economic processes. Given that there is a possibility of a great multiplicity of answers for any one question, it can be hard to quantitatively analyse the results, requiring some form of content analysis. So open-response questions need to be carefully asked in a manner to create a distinct passageway for the respondent to follow, without actually suggesting responses; for example, which is the farthest place from your home town which you have visited ever (Payne 1951)?

Gilbert (1998) made use of close-response and open-response questions to analyse strategies for survival among poor working women and their use of place-based social networks. The close-response questions produced data on the demographic and household characteristics of the women, while the open-response questions presented a deep understanding into women's socio-spatial patterns of networking as coping strategies of life circumstances.

Overall, a survey based on a combination of open- and closed-response questions provides both qualitative and quantifiable information for writing. Advantages of open-response questions include obtaining answers in natural spontaneity, freedom of expression and opportunity to probe ideas or awareness. Close-response questions generate results that can produce statistical information which can easily be summarised and clearly presented in quick-look summaries. Questions in both cases should be designed in such a manner that variables can be generated that could be properly analysed.

Question content and sequence: It is to be ascertained that all questions are relevant. These ought to be closely related to the purpose of research and personal experience of the respondent. Above all, questions should be neutral or secular in nature, not favouring any particular region, religion or viewpoint.

Another important rule of preparing questionnaire involves question sequence. It is essential to begin by providing a brief statement on the purpose of the questionnaire. The respondent should also be detailed as to the time the questionnaire will take to complete and to the confidentiality of the responses. A questionnaire would begin by an introductory section which seeks details about the respondent. Such details are often turned into explanatory variables in analysis. Then follow the main sections of the questionnaire. The question sequence has to be clear, coherent and concise. Questions should be grouped into sections and ordered in a progressive manner. The different sections may be made to align with the various chapters of the text of the thesis. At the end always thank the respondent for the cooperation given.

Length and presentation are other two important aspects of the questionnaire. The basic rule is that the questionnaire should not be too long and include only the most needed questions. It effectively means limit questions to as few as possible. Every question should have a distinct, unambiguous role and function. Questions should create and sustain the interest of the respondent. These should be presented with appropriate spacing and boxing. Normally it should take less than ten minutes to complete a questionnaire.

Question wording: Each question wording should be clear and precise to achieve reliable and valid results. Reliability and validity are two essential virtues of a question. Reliability indicates the consistency of a question. It is the chance of obtaining the same result even if the question is reproduced in some other form. Validity refers to the capacity of question to capture what was intended (Oppenheim 1993). Short, straight, simple questions in line with the respondent's ability to understand them would help achieve reliability and validity.

Payne (1951) and de Vaus (2002, 97–99) focus on some general issues related with question wording. These list the avoidables. Below are some illustrations:

- Combining two questions into one: have you retrieved landslide information from newspapers and the internet?
- Asking a question which is already settled: do you think the backward regions in India should be given a preference in development?
- The question has a negative tone: should we delink the planning of cities and countryside from each other?
- The question hurts the sensitivity of the respondent: do you agree that all people in your state are lazy?

74 Traversing the path: data management

In all such cases, rephrase the question if it is unavoidable.

Form of responses: Questionnaires should contain clear directions to gather individual responses. The questionnaire has to be self-explanatory for self-administered surveys since these do not involve an interviewer. For ease of filling the questionnaire without assistance, the instructions for respondents must be written in a simple, clear, explicit and direct language. Frame questions in a way that these call for short answers, in a word or two or a number or a tick on the checklist. There are well-tested guiding principles for crafting and formatting interviewer-administered questionnaires (Fowler 2002).

It is always helpful to pre-test the questionnaire over a small number of respondents. This is called a pilot survey. Pre-testing often reveals flaws in the questionnaire of which the researcher was not aware. This helps in catching and solving unforeseen problems in the administration of the questionnaire. A geographic flavour is an essential attribute of a questionnaire in our discipline.

Administering the questionnaire: There are several strategies to carry out a questionnaire survey. Traditional methods include in-person interviews, drop and pick-up questionnaire surveys, postal surveys and telephone surveys. Advances in computer technology have facilitated questionnaire survey via email or internet. A questionnaire is filled by the researcher or the respondent.

Survey strategies are decided by practical considerations like nature of the questionnaire, cost and time constraints and desired level of quality of responses. Some utilise self-administered questionnaires, while others require an interviewer. Each survey strategy has distinct advantages and disadvantages, and the 'best' choice depends upon the purpose of the research.

There are two types of surveys – the census and sample survey. The former covers all items in a survey while the latter goes by representative part of the whole. Census of India is a census survey, while National Sample Survey Organisation collects data on the basis of a sample. One of the basic concerns in the conduct of a survey involves sampling.

Sampling

A statistical population, technically referred to as a universe, is a finite or infinite collection of objects whose characteristics we wish to study (Kendall and Buckland 1960). A geographical population, by analogy, is a collection of objects with some common geographical characterisation, such as villages in a district or cities in the country. A sample is the subset of a population or of geographical objects to which the questionnaire will be administered to represent the whole or the universe. Falling in between is the sampling frame constituted out of the statistical/geographical distribution or universe from which the sample is chosen. In some situations, the sampling frame may be the same size as the population or universe on which it is based.

Typically, a sample of size (n) is selected to represent the characteristics of a large population (N). Effective sampling requires that the universe is clearly defined, and the sample is most representative by way of capturing the variability in the population as closely as possible. While trying to understand the conditions of slums in Indian cities, we may find it difficult to cover all 468 of them in the country. Here we go for a sample of 47 cities or 10 per cent of all cities to represent the universe. Likewise, we may intend to examine the residential quality of individual households in a city of half-a-million households. Covering all households may be a task requiring many years of surveying. Here we may choose a sample of 1 per cent of the households, or 5000 households in all. The basic assumption is that a reasonable and judicious selection of a sample is good enough to provide an authentic picture of the whole. The variability is taken care of, for example, if the proportion of large, medium and small units in the sample is about the same as in the population. A reliable sample is expected to represent the share of various segments of a universe in the same proportion.

The purpose of a sample survey, evidently, is to save on time, cost and effort. It also allows for the construction of a more detailed questionnaire for an intensive investigation. Survey data are used to make inferences or construct generalisations for the universe. At times, sampling is unavoidable. A geomorphologist interested in the dynamics of freeze or thaw weathering may find it difficult to access all the slopes in a region, and there is no alternative to sampling. Sometimes a complete survey may not be necessary – for example, the recording of the temperature in a small homogeneous tract. Confining this recording to a few select places is good enough in this case.

Theoretical basis of sampling: The fact that a sample is in a position to provide an approximately accurate idea about the characteristics of the whole population is based on the operation of two laws: statistical regularity and inertia of large numbers. The law of 'statistical regularity' has been taken from the theory of probability in mathematics. It states that a group of objects picked up at random from a larger group (referred to as population) tends to possess the characteristics of the larger group. Probability is the relative frequency with which an event occurs or can occur in the long run. The law of 'inertia of large numbers' implies that larger samples are more representative of the reality than the smaller ones. It is, in fact, a corollary of the law of statistical regularity.

Sampling design: Once it is decided to collect data by sampling, we should carefully devise a sampling design. This involves five steps:

(i)   Definition of the population
(ii) Construction of a sampling frame
(iii) Selection of the sampling method/technique
(iv) Fixation of the size of the sample
(v)   Conduct of a pilot or an exploratory survey

(i) *Definition of the population*: In the context of sampling, population means all the objects or the entire set of entities of interest out of which we are going to choose the sample. Here population carries a different meaning from the one we commonly understand. If our study proposes to go for a sample of houses in

76 Traversing the path: data management

a village for investigation, then all the houses in the village become population or universe for our purpose. At times, it becomes difficult to precisely define the population. If some houses in the village are lying vacant for years, should these be a part of the population or not. Here the researcher is expected to take an appropriate decision, with justification.

It is necessary that the sample is truly representative and is seen to be without bias. Representativeness is the degree to which the smaller set resembles the larger set (Montello and Sutton 2006, 144). Sampling representativeness is more critical for some research goals, such as exit polls. Methodological procedure rather than individual judgement of the sampler must be used to avoid bias. Truism is that since sampling is a model of reality and not the reality itself, sampling error is encountered, which measures the unavoidable distance of the model from the reality. The less the value, the more it is close to reality.

(ii) *Construction of a sampling frame*: Once we have defined the population, we must set up a sampling frame or population frame. Also known as a sources list, a sampling frame is an orderly list of all the objects out of which a sample is to be selected. An essential requisite of the sampling frame is to provide adequate representation to the population under study. Typical sampling frames are electoral lists, a numbered list of all households in the village and, most important from a geographical point of view, the map. In the case of the map, superimposition of a grid system can serve as the sampling frame. In another situation, a researcher might work on a particular vegetation type in a specific region of the Himalayas by driving along the major roads to make observations. The sampling frame in this case would comprise the vegetation types visible from all of the roads that the researcher might choose to drive along.

The sampling frame, therefore, depends on the way the researcher identifies and accesses potential cases for measurement. The nature of the frame is determined by the kind of population under study, the cost involved or the nature of the data to be collected. In a clustered or multi-stage design, sampling frames will be needed at each level of sample selection. Stratification can be used to ensure proportionate representation to each segment of a population. Multi-stage and clustered designs are usually used when the cost of data collection is high.

A sampling frame can either be spatial or non-spatial. In a spatial frame, fixation of the location of all the items is essential, as location is the fundamental base of the variability of individual observations. This is equally true of point, or line or area distributions. Each will call for its own specific sampling technique.

If, for example, one is sampling a map to determine the variation in the amount of rainfall in an area, or the extent of woodland in the map area or the relationship between vegetation and altitude in an area, one must ensure that all parts of the map are duly represented. This may be done in one of the following three ways:

(i) Point sampling, by a sample of grid intersections
(ii) Line sampling, by a sample of linear transects or cross-sections
(iii) Area sampling, by a sample of quadrats or grid squares

Sampling frames in these cases will be populations of all possible grid intersections, linear transects and quadrats on the map, respectively.

Besides spatial sampling frames, geographers frequently make use of non-spatial variety, where the locational variability of individual observations is not considered. The sampling frame is then simply the total collection of phenomena under consideration, such as all households in a village, all the slums in a town or all the shoppers in a shopping mall. Here it is important to capture the full range of variability within the population, but this can be done without reference to the location.

There is one other situation to consider. In a study of the climate in a region, we may target all places as our sampling framework, but data may be available for only those sites where meteorological stations are maintained. If we draw a sample of meteorological stations, we are not sampling our target population, but a given population. A target population is the set of all items relevant to a particular study while a select population consists of all the items for which data are available. It is desirable to have the target and select populations as nearly identical to each other as possible.

(iii) *Selection of sampling method/technique*: A researcher selects samples from the sampling frame following a proper sampling method or design. There are two main categories of sampling methods: probability (random) sampling and non-probability sampling. The former, codified in the 1930s by the Polish statistician, Jerzy Neyman, is more typical of quantitative research. The latter, the non-probability one, is more relevant to qualitative research.

Non-probability sample is one where the probability of a particular case being selected is unknown. The researcher cannot say in advance what would be exact chance of any particular case falling in the sample. There are around 16 different strategies for choosing a non-probability sample. The often used ones are purposive or judgemental sampling, convenience sampling, quota sampling, snowball sampling and self-selected sampling.

The *purposive sampling or judgemental sampling* is the most subjective sampling. Here the choice is based on the interviewer's personal knowledge and belief that the sample is representative of the whole. This method holds a great significance in geography in the spirit of 'case study' approach wherein the selection of a 'typical' or 'representative' unit is critical for an in-depth study. A typical city, a typical watershed, a typical village and so on tend to form the very basis of our understanding. The method is also frequently used in pilot surveys and qualitative research. If we have to select one village from each development block in a district, they could be the ones with the maximum number of households below poverty line.

Convenience sampling is based on ease or convenience in obtaining the sample. It is not uncommon to adopt a conveniently accessible village or town for a geographic study. Here expert judgment is not used to select a representative sample. No rigorous effort is involved.

In the *quota sampling*, we go by a pre-fixed number of respondents. In an exit poll, the first 50 respondents willing to participate may be adopted as a sample. The constituents of the sample may not be truly representative of the population. In

78 Traversing the path: data management

such a limited situation, where the universe is indefinite, this technique becomes necessary to adopt. It is easier and less expensive to work on and does not require construction of a sampling frame.

Snowballing is the process of 'using one contact to help you recruit another contact, who in turn can put you in touch with someone else' (Valentine 2005, 117). Initially, an appropriate contact that 'gets the ball rolling' is a must. This process is continued until the required number or a saturation point has been reached, in terms of the information being sought. Of course, the sampled cases are expected to meet the requirements of the research being conducted.

At times, a sample is *self-selected*. An announcement on the television often seeks viewers' response to a question. Here neither the sample frame nor the sample size is fixed. Those who care to respond form part of the sample.

The results from *non-probability* samples remain informed estimates. In some cases, as in exit polls, a large sample is initiated but is selectively processed to make it as representative of the population as possible. The stakes in the credibility of such surveys are very high.

In *probability sampling*, the size of the universe is known, and each element in the population has a chance of being selected through the use of a random selection procedure. Probabilistic samples are considered representative, and their error is calculable. These, however, require a known population to draw a sample frame.

Geographers use a variety of specific probability sampling methods, both spatial and non-spatial. The latter does not involve the issue of location. In geographic research, we are obliged to go by a spatial sampling technique. A range of sampling techniques is available in this case. These include random spatial sampling, systematic spatial sampling, stratified spatial sampling, stratified systematic spatial sampling, multistage spatial sampling and cluster sampling. All of these techniques are parallel to non-spatial techniques – random, systematic and stratified, and so on – with a necessary orientation to a locational bias. The nature of the data that is going to be sampled will suggest the method which is most appropriate in a particular case.

A brief description of spatial sampling techniques follows.

The most common is *simple spatial random sampling*. In this case, each member of the sampling frame has an equal chance of being selected into the sample. If 64 districts out of a total of 640 in India in 2011 are to be sampled, the first step would be to number all the districts in a serial order of 1 to 640. As a second step, go to a random number table, select any three digit column (because the serial number of a district in this case can go only up to three digits) and start following this column. The first number may emerge as 231, the second as 007, the third as 095 and so on until you reach the 64th number in this column. As a final step, look for the names of all the districts which coincide with these numbers in the primary list. All these districts will constitute the sample for the study we intend to carry out.

Here it may be understood that a random or chance spatial distribution is not without a pattern. The nearest neighbour statistic in a random distribution is always equal to one. A random distribution in itself is defined by three conditions: one, every object has a chance to get located anywhere in the area; two, every part of the area has an equal chance of getting an object; and three, the location of one object in the sample is not influenced by the location of other objects in the area.

With random sampling, a possible problem can arise when the distribution of items is highly uneven. Some parts of the study area may go unrepresented. Systematic spatial sampling is an answer to such situations.

In *systematic spatial sampling*, we number the items in a serial order. The first item in the sample is selected using random number tables. The subsequent items are selected systematically at a regular interval using this initially fixed number and the sampling interval. The 'sampling interval' is defined as the ratio of the size of the sampling frame to the size of the required sample. To select 64 districts from a sampling frame of 640 districts, the sampling interval is $640/64 = 10$. The first observation is randomly chosen from among the first ten items. Let us assume it is seven. Now we move systematically. The second district will be at number 17, the next one at 27 and so on until we reach the 64th district at number 637. All the districts identified in this manner will constitute the sample. Haining (1990) believes that systematic random sampling is more representative of the universe than the random sampling and even the stratified random sampling. It is more inclusive of diversity in any distribution.

Stratified spatial sampling involves partitioning or dividing the sampling frame into strata or segments and then sampling randomly within each. In a population made up of heterogeneous groups, it is far more efficient to use stratified sampling than simple random sampling, provided the strata identified are reasonably homogeneous within and heterogeneous among themselves. Stratification is a classification procedure which minimises within-group variance and maximises between-group variance. So it is often useful to precede a sampling design by some grouping procedure. An area under study could be stratified in terms of relief, caste groups, historical background or administrative arrangement. In his study of unemployment and underemployment in rural Punjab, Krishan (1986) used the technique of stratified sampling for a selection of sample villages for fieldwork. The state was taken as organised into 42 subdivisions, and from each subdivision, one village was chosen with the help of random number tables.

In stratified spatial sampling of districts in India, we may want to ensure that every state or union territory has at least one district in the sample. The size of the sample involved is 64 districts. As a first step, we randomly choose one district each in every union territory. There are 7 union territories with 21 districts in all. Now we are left with 619 districts in 29 states to contribute 57 districts to the sampling frame. We may distribute 57 districts among 29 states in proportion to the number of districts in each state. As a second step, we again go back to the three-digit column of the random number tables and start allocating districts to different states as per their entitlement in the list. In this process, we stop allocating districts to a state if the prescribed number has been attained. In the end, all the districts as identified in different states and union territories are made to constitute the sample.

In stratified spatial sampling, we may randomly select items proportionate to the size of the strata or opt for an equal number of items in each case. In case an equal

80 Traversing the path: data management

number of items from each stratum are taken, it helps in comparing the different stratified groups more effectively.

There may be a situation where we have to take into account two related variables — for example, altitude and vegetation. It would be desirable in this case to stratify the area first into bands of altitude and then choose a sample of the vegetation from each band. This will help in capturing the diversity of vegetation by altitude.

Geographers often opt for *multi-stage spatial sampling* wherein the areal extent of the sampling frame is divided into geographic areas of hierarchical order, such as states, districts and individual settlements. The sample is scattered to cover all the levels. Large-scale surveys, such as the National Family Health Survey, go by such a procedure. They are akin to stratified sampling, but based on geographic areas rather than thematic stratification variables.

The *multi-stage stratified spatial sampling* is resorted to when it is not possible to cover all the parts of an area under survey. Such a method is quite often adopted in the case of surveying cities. Herein a particular city is first divided into different kinds of localities, such as high income, middle income, low income and slums. Second, these are subjected to sampling within the group. Finally, the sample of households is taken from the sampled localities only.

Cluster spatial sampling is the one in which the primary sampling units are located in clusters. In the case of a city, for example, some representative localities are identified first, and within each, households are selected in clusters and not in scatter. This absolves the researcher from wandering all over in search of respondents. In spite of convenience and economy, cluster spatial sampling provides estimates that are less precise compared to that which could be obtained via simple or stratified random samples. The main reason for this loss is the inherent homogeneity of sampling units. These are physically located close to each other and tend to have similar characteristics. A special effort is to be made to generate heterogeneity. This may be done by sampling households by income level or occupation or caste within a cluster.

In *independent spatial sampling*, we choose a sample which as a group is displaying some special characteristics, such as fast-growing towns or laggard states. At times, geographers practise *non-independent sampling*. This is done when the area under study exhibits a great variability. That is why transects are placed at right-angle orientation across streams or rivers, up mountain sides rather than along them and so on (Montello and Sutton 2006, 150).

In physical geography, in contrast, sampling is very often done from entities, such as the terrestrial surface, soil layers, rivers and oceans and from the atmosphere, where elements such as temperature, precipitation and air pressure are continuously distributed in space. When sampling such continuously distributed phenomena, geographers divide the study area into mutually exclusive strata or different kinds of segments. From these strata, they obtain a sample using appropriate techniques. The choice will depend on the nature of spatial variability in the area. In case the area is relatively uniform, the simple random spatial sampling will do. If diversity is of high order, stratified spatial sampling becomes necessary. Geographers sampling from continuous fields must, therefore, answer questions about how many points are to be sampled, the locations from where these are to be picked and whether they should go in for interpolation.

There can be situations where geographers find anomalous situations more exciting, such as a limestone pocket in a volcanic topography. This peculiar feature itself becomes a sample. Sampling, in this case, is based on knowledge of the local area.

(iv) *Fixing the size of the sample*: While designing a sample, an important decision pertains to the size of the sample. The sample size required is a function of the criticality of what is being estimated. A sample for an opinion poll cannot be taken lightly. Another consideration involved is the size of the sampling frame itself. Issues of urgency, time available and resources at disposal are no less important.

Sample size is essentially a compromise between two competing considerations: benefits versus costs of a specific sample size. As a general rule of thumb, the larger the sample, the more confident we can be that the statistic derived from it will be similar to the parameters of the population. Larger samples, however, cost more money, time and effort.

A sample can be just one village or thousands of respondents for pollsters. In most cases, a sample of 3 to 10 per cent of items in the universe is considered good enough. It is desired that the mean and standard deviation of the sample should be proximate to those of the universe. Appropriate sample size depends essentially on the overall size of the universe. The election results projected through exit polls are based on contact with some thousands of voters' vis-à-vis hundreds of millions of voters in the country. The fact is that a small but carefully designed sample yields better results than a large sample with poor sampling design (Chatfield 1995).

(v) *Conduct of a pilot or exploratory survey*: The particular technique used for sampling must be rigorously defined and pretested by conducting a pilot survey. A pilot sample, or pre-test, is an additional sampling and data collection procedure in advance of the main data collection effort. A pre-test can help in revealing deficiencies for any of the following reasons: difficulty in locating the respondents; problems in questionnaire wording, question sequences or format; gaps in the questionnaire; or inadequately trained interviewers.

Then there are sampling errors which represent the departure of the mean and standard deviation of the sample from that of the universe. These decrease with an increase in sample size and are eliminated in census inquiry. The likelihood of these occurring is less when the population is homogeneous.

Sampling error has two components: sampling variance and sampling bias. Sampling variance is that error which results from the 'luck of the draw'. Herein a repetition of the sampling process results in different estimates. This can be controlled by sampling design factors, such as sample size, stratification and estimation procedures. Sampling bias can occur due to shortcomings in (i) construction of the questionnaire, (ii) expertise of the interviewer, (iii) behaviour of the respondent, (iv) mode of data collection and (v) a combination of any of these.

In practice, however, we do not take a number of samples but only one, and we do not know the population parameters but can only estimate them from our

82 Traversing the path: data management

one sample. By hypothesising sampling distributions based on a large number of imaginary samples, mathematicians have been able to provide us with a measure of the accuracy of parameter estimates based on a single real sample. This is based on a mathematical theorem called the *central limit theorem*, which states that the mean of a large number say, 30 or more, of independent random variables will be normally distributed about the population mean. If it is not, then our sample carries an error.

Nonsampling error is a catchall phrase that refers to all types of survey errors, other than the errors associated with sampling. These errors are linked to problems associated with measurement, nonresponse and data processing. Many people appear to think that nonsampling error applies only to research studies that use the survey method of data collection. The fact is that such errors are common to all types of social science research, be it qualitative or quantitative.

Some large-scale sample surveys

By way of illustration, here we provide a brief description of the methodology adopted for conducting three large-scale surveys in India. These include the Sample Registration System (SRS), the National Family Health Survey (NFHS) and the National Sample Survey Organisation (NSSO). The first focuses primarily on vital statistics, the second on health and the third on economy.

The Sample Registration System (SRS) in India is the largest demographic survey providing information on birth rate, death rate and infant mortality rate. The data are made available every six months. The 'SRS Statistical Report, 2016', based on the sample taken from Census 2011 gives a clue to the methodology of conducting this survey (www.censusindia.gov.in/vital_statistics/SRS_Reports__2016.html [accessed on 10.12.2018]).

For major states/union territory(ies) (population with ten million or more as per Census 2011), the estimates of population, births, deaths and infant deaths are generated for rural/urban areas separately at the level of natural divisions, which are contiguous administrative districts with distinct geographical and other natural characteristics. In 2016, the year for which the survey is based, the country had 85 natural divisions.

For smaller states, these estimates are generated for rural/urban areas separately at the state level.

Stratification in rural areas is done on the basis of the size of villages. Stratum I consists of villages having a population of less than 2000, and Stratum II contains villages with a population of 2000 or more. Smaller villages with a population of less than 200 were excluded from the sampling frame in such a manner that the total population of villages so excluded did not exceed 2 per cent of the total population of a state.

The villages within each size stratum were further categorised by the female literacy rate based on the Census 2011 data. Three equal size substrata were established. The sample villages within each substratum were selected at random with equal probability without replacement.

Two-stage stratification was applied in larger villages with a population of 2000 or more. Here each village was subdivided into two or more segments in a way that none of the segments cut across the Census Enumeration Blocks (CEBs), and the population of each segment formed by grouping the contiguous CEBs was approximately equal and did not exceed 2000. A frame of segments was then prepared, and the selection of segments was done at random at the second sampling stage for the SRS enumeration.

Urban areas were divided into four strata based on size classes. Stratum I included towns with a population of less than 1 lakh; Stratum II had towns/cities with a population of 1 lakh or more but less than 5 lakhs; Stratum III, had towns/cities with a population of 5 lakh or more; Stratum IV included four metro cities of Delhi, Mumbai, Chennai and Kolkata.

The sampling unit in an urban area is a CEB. The CEBs within each size stratum were ordered by the female literacy rate based on the Census 2011 data, and three equal size substrata were established. The sample CEB within each substratum was selected at random with equal probability. A simple random sample of these enumeration blocks was selected within each sub-stratum without replacement from each of the size classes of towns/cities in each state/union territory. In all, the number of sample units covered were 8779, 4909 and 3870 and the population covered included 7708, 5674 and 2033 (all in thousands) for the total rural and urban areas, respectively under the 2016 SRS survey.

The National Family Health Survey-4 (NFHS-4), 2015–16 sample was designed to provide estimates of all key health indicators at the national, state, and district levels for all 640 districts in India, as of the 2011 Census.

The NFHS-4 sample is a two-stage stratified sample with the 2011 Census serving as the sampling frame.

The first stage consists of identification of primary sampling units (PSUs). PSUs were clusters or small geographically defined areas: villages in rural areas and CEBs in urban areas. PSUs with fewer than 40 households were linked to the nearest PSU.

The second stage involved the selection of households in every selected rural and urban cluster, randomly selected through systematic sampling.

Each rural stratum had six approximately equal substrata created by crossing three substrata, each created on the basis of the estimated number of households in each village, and with two substrata, each created on the basis of the percentage of the population belonging to scheduled castes and scheduled tribes (SCs/STs). Within each explicit sampling stratum, PSUs were sorted according to the literacy rate of women age six plus years. The final samples of PSUs were selected with probability proportional to size (PPS).

In urban areas, CEB information was obtained from the Office of the Registrar General and Census Commissioner, New Delhi. CEBs were sorted according to the percentage of the SC/ST population in each CEB, and sample CEBs were selected with PPS sampling.

In every selected rural and urban PSU, a complete household mapping and listing operation was conducted prior to the main survey. Selected PSUs, each with an

84 Traversing the path: data management

estimated number of at least 300 households were segmented into approximately 100–150 households. Two of the segments were randomly selected for the survey using systematic sampling with probability proportional to segment size. Therefore, an NFHS-4 cluster is either a PSU or a segment of a PSU.

In the second stage, in every selected rural and urban cluster, 22 households were randomly selected through systematic sampling.

In all, 28,586 PSUs were selected across the country in NFHS-4, of which fieldwork was completed in 28,522 clusters (see for details file:///D:/sampling/NFHS%204%20Sampling.pdf).

The National Sample Survey Organisation (NSSO), in its 68th round (July 2011–June 2012), conducted surveys on 'household consumer expenditure' and 'employment and unemployment'. It had also adopted a stratified multi-stage design. For details of the surveys, see http://mospi.nic.in/sites/default/files/publi cation_reports/nss_report_554_31jan14.pdf (accessed on 22.04.2019).

Each district was divided into two strata: rural and urban. The villages, panchayat wards in the case of Kerala, as per the 2001 Census, consisted of the *First Stage Units (FSU)* in the rural sector and *Urban Frame Survey (UFS)* blocks in the urban sector.

The *Ultimate Stage Units (USU)* were the households in both sectors. In the case of large FSUs, one intermediate stage of sampling will be the selection of two hamlet groups (hgs)/sub-blocks (sbs) from each rural/urban FSU.

The rural and urban sectors are further sub-stratified. In the case of the rural sector, if 'r' is the sample size allocated for a rural stratum, then the number of sub-strata formed will be 'r/4'. The villages within a district, as per frame, will be first arranged in ascending order of population. Then sub-strata 1 to 'r/4' will be demar-cated in such a way that each sub-stratum will consist of a group of villages having more or less equal population.

In respect to the urban sector, if 'u' is the sample size for an urban stratum, then 'u/4' number of sub-strata will be formed. If u/4 is more than 1, implying the formation of two or more sub-strata, this will be done by first arranging the towns in ascending order of the total number of households in the town as per UFS phase 2007–12 and then arranging the four units of each town and blocks within each of the four units in ascending order of their numbers. From this arranged frame of UFS blocks of all the towns/million plus city of a stratum, the 'u/4' number of sub-strata will be formed in such a way that each sub-stratum will have a more or less equal number of households per UFS 2007–12.

The 68th round covered 8548 villages chosen for a state sample (which makes a sample of 1.4 per cent) and 7516 for a central sample (a sample of 1.3 per cent) of 593,615 inhabited villages in India.

Apart from questionnaire-based surveys, there are several other ways to collect primary data. Notable among these are interactive methods of data generation, such as interviews or focus group discussion, protocol analysis and online access. A brief note on each of these will be in order.

Other methods

Conducting interviews: Interview is defined as 'a conversation with a purpose' (Burgess 1984, 102). This approach is mutual and empathetic and allows the interviewee to share life experiences or set of ideas in one's own words. It is a dialogue or social interaction rather than an interrogation. A rich, detailed and multi-layered material is generated in this way (Burgess 1984). Interviews produce rich data on people's experiences, encounters, feelings, values, aspirations and opinions; in other words 'a deeper picture' than a questionnaire survey (Silverman 2001, 15). The contents of an interview are analysed by using a textual approach, which leans on words, messages and meanings, rather than statistics.

Interviewing has become one of the most popular methods for research in human geography (Cloke *et al.* 2004). This is in the nature of case study method. The intent is to learn about an individual's experience or thoughts on a specific topic as also how they make sense of their own lives (Valentine 2005, 111). This method is challenging in terms of locating the appropriate respondents and designing the interview format. Normally around 30 respondents are considered as a good enough number to yield material for an authentic research. For understanding the most critical development problems of a block, a researcher may first sample ten villages and interview three responsible persons, the *sarpanch*, a scheduled caste member of panchayat and a respected non-political person in each village.

Interviews can be structured or formal and unstructured or informal. In the structured interview the researcher works through a series of standardised questions, that is an interview schedule. All respondents are exposed to the same set of questions. The information gleaned from structured interviews is usually quantifiable. The unstructured or informal interview requires the researcher to have a list of discussion points that need to be taken up; there are no predetermined questions that have to be canvassed. This interview is more like an informal conversation. Open-ended questions are asked and the emphasis is on the respondents 'speaking for themselves'. Unstructured interviews produce qualitative data and use small samples. These are more typical of ethnographic research. A research on the group of displaced Kashmiri *pundits* settled in Delhi and subjected to an unstructured interview will fall in this category.

One increasingly popular technique is to conduct interviews on telephone. These are oral–verbal responses to oral–verbal stimuli and are best taped. Through an interview on telephone we can conduct a large-scale survey within a few hours of the occurrence of a traumatic event like an earthquake or a riot. There is an added advantage of relative anonymity in such interviews, this being the case of exit polls. This technique is advantageous when the respondents are highly scattered. One major disadvantage of telephonic interview is that people using telephone/mobile may not be representative of the total population, or they may be categorically reluctant to respond.

Focus group discussion: Carried out with a small group of respondents, optimally eight to ten, led by a moderator, this is a subtype of unstructured interviews. The

86 Traversing the path: data management

discussion develops into a group dynamics in an informal setting, especially on a point of debate, for example should Uttar Pradesh be carved into four states or not. It produces a good deal of qualitative data expressed in the words of the participants, effective in capturing the experiential knowledge of a group rather than of an individual (Hoggart, Lees, and Davies 2002, 214). Focus group discussion technique can be used as a part of an ethnographic study (Hay 2000). This could be in the form of a discussion on the mode of resettlement of displaced Kashmiri pandits in their native land of Kashmir. The question here is whether they should be settled in a separate township or within the existing Muslim localities.

Qualitative information gathered through a focus group discussion is utilised by way of a 'condensed summary' or content analysis, in which themes, words, and phrases are tracked and interpreted, or through narrative analysis, where the researcher reviews and synthesises stories told by the participants. A geographer would be interested in assessing the degree to which the discussion happened to be geographical in nature.

Focus group discussion, along with interviewing, participant observation and filmed or visual approach, are among the 43 different ways of conducting ethnographic research (Tesch 1990). Ethnographic methods, as a mix up of 'reading, doing and writing', are employed in humanistic or cultural geography (Cook and Crang 1995, 4). These are in contrast to the 'conventional read-then-do-then-write sequence' of other approaches.

Protocol analysis: It is a procedure in which the participants are made to think and share whatever is going within in their mind. A researcher may take a group of his or her friends to a hill station and ask them to share individually their response to the landscape around. This gives him insight into diversity of mental responses to the same geographical setting. Evidently, protocol analysis is also a subtype of unstructured interviews.

Online access: Researchers are also increasingly making use of internet, including the World Wide Web, to seek responses to a questionnaire in addition to plucking available data. The major benefits of this approach, whether emailing surveys or making people respond to a Web form, is its efficiency and low cost. Data entered on Web surveys are also available in a digital form; for example data regarding the number of emigrants from India to different countries of the world can be readily accessed online from the website of the Ministry of External Affairs, Government of India.

Gathering of secondary data

Secondary data are the ones created earlier by someone other than the researcher. These are collected for a general purpose unlike the primary one which are generated in a specific context and for a particular reason. Landsat imagery used by a geographer to study land use change in any city is an instance of this kind. Obviously, the imagery was not produced by that researcher, nor was it mainly intended for a land use change study specifically. The data which a geographer may produce out of Landsat imagery are in the nature of primary data while the Landsat imagery remains in the category of secondary data.

The fact that secondary data are not customised to the geographer's explicit research question influences the kind of research undertaken by geographers. Most often they gear their research to the available data. Usually such data are published for large spatial units, such as countries, subnational units and districts. Hence most geographic research happens to focus on macro- or meso-spatial scales. Secondary data for micro-spatial units are scanty and this constrains geographic studies at the local level. Fieldwork is an alternative but is deemed as expensive. Secondary data are certainly more economical than primary data in monetary terms besides saving on time and effort.

There are three main considerations that impel an access to the secondary data sources in research. First, the nature of some studies, as in historical geography, is such that one cannot do without an exclusive dependence on secondary sources. Second, secondary data enables parallel analysis of the same data by different scholars and one can make a comparison of varying findings arrived at. Finally, the dictates of economy are such that it induces a researcher to explore secondary sources of data, especially when a large area is to be covered by a study.

Today secondary data are used by both human and physical geographers. Its availability in digital form, in addition to in print, is of special value. Much of secondary data is now created, stored, analysed, represented and distributed digitally. The digital data can easily be analysed with various software packages that include statistical analytical programmes and GIS. Today, exploration of digital data through GIS is a new wave of research direction in geography. New geo-visualisation approaches allow for the recognition of spatial patterns in secondary data. Exploratory spatial data analysis (ESDA) involves advanced data displays that combine maps with graphs and tables. This helps the researcher to visually observe the data and identify new spatial patterns (MacEachren 1995; Longley *et al.* 2005).

In making use of secondary data, however, the researcher needs to be aware of its limitations. Such data tend to be dated. Census of India, for example, is conducted only after a gap of ten years. Also one cannot be very sure about the precision of such data since it has been collected by someone else. At times, the requisite secondary data for a specific research study is not available. Per capita income of different districts in India is hard to find. Above all, secondary data do not carry the personal feel of the researcher which primary data do.

Sources of quantitative secondary data

Governments make massive financial investment in collecting the data and therefore are eager to disseminate it. Volumes of government-generated data in India, whether in the form of Census of India or data sheets of different ministries, are today easily available to all via the internet, if not in printed form in all cases. Some government institutions like National Sample Survey Organisation and Reserve Bank of India bring out data on a regular basis. The technical documents of the government bodies, such as Reports of the Finance Commission, do contain very useful data. At the state level, *Statistical Abstracts* are published annually by the respective governments. At the village level, there are *Lal Kitabs* or Village Record books that provide a variety of unpublished data. National Informatics Centre of the Government of India likewise disseminates detailed village-wise data, in addition to data at the district, state and national levels.

The Centre for Monitoring Indian Economy is a famous private organisation that compiles and commercially makes available an immense array of data. Books and research journals are other sources of data in the form of tables. Several research articles based on primary data are also a source of data.

Secondary data thus encompass disparate information that originates in a variety of ways. These data vary greatly in terms of nature (quantitative or qualitative), type (official and unofficial), coverage (in spatial or temporal terms) and with reference to categories or classifications through which it is organised. Since the information is stored as a database, the qualitative information remains somewhat limited.

A research student is generally not aware of several sources of data and the spatial scales at which it is available. Hence it will be worthwhile to provide an extended note on the major sources of data. In a geographic spirit, these data sources are being described at international, all India, subnational or state and local levels. Here it will not be enough to give an idea of only the kind of data each source makes available but also to tell the hierarchical levels of spatial scale for which data have been provided. For a geographer, this kind of knowledge is most essential.

At international level

Internet has enabled large amount of data of organisations like the United Nations, United Nations Habitat Center and World Bank to disseminate information of a large variety. UN data are made available via internet-based data service. Through a single entry point (http://data.un.org/), users have an easy reach to UN statistical databases. Data pertain to indicators of overall development, human development, population, economy, environment, defence, education, health, tourism and gender, among others. Such data are available by individual countries.

Country Data (http://data.un.org/countryData) enables different nations to share official development data on priority development indicators identified by their national statistical systems. These data are now shared with the global user community via Country Data. The data are based on specific country context. It enables succinct comparisons of development indicators between national and international estimates. Difference, if any that exists between national and international series, is mentioned. The reasons for these differences are fully explained. Users can hand pick data that suit their requirement. Data on a specific country, say for India, can be located on http://data.worldbank.org/country/india.

If one is searching for information on climate change, visit the website http://www.un.org/climatechange/publications/. The site provides further links to access various United Nations reports, documents, conventions and records on climate change. Examples of reports include 'Turn Down the Heat: Why a 4°C Warmer World Must be Avoided' (2012) and 'Special Report on Managing the Risks of Extreme Events and Disasters to Advance Climate Change Adaptation' (SREX) (2012).

The Climate Change Knowledge Portal (CCKP) of the World Bank group (http://sdwebx.worldbank.or/climateportal/) is where all the data, related information and world reports about climate change are available. It enables you to query, map, chart, compare and summarise key climate and climate-related information.

Some of the important UN publications that provide country-level data include *Demographic Year Book*, *Population and Vital Statistics Report* (quarterly), *Human Development Report* (annual) and *State of the World's Cities*, among others. Several international agencies, such as the Food and Agriculture Organization (FAO), International Labour Organization (ILO), United Nations Department of Economic and Social Affairs, United Nations Education, Social and Cultural Organization and World Health Organization bring out publications regularly. These are like FAO *Statistical Yearbooks*, *Year Book of Labour Statistics*, *Statistical Yearbook* and *World Health Statistics Annual*. The FAO provides information on world food and agriculture, ILO on economically active population, UNESCO on education, literacy and school attendance for different countries of the world and WHO on a variety of health parameters.

World Bank (http://data.worldbank.org/) website can be freely accessed for data on development parameters in countries around the globe. The open access to data is a great support to researchers. It enables access to some 7000 indicators with time series data for more than 200 countries for over 35 years; 'http://go.worldbank.org/CPZ0FF0FU' is a permanent URL for World Bank publications and reports. There are in addition country-specific websites. The website for India is http://www.worldbank.org/en/country/india. The World Bank also brings out an annual publication focusing on a specific theme. As an annexure, it carries a number of informative tables giving country-wise data.

Thus, at the international level, agencies such as the United Nations Development Programme or The World Bank and their associated organisations document data at the country level relating to different aspects of economy, society, governance and environment. These data are produced at regular intervals and made available through internet-based services or in electronic or print form.

At all-India level

Enormous amount of data are available in India covering myriad aspects of society, economy, polity and environment. These data are stored in databases of some sort – demographic characteristics, social attributes, economic activity, employment–unemployment, financial transactions, consumption patterns, consumer expenditure, voter turnout and voting pattern, housing and household amenities, climate etc. These are available in print or digital form and can be accessed. Such data are collected by government/quasi-government, corporate sector and institutions.

90 Traversing the path: data management

The secondary data are at different spatial scales, ranging from the country as a whole to the smallest level of hierarchy, such as *ward* in a town or an agricultural landholding in a village. Some data are in the form of full coverage while others are on sample basis. Several data are published, some unpublished, as will be detailed in ensuing discussion.

An obvious starting place for many research works is the websites of the various departments and organisations of the Government of India. A few minutes of browsing the web addresses shows that there is an enormous range of data available to a researcher without leaving the desk. Much of this information is free to access. The web address starts http://www. In India, 'india.gov.in', the National Portal of India, is an important site that provides useful link to other sites such as 'Districts of India'. The data are disaggregated by spatial scale, residence, gender and social groups.

Information in the form of reports, such as *Report of the National Committee on the Development of Backward Areas, State Development Reports* and *State Human Development Reports*, are also available. These reports also contain data related to economy, demography and social sector, among others. Such data are at both all-India and state levels.

The National Informatics Centre develops sites with the contents provided and maintained by various ministries, such as the Ministry of Rural Development, Government of India. Salient data on rural development can be accessed from http://rural.nic.in/sites/IDFC.asp. The Ministry of Home Affairs (http://mha.nic.in/) makes available information in the form of documents, reports and state-level data through their websites and related links. The website http://www.ndmindia.nic.in/ is the one providing data on national disaster management. A link to Central Water Commission (http://www.cwc.nic.in/) enables an independent access to information on water resources. Several other official portals, such as the Geological Survey of India (http://www.portal.gsi.gov.in/portal/page?), India Meteorological Department (http://www.imdpune.gov.in/) and Census of India (http://censusindia.gov.in/) provide access to a large variety of data and map products.

The Census of India yields extensive data on demographic situation of the country. The first census in India was carried out in 1872 but neither did it cover all parts of India nor was it confined to a uniform period. The first synchronous census over the whole of India was held in 1881. Thereafter, censuses have been held continually every tenth year. The population census is a Union Subject (Article 246). The Seventh Schedule of the Constitution of India lists it at serial number 69. The Census Act 1948, an instrument of Central legislation, forms the legal basis for conduct of censuses over the country. The state governments through their Directorates of Census Operations execute and engage in actual conduct of survey. The census data are brought out in different volumes or tables published at two levels: the Office of the Registrar General and Census Commissioner, India that publishes 'All-India' volumes detailing state-wise data; and Directorate of Census Operations of respective states that publish data pertaining to lower order administrative divisions, that is districts, *tahsils* and *blocks*. The data are aggregated at various

Data collection **91**

spatial scales that include states/union territories, districts, *tahsils/taluks/community development* (CD) blocks and villages/towns as well as their wards.

Census is the most important source of data for geographers since it provides, in temporal frame, attribute data for successive spatial scales ranging from the country as a whole to individual villages and towns. The data are collected and compiled by residence. Number of houses, households and population, sex composition, literacy, scheduled caste/tribe status and workers are the focus of primary abstract. Valuable information is made available at the household level on the housing stock, amenities and assets for India and all the states/union territories down to individual districts, sub-districts and towns. Special tables are brought out for data pertaining to scheduled castes and scheduled tribes. Census is the single most detailed source of data on religion and language. Migration data are presented for both the place of origin and place of destination on the basis of 'place of birth' and 'place of last residence' for individual states/union territories and districts within each. This information is not compiled or published at the level of towns and villages. This is to add that with the exception of the Census of India, all other sources provide data based on sample basis.

Geographers evince a special interest in maps. Many organisations have been since long engaged in bringing out maps in a variety of forms. The quality of maps and efficiency in production has improved considerably over time with the adoption of digital mapping system.

Survey of India set up in 1767 at Calcutta (present Kolkata) is the main source of map information working under the Department of Science and Technology. It has its headquarter at Dehradun. The organisation provides user-friendly reliable geo-spatial data and publishes a wide variety of maps – topographical maps (open series and defence series), general wall maps, plastic relief maps, state maps, tourist map series, outline maps for educational use etc. Thematic maps are prepared by National Atlas and Thematic Mapping Organisation.

Geological Survey of India set up in 1851 is another organisation involved in producing and disseminating geo-scientific data and maps in matters of earth science. The data are collected from various field and laboratory-based investigations.

Census of India is a large repository of mapping activities since 1872. Its Map Division prepares maps by administrative units at different spatial scales. Major shift in mapping census data took place in 1961 and later in 2001. The former saw the emergence of Census Atlas for India followed by its constituent states and union territories. Likewise, district and tahsil-level maps showing infrastructural facilities began to be prepared for District Census Handbooks. In 2001 another endeavour began to bring out 'map products' for Census of India using GIS technology. It led to generation of thematic maps based on Census data on an interactive basis.

Maps are prepared for use in both phases of the conduct of Census (pre-Census) and in data dissemination (post-Census). These are in the nature of administrative and thematic maps and atlases. Examples include The Indian Census Centenary Atlas, India Administrative Atlas 1872–2001 – A Historical Perspective, and Administrative Atlas of India and of its all states and union territories.

92 Traversing the path: data management

Beginning its journey as National Atlas Organisation in 1956 and renamed as National Atlas and Thematic Mapping Organisation in 1978 to work in thematic cartography and geographical research, the organisation is engaged in compilation of National Atlas of India, Atlases for different states of India and thematic maps and atlases.

Indian Meteorological Department working under the ambit of Ministry of Earth Sciences brings out weather maps.

All these government organisations charting out different map products have their own unique selling points.

Sample Registration System (SRS) initiated by the Office of the Registrar General, India provides information on vital parameters of fertility and mortality on a regular basis since 1971. Data on reliable estimates of birth rate and death rate are made available for rural and urban areas separately at the national and state/union territory levels. From 1990 onwards tabulations on additional items of demographic interest, such as mean age at effective marriage for females, maternal mortality rate and causes of death are also being published. Data are also being generated on sex ratio at birth for India and bigger states, to monitor the gender bias. The system of sample registration of births and deaths in India began in 1964–65 on a pilot basis and on full scale from 1969 to 1970.

National Sample Survey Organisation (NSSO), now known as the National Sample Survey Office, established in 1950 is presently functioning under the *Ministry of Statistics and Programme Implementation (MOSPI)*. It is a vital source of data on various themes namely, socio-economic, demographic, agricultural and industrial for Government of India and state governments, in particular, for development planning. It conducts surveys to collect data from households and enterprises in both rural and urban areas on a sample basis. Large-scale sample surveys are conducted on topics like employment and unemployment, household consumer expenditure, health and medical services and estimates of agricultural production in India.

NSSO regularly conducts socio-economic surveys on themes to be covered in different rounds – one year, two years, quinquennial surveys and remaining two years of open rounds decided on the basis of a ten-year time frame. The surveys are conducted on land and livestock holdings; debt and investment, social consumption (education and health care etc.); household consumer expenditure, employment and unemployment situation; non-agricultural enterprises, namely, manufacturing, trade and services in unorganised sector; and subjects of current/special interest on the demand of central ministries, state governments and research organisations are covered.

The surveys by the NSSO are conducted in all the states and union territories with the participation on an equal matching basis proportionate to their population. Andaman & Nicobar Islands, Dadra & Nagar Haveli, Chandigarh and Lakshadweep, interior villages of Nagaland situated beyond 5 km of the bus route and villages in Andaman & Nicobar Islands which remain inaccessible throughout the year do not form part of the survey. Data are collected through enquiry method, using the same methodology and schedules that are specially designed. At present, India is organised into 88 NSSO regions for the purpose of data collection.

Reserve Bank of India (www.rbi.org.in/) annually publishes *The Handbook of Statistics on the Indian Economy* containing data on financial and economic indicators. These are long historical time series data at All-India and State levels. Database on Indian Economy (DBIE) can be accessed online on the Reserve Bank's website (http://dbie.rbi.org.in). It is also available in print and electronic form containing data tables. The coverage of data in print version is available only for the latest time periods, while the electronic form provides copious time-series data.

Reserve Bank of India also publishes monthly, quarterly, annual bulletins, comprising data on various indicators. This database is categorised under three subheadings: (i) Current Statistics, (ii) Handbook of Statistics on Indian Economy and (iii) Database on Indian Economy. Within it, the data on Public Finance are listed under the three subheadings of Central and State Government Finance (combined), Central Government Finance and State Government Finance. The data series on major components of receipts and expenditure of all states combined are available since 1970.

Central Statistical Organisation (CSO), which functions under the purview of the Ministry of Statistics and Programme implementation (mospi.nic.in/), brings out some regular publications, such as the Annual Statistical Abstract, Annual Survey of Industries, Monthly Abstract of Statistics and Estimates of National Income, to list some. It also provides data on Indian economy, wherein state-wise public finance data are placed on the website. State-wise statistics related to climate change can also be retrieved from the website of the CSO.

Planning Commission of India, revamped since January 2015 as the National Institution for Transforming India (*NITI Aayog*), was set up by the Government of India in March 1950. The objective was to improve the quality of life of people through an efficient use of the country's resources, increase in production and creation of employment. *NITI Aayog*, constituted to serve as a think tank of the government, comprises of a Governing Council with the prime minister as the chairman. The Governing Council of this institution comprises of the chief ministers of all the states and constitutional heads of all union territories and other members. It is tasked to provide advice to the governments at the central and state levels on a number of policy issues of strategic and technical nature confronting the nation. A variety of data are made available by it under the title: Data and Statistics, which is further categorised as Central, State and Non-Governmental Organisations (NGO) data tables. Data tables cover Indian economy, including public finance; social sector including health and family welfare, education and drinking water; state plans; world economy, and the census-based demographics.

Finance Commission of India is a constitutional body formed under Article 280 of the Indian Constitution. It recommends the devolution of non-plan funds from the central government to the state governments. These recommendations are finalised by a group of members, under a chairperson, duly appointed by the Government of India, after every five years. The reports of the Finance Commission carry

94 Traversing the path: data management

useful data by states in the form of tables. Recently the recommendations of the 14th Finance Commission of India have been accepted by the Union Government.

Indian Public Finance Statistics is an annual publication of the Economic Division of the Department of Economic Affairs, Ministry of Finance. It provides a detailed overview of the budgetary transactions of the central and state governments. State-level data on budgetary transactions, domestic savings and investment, net domestic product of states and their tax revenue are also made available. The reports of this institution, thus, contain a variety of useful data at the state level.

The Economic Division of the Department of Economic Affairs in the Ministry of Finance also prepares an Economic Survey that is presented by the Finance Minister one day before the announcement of the Annual Budget. A similar procedure is carried out at the level of different states. A much-awaited document every year, the Economic Survey focuses on the government's performance, programmes, policies and prospects. It makes an overall review of the development scenario in the closing year. It reviews the performance of the major development programmes, focuses on the policy initiatives of the government and sets forth short- to medium-term prospects of the economy. As an annexure to the Economic Survey document, a large number of statistical data covering all aspects of the economy at macro level as well as sectoral level are provided. These cover items like national income and production, budgetary transactions, monetary trends, prices, balance of payments, foreign trade, external assistance, human development indicators and employment. Most of these data are for the country as a whole.

National Family Health Survey (NFHS) is a large, multi-round household-level sample survey conducted throughout India, both at the national and the state levels. It is equivalent of the Demographic Health Surveys (DHS) conducted across many developing countries from time to time. The survey provides information on a wide spectrum of demographic attributes such as marriage and fertility, infant and child mortality, maternal and child health, reproductive health, nutritional status, the practice of family planning, utilisation and quality of health and family welfare, knowledge of HIV/AIDS among adults, women's empowerment and gender-based violence, tobacco use and alcohol consumption among adults and so on. For adults the data are for the age group 15–49 years. Four rounds of survey have been conducted since the first survey in 1992–93 with the twin purpose of providing essential data on health and family welfare to the government and other agencies for formulation of policies and programmes and update on emerging health and family welfare issues. NFHS-4 for the first time has produced district-level estimate data for the indicators at the state level. Besides generating data, it brings out technical reports at the national level and also for individual states.

The International Institute for Population Sciences (IIPS), Mumbai works as the nodal agency for the conduct of the survey with technical assistance on specific issues provided by ORC Macro (USA) and other organisations. NFHS is perhaps a fine example wherein sample survey on a large scale is undertaken with funding for different rounds being provided by international agencies besides the Government of India. See more at http://dhsprogram.com/publications/publication-OF31-Other-Fact-Sheets.cfm#sthash.Hf18xoq1.dpuf.

National Data Centre (NDC) is the central agency of all meteorological data in India. The data available for more than 125 years are quality-controlled and used by researchers of various institutions and universities for the purpose of weather prediction, aviation, shipping, agriculture and environmental studies.

Centre for Monitoring Indian Economy (CMIE) is a leading private business and economic database and research company. It has created a large integrated database of the Indian economy. Their products include Economic Outlook, Industry Outlook, Prowess, CapEx, Commodities, Consumer Pyramids and States of India. The customer range is equally wide – banks, financial markets, governments, corporates, business schools, academia. Its applications are in sales, management, appraisal, prospecting, finance and taxation, strategic planning, policy making, administration, real-life experiences in class-room teaching and research. The database and all research work are delivered to customers through subscription services.

The database 'States of India' provides a comprehensive data of all the states and union territories of India in time-series and official statistical documents from state governments for different years. The data are on demographic, economic, industrial and socio-economic indicators compiled from official documents and organised under broad categories. Themes on which the data are available are snapshot, state domestic product, inflation, banking, public finance, agriculture, energy, infrastructure, industry, investments, households, population, education, employment, health, crime, elections. Data on select indicators such as state domestic product, banking, agriculture, investments, households, population and demography and education are also provided for the district level. Evidently CMIE saves a researcher from visiting a large number of official sources of data but at a price which is quite high.

At state level

Government websites of different states provide access to documents, such as Statistical Abstracts, State Five Year Plans and Economic Surveys in electronic form. The Statistical Abstract is an annual publication providing data at the district level and at times up to block and municipality levels. It is a compendium of all varieties of data, much beyond economic and social sectors. These may cover the list of the members of legislative assembly, area and population of every district, temperature and rainfall figures and so on. The release of the State Statistical Abstract has to meet the approval of the state assembly at its Budget Session. It is the time when Economic Survey of the state is also presented. The Economic Survey gives a view of key socio-economic activities and achievements in different sectors of the state's economy. Annexures to the Economic Survey are a rich source of data, especially on state finances.

Under the provisions of the 73rd and 74th Constitutional Amendments, each state is required to constitute a State Finance Commission (SFC) every five years. These commissions are mandated to make recommendations on the sharing of the state revenue with the *panchayats* and municipalities, identifying taxes, duties, tolls, fees etc. which local bodies can levy, and suggest measures to improve their financial status. The reports brought out by State Finance Commissions carry data on public finance comprising development profile, fiscal scenario of state, financial position of local bodies, norms and standards of expenditure on public health services and district-wise allocation of funds for *panchayats* and municipalities.

At village level

For micro-level geographic studies, village-level data are the prime necessity. In this context, *Lal Kitab* or the village record book is a highly valuable document. This document is accompanied by a village map, showing the field and settlement boundaries and ownership status of the fields. The data contained in *Lal Kitab* pertain to land use, crops grown, mode of irrigation, agricultural implements and livestock, among other things. All such information is unpublished and has to be personally noted down by the researcher.

Scholars generally agree that technology and rapid telecommunications have brought a revolution in all aspects of data generation, collection and storage. Remote sensing, GIS and GPS have led to a decreased cost of data collection, availability of 'Big data', feasibility of data collection over larger areas and repeatedly through time and better systems of data organisation and storage. Advances in remote sensing capabilities and availability of inexpensive computing capabilities, sophisticated workstations, GIS and GPS have enhanced the ability to process the digital data. The availability and accessibility to large sets of spatial data will help to sustain the exploration of new geographically explicit questions (Lim *et al.* 2003; Wulder, Niemann, and Goodenough 2000). Not only this, data are increasingly being viewed as public properties. Spatial data browsers, such as Google Maps, are transforming how society understands spatial data (Miller 2006).

Sources of qualitative secondary data

Archival sources, both formal, such as historical inventories, and informal comprising transcripts, field notes, documentary evidence like diaries, memoirs, letters and paintings, photographs, comprise an important source of qualitative secondary data. Such data may have been recorded by those who actually witnessed an event, such as the survivors of *Bhuj* earthquake in Gujarat or of tsunami along the Tamil Nadu coast, or may have been generated by government employees and non-government volunteers who visited the site to make an assessment of the damage occurred. Such data remain secondary in nature because those who recorded these were not the ones to experience the event. They were, of course, witness to it. Information in public or private domain may be 'closed (unobtainable), restricted (special permission needed), open-archival (no permission needed but sources are archived at one site) and open-published (freely available)', so to say (Scott 1990).

Travelogues constitute a veritable source of qualitative data for geographers. Based on newspaper reports landslide studies have been conducted in geography. The novels of Thomas Hardy or Paulo Coelho can be tapped for a lot of geographical knowledge through their purposeful reading.

Secondary data: some issues

There are three issues of concern to contend with for geographers using secondary data. First, large-scale data collection practices do not stay consistent and researchers using them have no control over these changes. The definition of literacy or urban place or a worker in the Census of India, for example, has changed over time and this fact has to be reckoned with while making a long-term analysis of the Census data. Second, boundaries of spatial units, such as districts quite much change from one decade to another. There were 310 districts in India at the time of 1951 Census but by the 2011 Census their number had increased to 640. These changes are often not by way of subdividing or unifying the existing units but by merging parts of a number of existing units into fresh ones. This creates the problem of spatial adjustment of data over time, a situation that is technically described as Modifiable Areal Unit Problem (Wong 2004). Finally, in some cases the existing categories are modified or clubbed together, again leading to additional problems of comparison. The previous nine industrial categories of workers in Census of India were clubbed into four in the 1991 Census, and in the 2011 Census plantation workers were deemed as non-agricultural in place of earlier being categorised as agricultural workers. Such situations demand extra care in data adjustment and analysis.

There is then an ecological fallacy as well. It refers to the assumption that all individuals in a group share the average characteristics of that group. We should be careful in assuming that all people residing in a particular geographical area, such as a census district, have properties identical to the average for the area as a whole. At times, the nature of the spatial unit may not be suited to the variable under study. This is the case with migration data by districts as made available by the Census of India (Martin and Pavlovskaya 2010, 180–181). Such data by individual settlements would have carried real great relevance. Then there are situations when requisite data may not be available by the desired spatial units. Census of India data are provided by administrative units and not by parliamentary or state legislature constituencies. Adjustment of data pertaining to different spatial frameworks is a highly demanding task.

Above all, the researcher has to be aware of the fact that the scale at which data are presented and analysed can affect one's results. Analysing the urban data by states may show Maharashtra as a fairly urbanised state, but an analysis at district level may reveal the contrast between the highly urbanised western Maharashtra and predominantly rural eastern Maharashtra. Hence analysis at multiple spatial scales is necessary to obtain a realistic picture.

Gleaning of tertiary data

A tertiary source is a digest of primary and secondary sources. This may be in the form of dictionaries, encyclopaedias, bibliographies and reviews. Included herein is the information gathered from primary or secondary sources.

In research we may be required to access information documented in a journal, captured in a song, painting or poem, or placed in Facebook or shared through emails. Folk songs can be a source of data to infer how people in different parts of India highlight the geographical beauty of their regions or represent their contemporary society. If we conduct a research based upon all such information, this will amount to a use of a tertiary source. You have to learn the technique of processing such information as relevant to research in geography.

At times the distinction between primary, secondary and tertiary sources of data can be ambiguous. Data generated by a research student for a personal study are primary but if used by some other scholar they become secondary. An encyclopaedia is a tertiary source of information, but if adopted as an item of research in itself it becomes a primary source. It all depends on who produces the data and who uses it and in what form.

Hypothesis and data collection

Explanation is an essential task in any scientific study. The possible explanations have to be verified. This is achieved through formulation and testing of hypothesis. It provides a connection between what is known and what in relation is unknown.

Geography as a discipline is distinguished for its spatial perspective. This impels geographers to seek explanations with a spatial bearing. Hypotheses are central to this task. Some hypotheses necessitate generation of primary data while others depend upon already existing secondary data.

What is hypothesis?

In terms of its etymology, *hypothesis* is made up of two parts: 'hypo' (under) and 'tithenas' (to place). It is an underlying explanatory statement of relationships, the validity of which is to be tested. Braithwaite (1960, 2) asserts that a hypothesis is an empirical proposition, subject to its verification. In a similar vein, Johnston *et al.* (2000, 365) identifies hypothesis as a provisional and not firm statement that guides empirical work in several scientific inquiries. A hypothesis is, thus, a proposition whose truth or falsity is capable of being asserted (Harvey 1969, 100). In deductive research, hypothesis links theory and practice and is used to assess the truth of a theory.

Research proceeds by observing the patterns of relationship among variables being examined. An indication that there is some positive or negative relationship may be stated as a hypothesis. Hypotheses are therefore the core elements of structured empirical research programmes. Such an idea was strongly promoted during Quantitative Revolution in geography.

Whereas in positivism hypotheses are devised to be verified as validated or otherwise, in Critical Rationalism (proponent Karl Popper) they are designed to be falsified rather than validated. Science advances, it is argued, not by accumulating evidence of verified hypotheses but by discarding false hypotheses. This is the principle of falsification. The two other formulations of critical rationalist view of science are the principle of criticism which believes that scientific knowledge grows only when open to criticism, trial and error; and the principle of demarcation which stresses that the characteristic of scientific statements are that they can be empirically tested and refuted if they are false (Haines-Young and Petch 1986, 44). The logic of established ideas is to be questioned. This applies equally to human geography (Bird 1993) and physical geography (Haines-Young and Petch 1986).

Most simply stated, a hypothesis is a proposition put forth as an explanation for some fact under consideration. It is basically a potential answer to a question. Its formulation is significant in the research process, following the selection and definition of the research problem.

Hypothesis, in fact, serves a variety of purposes. It stimulates conceptualisation on the theme and takes us to its fundamentals. It equips the researcher with verified idea for making a confident statement. One critical role of a hypothesis lies in channelising the flow of research and keeping it within the defined limits. Finally, it provides a strong base for making some firm statement towards the end. It is advisable to place the results of a hypothesis testing as a tailpiece of the concluding remarks.

Formulation of hypothesis

There are no precise rules for formulating a hypothesis. The process is guided by the nature and requirements of the study. There are, of course, certain considerations that can be helpful. First, the researcher is expected to be well versed with an overall knowledge of what he or she is examining. Some prior understanding of explanatory variables vis-à-vis that item is expected. The message here is that the researcher is not to go with a blank mind while formulating a hypothesis. Second, hypothesis construction can follow either or both procedures of inductive and deductive reasoning. In inductive procedure, we assume an existing support of quantitative data; for example, males migrate over longer distances as compared to females. In deductive procedure, we go by an existing theory; for example Christaller's theory is not applicable to mountainous regions. The induction and deduction procedures are not antithetical of each other but complement each other. Finally, consultation with experts can help a research student in formulation of a meaningful hypothesis.

Statement of the hypothesis

A research hypothesis, for its proper estimation, must be stated in a testable form. The relationship that is to be validated or otherwise must be put in a clear, concise and logical manner. Also in geographic research a hypothesis must have a spatial flavour. 'Income and happiness are positively correlated with each other' is not strictly a geographical hypothesis but 'people in developed countries are happier than those in developing countries' is a hypothesis in geographic spirit.

A research hypothesis can be directional or non-directional. A directional hypothesis proclaims a direct relationship between two variables. There is a positive relationship between irrigation intensity and cropping intensity. It is a case of directional hypothesis. Non-directional hypothesis does not specify the nature of relationship. Poverty exists in both developed and backward regions. Here the direction of relationship is not specified.

Research hypotheses differ in their expression. They assume one of three forms: declarative, null and explanatory. Details are as follows.

Declarative hypothesis: Herein a researcher makes an assertive assessment about the outcome of the study. The statement 'urban areas carry far higher population densities than the rural' is a hypothesis in declarative form. This is also known as alternate hypothesis, which is an alternate to null hypothesis. It is symbolised as Ha.

Null hypothesis: This is the one 'suggesting that the difference between statistical samples does not imply a difference between populations' (*The Reader's Digest* and Oxford 1993, 1040). A 'null hypothesis' thus takes a negative position on a proposition. It is the starting point of most statistical tests and is called testing hypothesis. It is symbolised as Ho. That 'there is no significant difference in cost of living in different metropolitan cities of India' is an example of null hypothesis.

In hypothesis testing you generally proceed on the basis of null hypothesis keeping the declarative or alternative hypothesis as standby. Why is this so? The assumption is that if null hypothesis is validated, one starts doubting the sample chosen and restarts the whole process to confirm firmly the result obtained. This is not possible if we start with the alternative hypothesis. There is an additional advantage as well. Since every hypothesis is to be reasoned out beyond its statement, a null hypothesis compels the researcher to reflect on situations which contradict a popular impression. Therefore, the use of null hypothesis may at times seem a cumbersome procedure, but it ensures that a suitably impartial attitude is adopted.

Normally it is the research hypothesis that is transformed into a null hypothesis for verification. It also means that null hypothesis is reverse of research hypothesis. Null hypotheses do not exist in reality but are used to test research hypothesis. Its rejection would mean acceptance of research hypothesis.

Exploratory hypothesis: Many research problems in geography are still so little understood that it is difficult to advance a hypothesis which can be directly validated or otherwise. In such situations, an exploratory hypothesis can be framed in a question form. How is it that the British developed more hill stations in North India than in South India? It is a case of exploratory hypothesis. It indicates a kind of spatial relationship but does not have a ready answer. Exploratory hypotheses in fact reflect paucity of theory in geography. In case a theory was available to explain frequency of hill stations in different regions, there was no need for this kind of exploratory hypothesis.

Finally, a special care is necessary while formulating a hypothesis in geographic research. It should have a spatial complexion. The spatial logic underlying the hypothesis is also to be spelt out.

Indicators and data collection

In overall terms research displays two special tendencies: (i) it places a premium on empirical research directed at conceptual themes, such as ethnicity, gender bias and development level and (ii) it seeks comparisons at different scales, such as international, inter-regional within a country and inter-locality within a region (Krishan 1999). Normally a theoretical framework is constructed around the theme of a study, its constituent elements are identified and appropriate information is sought for each item. Invariably direct data on the various concepts involved are not available. This leads to a search for indicators that could represent what is being examined. Sometimes data are generated anew; more often the existing data are fabricated to serve the purpose.

The above observations raise a number of questions. How do we define indicators? In what way do these differ from variables or criteria? How are these distinguished in their functional forms? Which are the basic essentials for selection of indicators? Here we deliberate over these questions. Some illustrations by way of selecting a few studies which deal with the question of indicators are also listed.

On indicators

Indicators are the quantitative representation of qualitative concepts. These are statistics which articulate descriptive as well as normative aspects of any theoretical formulation (Kundu 1980, 30). In descriptive terms, the average number of married women per household in a region may give an idea about the incidence of joint family system. The ratio between the widowed and married women in an Indian city may represent the persistence of tradition, while the percentage of never married females in the 30 plus age group may give a clue to the degree of its modernity. Per capita income of municipalities is an index of their economic dynamism, whereas percentage of vacant houses points to stagnation. Energy crisis in a country may be referred to the difference between the increase in the rate of petrol prices and the overall inflation rate. Inflation rate plus unemployment rate would yield the misery index of a country.

Indicators always give an operational meaning to an abstract idea. They combine fact with theory and are placed in the context of a specific time. Universality is not their virtue. This impact, however, can be minimised by ensuring that a diversity of situations are represented (Land 1978, 14). The elite (change promoters) and masses (change recipients and actors) will sharply differ on the choice of indicators having a bearing on the quality of life. Ironically the former would emphasise needs, such as calories consumed per capita, and the latter would give voice to wants, such as cars per 100 persons (Mukherjee 1989, 45).

One must distinguish between a variable and an indicator as also a criterion and an indicator. A variable is a secular term without any special meaning. The

102 Traversing the path: data management

percentage of literate females is one such case. This variable takes the form of an indicator if it is used to represent the status of women.

A criterion and an indicator differ from each other in the mode of their expression. The former is qualitative and the latter quantitative. Taking the same example, the educational level, as one of the components of the status of women, is a criterion but the percentage of literate females, as one of the measures, is an indicator.

Indicators can be classified in several ways. Important categories can be listed as (i) spatial (average distance from which perishable commodities of daily use are obtained) and non-spatial (per capita consumption of milk); (ii) input (percentage of irrigated area) and output (agricultural produce per hectare); (iii) descriptive (share of budget allocated to education) and performance (share of allocated funds utilised); (iv) direct (per capita income in a village) and surrogate (percentage of *pucca* houses in the village); (v) limiting (percentage of literate persons with an absolute limit of 100) and open (per capita income which can rise to any figure); and (vi) static (population density) and dynamic (inflation rate).

The functional form of indicators, that is the manner in which these are calculated, also displays a variety. The frequency of schools is one of the indicators of educational development. In actual measurement, the number of schools can be compared to the size of the population being served, or to the extent of area being catered to, or to the proportion of settlements in the neighbourhood of this facility. The underlying purpose differs in each case. The school/population ratio represents the adequacy of this facility; the school/area ratio gives an idea about the accessibility of this facility; and school/settlement ratio is an expression of local availability of this facility. The first case will be pertinent to urban areas, the second to rural areas and the third to situations where there are cultural constraints to mobility outside the settlement, as for female children in some parts of India. It is imperative that such distinctions are kept in mind while operationalising indicators.

As it emerges, indicators help us in understanding the evolving scene of social reality, enable us to evaluate the impact of specific programmes and guide us in formulation of policies (Smith 1973, 135–130). They call for a sound conceptualisation in their construction. One has to clearly define the objective of the study in terms of its spirit and substance. In a situation of data constraints, an operational definition may be adopted. Indicators must flow from these definitions. An effort should be made to identify more comprehensible and expressive indicators. The fewer, the better.

Some illustrations

A sample of select indicator-based thematic studies is presented below. These pertain to different spatial scales: international, national and regional. They demonstrate the basic ideas set forth in this chapter.

Human development

The United Nations Development Programme maintains that human development is a process of building people's capabilities for the purpose of enlarging their opportunities and choices. This goal can be achieved if people are healthy and live long, are educated and take rational life decisions and have necessary resources for a decent living. As such, the three indicators adopted for measurement of the relative level of human development include (i) life expectancy, (ii) adult literacy rate and (iii) per capita gross domestic product (United Nations Development Programme 1997, 122). A crucial finding is that though the economic development index and the human development index are positively related to each other, there are several glaring exceptions to this generalisation. The country pairs of Sri Lanka and South Africa, Greece and Germany, and Hungary and United Arab Emirates have their per capita gross domestic product roughly in the ratio of 1 to 4, but they are almost at the same level of human development within their respective group.

Status of women

The comparative status of women vis-à-vis men within the same country and vis-à-vis each other across countries has been the subject of stimulating research at the global level. The status of women is judged from their access to and control over material resources, such as land, house, income, food, and to social resources, such as education, power and prestige, in comparison to that of men. With this kind of conceptualisation, the Population Crisis Committee, Washington, DC (1990), produced a map showing the differential status of women in various countries of the world. Five criteria and 20 indicators adopted for the purpose were as follows:

Health
- **Female infant and child mortality**
  Percentage of girls who survive to their fifth birthday

- **Female mortality during child-bearing years**
  Percentage of women aged 15 surviving to age 45

- **Female life expectancy at birth**
  Average number of years a woman may expect to live

- **Gender gap: female/male differential in life expectancy**
  Difference in years between female and male life expectancy at birth

Marriage and Children
- **Teen marriage**
  Percentage of women aged 15–19 who are married

104 Traversing the path: data management

- **Total fertility rate**
  Average number of children per woman

- **Contraceptive prevalence**
  Percentage of married women using contraceptives

- **Gender gap: female/male differential in marital status**
  Widowed, divorced or separated women per 100 widowed, divorced or separated men

Education

- **Secondary school teachers**
  Percentage of secondary school teachers who are women

- **Primary and secondary school children**
  Percentage of girls attending primary and secondary schools to total number of girls in their age group

- **University enrolment**
  Percentage of university-level females to the total number of women in the 20–24 age group

- **Gender gap: female/male literacy differential**
  Difference in the literacy rates of women and men in the age group 25–45 years

Employment

- **Self-employed**
  Women, who operate their own business or are engaged independently in a profession or trade, whether or not they hire employees, as a percentage of women aged 15 years and above

- **Paid employees**
  Women, who work for a public or private employer in exchange for remuneration as wages, salaries, commission, tips or piece rates, as a percentage of women aged 15 years and above

- **Professionals**
  Women, working in professional, technical, managerial and administrative occupations, as a percentage of women aged 15 and above

Social Equality

- **Economic equality**
  The degree to which women have equality in the workplace and have equal participation in economic life

- **Political and legal equality**
  The degree to which women have equal political rights and legal protection against discrimination on the basis of sex

- **Equality in marriage and family**
  The right to freely enter into marriage, equal rights in divorce and equal rights and responsibilities between husband and wife in marriage

- **Gender gap: female/male societal equality**
  The absence of discrimination against women in society

The exercise revealed that in no country was the status of women equal to that of men. In a comparative sense, Sweden ranked first with a status score of 87 for women against 100 for men. The score was 82.5 for United States, 68.5 for Japan, 60 for Sri Lanka, 58.5 for China, 43.5 for India, 28.5 for Pakistan and 21.5 for Bangladesh. Scandinavian countries were noted for the relatively high status of women and the African countries for the comparatively low status of women.

Backward classes

Backwardness is always with reference to some forwardness on certain parameters. It was with this conceptualisation that the Backward Classes Commission (Government of India 1980) tried to identify the backward classes in India. The criteria for judging the relative backwardness of various castes or occupation groups were described as social, educational and economic, in that order of importance.

The criteria and indicators used by the commission were as follows:

Social
- Castes/classes considered to be socially backward by others
- Castes/classes which mainly depend on manual labour for their livelihood
- Castes/classes where at least 25 per cent females and 10 per cent males, above the state average, get married at an age below 17 years in rural areas or at least 10 per cent females and 5 per cent males do so in urban areas
- Castes/classes where participation of females in work is at least 25 per cent above the state average

Educational
- Castes/classes where the number of children in the age group 5–15 who have never attended school is at least 25 per cent above the state average
- Castes/classes in which the student drop-out rate in the age group 5–15 is at least 25 per cent above the state average
- Castes/classes among whom the proportion of matriculates is at least 25 per cent below the state average

Economic
- Castes/classes whose average value of family assets is at least 25 per cent below the state average
- Castes/classes in which the number of families living in *kutcha* houses is at least 25 per cent above the state average
- Castes/classes for whom the source of drinking water is located at a distance of more than half kilometre for over 50 per cent of the households
- Castes/classes where the number of households which had taken consumption loan is at least 25 per cent above the state average

---

The commission worked out that 52 per cent of India's population belonged to the backward classes. Scheduled Castes and Tribes made another 22.6 per cent. Forward castes and communities were placed at 25.4 per cent (17.6 per cent

106 Traversing the path: data management

among the Hindus and 7.8 per cent among other religious groups) of the total population.

Urban–rural relations

Despite their conspicuous difference and disparity, urban and rural areas are invariably interlinked in India, as anywhere. These linkages are manifold: economic, socio-cultural and politico-administrative. On the economic plane, the city functions as a marketplace for surplus agricultural produce, a retail centre for manufactured goods and an employment avenue for rural commuters. Socially, it provides educational, health, recreational and a variety of other services. Above all, it is often an administrative centre, a cultural focus and a transport node for its surroundings.

The intensity of urban–rural relations, however, differs from one part of India to another. To demonstrate this, Krishan (1991) took five indicators of urban–rural relations for his analysis. These included:

1. Percentage of non-agricultural workers in rural areas
2. Percentage of villages connected by pucca road
3. Per cultivator agricultural produce
4. Number of towns per thousand km^2
5. Percentage of rural to urban and urban to rural migrants in total population

Indicators 1 and 2 were meant to represent the rural–urban commuting; indicators 3 and 4 took care of commodity and service exchange; and indicator 5 captured that segment of the population which sustains and strengthens the urban–rural nexus.

Kerala, Punjab and Haryana were noted for the strongest urban–rural interaction. By contrast, this relationship was the weakest in Madhya Pradesh, Rajasthan and Bihar.

Development process

In her study of Haryana, Singh (1998) adopted the definition of development as the quality of a regional system in terms of economic growth, social advancement, political maturity and ecological balance. She selected a large number of indicators for her analysis. The list of criteria and indicators worked out was as follows:

Criterion/Sub-criterion/Indicators

Economic Development

a   **Net state domestic product**
1   Per capita net state domestic product

	Criterion/Sub-criterion/Indicators
b	**Agricultural development**
2	Percentage of net area irrigated
3	Fertiliser consumption per hectare of cropped area
4	Percentage of area under high yielding variety of seeds
5	Tractors per thousand landholdings
6	Power consumption per thousand hectares of cropped area
7	Agricultural produce per hectare
8	Agricultural produce per cultivator
c	**Industrial development**
9	Registered working factories per thousand population
10	Number of large and medium-scale industrial units per thousand km^2
	Social Development
a	**Infrastructural facilities**
1	Percentage of villages with safe drinking water
2	Percentage of electrified villages
3	Educational institutions per thousand km^2 and per thousand population
4	Health institutions per thousand km^2 and per thousand population
5	Percentage of villages connected by metalled road
6	Post offices per thousand km^2
7	Percentage of rural households living in pucca houses
b	**Demographic patterns**
8	Percentage of urban population
9	Percentage of literate persons
10	Percentage of rural non-agricultural workers
	Political Development
a	**Decentralisation of power**
1	Per capita devolution of funds at district and block level
b	**Administrative efficiency**
2	Change in per capita cost of administration
	Ecological Development
a	**Concern for ecology**
1	Percentage of state budget allocated to environmental subjects
b	**Ecological improvement**
2	Change in percentage of forest area

The study brought out that the Haryana experience was a story of socio-economic transformation of an erstwhile underdeveloped periphery of the former composite Punjab. The state now has its own less developed western half vis-à-vis the developed east. The former is, of course, not a periphery as it has been a beneficiary of political patronage. Practically every chief minister of the state hailed from this area and tried to strengthen its infrastructure base. Its overall

108 Traversing the path: data management

development, however, remained at a lower level due to physical constraints of semi-dry climate, less fertile soils and lack of water resources. Infrastructural provisions, such as roads, schools and hospitals, could not fully compensate for its natural handicaps.

Wood (1977) makes a strong case for adoption of truly geographic indicators in development studies. He would like to set aside the traditional development indicators of production for economists, of equity for sociologists and political scientists and of health for students of medicine. Instead he recommends the use of geographic criteria, such as local production share of essential items, sense of territoriality, efficiency of the transport system, maintenance of ecological balance and adequacy of recreational areas for measuring the development level of any area. Indicators in every case are also spelt out. He stresses that there is a need to bring geography to the core and not to keep it on the periphery in such exercises.

In that light, one could recommend the following as indicators of development: (i) mean distance from which perishable goods of daily use originate, (ii) intensity of macro- versus micro-territorial loyalty, (iii) time involved in travelling per unit distance, (iv) percentage of land free from ecological degradation and (v) per capita land developed for recreation.

All these indicators are spatial in nature. Statistical scores worked out in every case are positive to development.

Construction of indicators is indeed a very stimulating exercise in social science research. It impels any scholar to conceptualise on themes which remain vague in terms of their meaning and significance. It also strengthens the empirical base of any study. Comparisons become credible, issues get defined and areas requiring social attention get highlighted. One of the essential skills which any social scientist should cultivate is that of 'indicatorsmithy'. This craft is to be perfected.

References

Bird, James H. 1993. *The Changing Worlds of Geography: A Critical Guide to Concepts and Methods*. 2nd ed. Oxford: Clarendon Press.

Braithwaite, R.B. 1960. *Scientific Explanation*. New York: Harper Torchbooks.

Bunge, W. 1979. "Perspective on Theoretical Geography." *Annals of the Association of American Geographers* 69 (1): 69–174.

Burgess, J., and P. Jackson. 1992. "Streetwork: An Encounter with Place." *Journal of Geography in Higher Education* 16 (2): 151–157.

Burgess, R.G. 1984. *In the Field: An Introduction to Field Research*. London: Allen and Unwin.

Chatfield, C. 1995. *Problem Solving: A Statistician's Guide*. London: Chapman and Hall.

Chuan, G.K., and W.P. Poh. 2000. "Status of Fieldwork in the Geography Curriculum in South East Asia." In *Fieldwork in Geography: Reflections, Perspectives and Actions*, edited by R. Gerber and G.K. Chuan, 99–118. Dordrecht, Boston and London: Kluwer Academic.

Cloke, Paul, Ian Cook, Philip Crang, Mark Goodwin, Joe Painter, and Chris Philo. 2004. *Practising Human Geography*. London: Sage.

Cook, Ian, and Mike Crang. 1995. *Doing Ethnographies, Concepts and Techniques in Modern Geography*. Norwich: School of Environmental Sciences, University of Easy Anglia.

Cosgrove, Dennis. 1984. *Social Formation and Symbolic Landscape*. London: Croom Helm.

Crang, P. 1994. "It's Showtime! On the Workplace Geographies of Display in a Restaurant in Southeast England." *Environment and Planning D: Society and Space* 12: 675–702.

Daniels, Stephen. 1993. *Fields of Vision: Landscape Imagery and National Identity in England and the United States*. Cambridge: Polity.

Davies, Andrew D. 2009. "Ethnography, Space and Politics: Interrogating the Process of Protest in the Tibetan Freedom Movement." *Area* 41 (1): 19–25.

de Vaus, D.A. 2002. *Analyzing Social Science Data: 50 Key Problems in Data Analysis*. London: Sage.

Dodge, Martin, and Rob Kitchin. 2006. "Net: Geography Fieldwork Frequently Asked Questions." In *The International Handbook of Virtual Learning Environments*, edited by J. Weiss, J. Nolan, J. Hunsinger, and P. Trifonas, 1175–1202. Dordrecht: Springer.

Dunkerley, D.L. 2003. "Determining Friction Coefficients for Interrill Flows: The Significance of Flow Filaments and Backwater Effects." *Earth Surface Processes and Landforms* 28 (5): 475–491.

Fowler, F. 2002. *Survey Research Methods*. 3rd ed. Thousand Oaks, CA: Sage.

Gilbert, Melissa R. 1998. "'Race', Space and Power: The Survival Strategies of Working Poor Women." *Annals of the Association of American Geographers* 88 (4): 595–621.

Gold, J.R., A. Jenkins, R. Lee, J. Monk, J. Riley, I. Shepherd, and D. Unwin. 1991. *Teaching Geography in Higher Education: A Manual of Good Practice*. Oxford: Blackwell.

Government of India. 1980. *Report of the Backward Classes Commission*. New Delhi.

Haines-Young, R.H., and James R. Petch. 1986. *Physical Geography: Its Nature and Methods*. London: Paul Chapman.

Haining, R. 1990. *Spatial Data Analysis in the Social and Environmental Sciences*. Cambridge: Cambridge University Press.

Hammond, Michael, and Jerry Wellington. 2013. *Research Methods: The Key Concepts*. Abingdon, Oxon: Routledge.

Harris, C. 2001. "Archival Fieldwork." *Geographical Review* 91 (1–2): 328–334.

Harris, C., M.C.R. Davies, and B.R. Rea, 2003. "Gelifluction: Viscous Flow or Plastic Creep?" *Earth Surface Processes and Landforms* 28 (12): 1289–1301.

Harvey, D. 1969. *Explanation in Geography*. Oxford: Blackwell.

Hay, I., ed. 2000. *Qualitative Research Methods in Human Geography*. Oxford and Melbourne: Oxford University Press.

Heron, J., and P. Reason. 2006. "The Practice of Co-Operative Enquiry: Research 'with' Rather Than 'on' People." In *Handbook of Action Research: Participative Inquiry and Practice*, edited by P. Reason and H. Bradbury, 179–188. London: Sage.

Hoggart, K., L. Lees, and Andrew D. Davies. 2002. *Researching Human Geography*. London: Arnold.

Hope, M. 2009. "The Importance of Direct Experience: A Philosophical Defence of Fieldwork in Human Geography." *Journal of Geography in Higher Education* 33 (2): 169–182.

Johnston, R.J., D. Gregory, G. Pratt, and M. Watts, eds. 2000. *The Dictionary of Human Geography*. 4th ed. Malden, MA: Blackwell.

Kendall, M.G., and W.R. Buckland. 1960. *Dictionary of Statistical Terms*. Edinburgh: Oliver and Boyd.

Kindon, S., R. Pain, and M. Kesby, eds. 2007. *Participatory Action Research Approaches and Methods*. London: Routledge.

Kitchin, Rob, and Nicholas J. Tate. 2000. *Conducting Research into Human Geography: Theory, Methodology and Practice*. Harlow, UK: Prentice Hall.

Krishan, Gopal. 1986. *Spatial Dimensions of Unemployment and Underemployment*. New Delhi: Concept Publishing Company.

110 Traversing the path: data management

————. 1991. "Urban-Rural Relations in India: A Critique." *Indian Association of Social Science Institutions Quarterly* 10: 92–104.

————. 1999. "Indicators in Social Science Research." *Indian Social Science Review* 1 (1): 181–191.

Kundu, A. 1980. *Measurement of Urban Processes.* Bombay: Popular Prakashan.

Kwan, T. 2000. "Fieldwork in Geography Teaching: The Case in Hong Kong." In *Fieldwork in Geography: Reflections, Perspectives and Actions,* edited by R. Gerber and G.K. Chuan, 119–130. Dordrecht: Kluwer Academic.

Land, K.C. 1978. "Theories, Models and Indicators of Social Change." *International Social Science Journal* 27: 7–37.

Laurier, Erich. 2003. "Participant Observation." In *Key Methods in Geography,* edited by Nicholas J. Clifford and Gill Valentine, 133–148. London: Sage.

Lim, K., P. Treitz, M. Wulder, B. St-Onge, and M. Flood. 2003. "LiDAR Remote Sensing of Forest Structure." *Progress in Physical Geography* 27 (1): 88–106.

Longley, Paul A., M.F. Goodchild, D.J. Maguire, and D.W. Rhind. 2005. *Geographical Information Systems and Science.* 2nd ed. Chichester, UK: Wiley.

MacEachren, A.M. 1995. *How Maps Work: Representation, Visualization, and Design.* London: Guilford Press.

Martin, Kevin St., and Marianna Pavlovskaya. 2010. "Secondary Data." In *Research Methods in Geography: A Critical Introduction,* edited by Basil Gomez and John Paul Jones III, 173–193. West Sussex, UK: Wiley-Blackwell.

McLafferty, Sara L. 2003. "Conducting Questionnaire Surveys." In *Key Methods in Geography,* edited by Nicholas J. Clifford and Gill Valentine, 87–100. London: Sage.

Miller, C. 2006. "A Beast in the Field: The Google Maps Mashup as GIS/2." *Cartographica* 41: 187–199.

Montello, Daniel R., and Paul C. Sutton. 2006. *An Introduction to Scientific Research Methods in Geography.* London: Sage.

Mukherjee, R. 1989. *The Quality of Life: Valuation in Social Science.* New Delhi: Sage.

Oppenheim, A.N. 1993. *Questionnaire Design, Interviewing and Attitude Measurement.* 2nd ed. Aldershot: Gower.

Ostuni, J. 2000. "The Irreplaceable Experience of Fieldwork in Geography." In *Fieldwork in Geography: Reflections, Perspectives and Actions,* edited by R. Gerber and G.K. Chuan, 79–98. Dordrecht: Kluwer Academic.

Payne, Stanley L. 1951. *The Art of Asking Questions.* Princeton, NJ: Princeton University Press.

Phillips, Richard, and Jennifer Johns. 2012. *Fieldwork for Human Geography.* London: Sage.

Population Crisis Committee. 1990. "Country Ratings of the Status of Women: Poor, Powerless and Pregnant." *Population Briefing Paper No. 20 (June).* Washington, DC.

Pratt, G. 2000. "Research Performances." *Environment and Planning D: Society and Space* 18 (5): 639–651.

The Reader's Digest and Oxford. 1993. *Complete Wordfinder,* edited by Sara Tulloch. London: The Reader's Digest Association Limited.

Rhoads, Bruce L., and David Wilson. 2010. "Observing Our World." In *Research Methods in Geography: A Critical Introduction,* edited by Basil Gomez and John Paul Jones III, 26–40. West Sussex, UK: Wiley-Blackwell.

Sauer, C. 1956. "The Education of a Geographer." *Annals of the Association of American Geographers* 46 (3): 287–299.

Scott, J. 1990. *A Matter of Record: Documentary Sources in Social Research.* Cambridge: Polity.

Silverman, D. 2001. *Interpreting Qualitative Data: Methods for Analysing Talk, Text and Interaction.* 2nd ed. Thousand Oaks, CA: Sage.

Singh, Nina. 1998. *Administration and Development of Indian States*. New Delhi: Anmol Publications.

Smith, D.M. 1973. *The Geography of Social Well-Being*. New York: McGraw-Hill.

Stoddart, D.R., and W.M. Adams. 2004. "Fieldwork and Unity in Geography." In *Unifying Geography: Common Heritage, Shared Future*, edited by J.A. Matthews and D.T. Herbert, 46–61. London: Routledge.

Tesch, R. 1990. *Qualitative Research: Analysis Types and Research Tools*. Brighton: Falmer.

United Nations Development Programme. 1997. *Human Development Report*. Oxford: Oxford University Press.

Valentine, G. 2005. "'Tell Me About . . .' Using Interviews as a Research Methodology." In *Methods in Human Geography: A Guide for Students Doing a Research Project*, edited by R. Flowerdew and D. Martin, 110–126. 2nd ed. Edinburgh Gate: Addison Wesley Longman.

Viles, Heather A. 2003. "Laboratory Work." In *The Student's Companion to Geography*, edited by Alistair Rogers and Heather A.Viles, 225–229. 2nd ed. Oxford: Blackwell.

Wong, D.W.S. 2004. "The Modifiable Areal Unit Problem (MAUP)." In *Worldminds: Geographical Perspectives on 100 Problems*, edited by D.G. Janelle, B. Warf, and K. Hansen, 571–578. London: Kluwer Academic.

Wood, H.A. 1977. "Toward a Geographic Concept of Development." *Geographical Review* 67: 462–468.

Wulder, M., K.O. Niemann, and D.G. Goodenough. 2000. "Local Maximum Filtering for the Extraction of Tree Locations and Basal Area from High Spatial Resolution Imagery." *Remote Sensing of the Environment* 73: 103–114.

Young, L., and H. Barrett. 2001. "Adapting Visual Methods: Action Research with Kampala Street Children." *Area* 33 (2): 141–152.

8

DATA ANALYSIS

Analysis refers to the process of ordering (systematising), structuring (classifying) and treating (subjecting to an analytical method) data to obtain statistical results. It addresses key features of the data and their use and involves application of some quantitative or qualitative technique. It is part of the chain between data collection, representation and interpretation. GIS and computers are technological tools for data display and analysis. Here we shall focus on data analysis activity.

Fundamentals of data analysis

The raw material for geographical analysis consists of information on a wide range of topics, from land values, ethnic composition, trade flows, gully erosion to air pollution in a city. We refer to such raw material for statistical analysis as data. It provides information about characteristics of objects. The information sources can also be in a form other than numbers. These may include newspapers, television broadcasts, memos we receive at work, text messages we exchange via mobile phones, graffiti we see in the streets.

In geography we deal with spatial data. Spatial data combines attribute information with locational information. Thus geographical data typically consist of information about characteristics of places or areas, for example population of cities or per capita income of states, or gradient of land. The data may also be textual, audio or visual information, as typical of National Geographic channel.

In the last quarter of the twentieth century, human geography got driven by 'isms' such as Marxism, post-modernism and post-structuralism, which resulted in less focus on quantitative analysis. A resurgence of the new quantitative geography with its focus on spatial data analysis in human geography is, however, on the cards with increasing popularity of online tools. Quantitative methods are, of course, an essential component of research in both physical and human geography.

The data can be put to extremely varied uses, including description, comparison and analysis. A variety of statistical methods are used for the purpose. For a geographer, it is imperative that such methods capture spatial parameters through an adaptation or reinvention of the standard statistical techniques. The usage of mean centre as a location, for example, is to be more in the trade of a geographer than a simple usage of a statistical mean as a number.

In statistical approach to any data, including spatial data, three basics are involved: classification, ordering and variable precision.

Classification basic is the simplest. This involves identification of objects in terms of classes or categories. Geographers use classificatory concepts in their systematic studies, ranging from weather types in climatology to functional classification of towns in urban geography, to land use categories. Categories are subparts of a class. In spatial analysis, we can consider shape as a classificatory concept; for example, shape of settlements classified as circular, linear or starlike.

Ordering basic is often found in research problems involving hierarchies. An urban geographer, for instance, might be concerned with a central place system for allocating towns not by general function, such as industrial, commercial or administrative, but by hierarchical status ranging downwards from metropolitan centre to market town. In a strictly spatial analysis, focusing on degree of circularity of cities, all shapes could be computed and allocated to ordered classes from negligible circularity to very high circularity or compactness.

Variable precision basic refers to exact measurement of any phenomenon. Monthwise amount of rainfall at New Delhi, the volume of traffic flow on its different roads and number of crimes in a year in its different localities are examples of data in the nature of variable precision basic. In geographic research, we are more often involved in treatment of such data for identification of patterns relating to areal differentiation or spatial analysis or spatial diffusion.

The quantitative and qualitative data could be analysed manually or using computing software. However, computer software does not perform data analysis in an automatic way. It depends on the researcher to sieve out important ideas, define the analytic issues to be explored and identify most appropriate modes of representation (Coffey and Atkinson 1996, 187). Software like Qualitative Data Analysis (QDA) is more like a word processor, an enabler to your text writing but not itself writing it (Flick 2009, 359).

At this stage the idea is to introduce the researcher to a variety of most commonly used techniques of data analysis. Some of these techniques have a detailed body of literature devoted to them. The choice of technique whether quantitative, qualitative or mixed has to be judicious backed by theoretical proposition. Here our intention is to provide you with an overview rather than an exhaustive treatment of major techniques.

114 Traversing the path: data management

Techniques of analysis

Quantitative techniques

These refer to mathematical or statistical treatment of data, and in geography are essentially adaptations of mathematical or statistical techniques to the purpose of the discipline. Parallel to centrographical techniques of mean, median and mode in statistics, for example, we have mean centre, median point and point of minimum aggregate travel distance in geography. Likewise, geography uses some other very specific techniques of data analysis, such as population potential and nearest neighbour analysis, dealing with point distributions; network analysis pertaining to line distributions; and cluster analysis in respect of area distributions. A detailed discussion on these and other such techniques is reserved for forthcoming pages.

Qualitative techniques

Qualitative research frees itself from the quantification process (Nkwi, Nyamongo, and Ryan 2001, 1). It concerns gathering and/or working with text, images or sounds. The information is commonly generated from interviews, survey questions, journals, recorded observations, existing documents, field notes, conversations, photographs, recordings, memos and diaries. The major deciding factor is the specific type of information generated and/or used.

In the process, enormous amounts of data are collected in the form of interview transcripts or narrative (text) scripts. From the pile of transcripts a qualitative analyst is required to identify themes, code the data or memoing, work out what it all means and tell it like it is. The idea is not to seek causes and explanations.

Geographers have analysed such material in the past by coding it manually with pen and paper. Coding is a process wherein ideas, words, phrases and interpretations are flagged within and across the recorded transcripts. For example, interview and focus group discussions are recorded, coded and recoded throughout the process of research.

In recent years computer packages, such as Computer Assisted Qualitative Data Analysis Software (CAQDAS), have come into use for the purpose. In fact a range of packages with nearly same functions are now easily available. These assist in three elements of the analytical process – data ordering, interpretation and project management.

Data ordering includes data file storage of documents, pictures, sound files, transcripts. It allows demographic information of the interviewees to be attached to the files. An analytic structure to group similar data from across cases is developed. The data are finally coded. All this is possible manually also but the main benefits of using computer-assisted packages is their ease, speed and power to handle large sets of data, accessibility of data, systematically search, arrange and filter data, and consistency of approach, to mention a few.

Interpretation of the data is enabled by the ability of the computer program to search for words or phrases in context, automated filtering and reorganisation of the data set, reorganisation of themes into concepts or categories, allow the user to draw diagrams and maps and envision their emerging patterns about the relationships between codes or categories, which can help them in developing typologies, explanations or theories.

Finally, CAQDAS packages are used as project management tools in situations where researchers are working on a project in different locations. This is done using certain functions in the program.

Qualitative analysis of data is done using different approaches with no clearly agreed rules or procedures for such an analysis. Many of the research traditions have their disciplinary origins in sociology, anthropology, philosophy, linguistics, psychology and so on. However, the results from qualitative research can divulge more insightful geographical thinking. Ritchie *et al.* (2014, 270–271) have condensed the main qualitative analysis traditions. Some of these are given below:

Analytic induction**:** Coined by Znaniecki (1934), analytic induction is logic in qualitative research to collect, analyse and arrange presentation of research findings of data in ethnographic research. The aim is to generalise through a systematic study of a limited number of cases. The research problem could range from a macro-social event to a mid-scale phenomena or everyday micro-social event (Katz 2001). Examples of the research problem at different scales could be an analysis of mass gathering at *Kumbh Mela in Haridwar or Allahabad*, or peasant uprising in north-west Uttar Pradesh; ongoing ways of reviving the dried up rivulets in the states under the Mahatma Gandhi National Rural Employment Guarantee Scheme; and expressive gestures visible only when videotape showing disaster-hit area is reviewed repeatedly.

Identifying the procedure wherein cases are examined, the phenomenon redefined, hypothesis reformulated until a universal relationship is established, Cressey (1953) lists five stages of analytic induction. A researcher begins by defining the field, formulating a hypothesis, studying one case to see if it fits the facts, modifying the hypothesis or the definitions in the light of this and thereafter reviewing further cases.

Condense analysis**:** It is by way of summarising of the recorded material. By that nature it is a descriptive and explorative method. Following a pragmatic approach condense analysis aims at cross-case analysis of themes of qualitative data based on interviews, observations and analysis of written texts. The generalisation procedure is a systematic text condensation and involves moving in an upward scale from chaos to concepts through the levels of themes, codes, meaning and description. An initial holistic impression is made which is followed by identifying and sorting meaning units to condensation and finally synthesis (Malterud 2012).

Content analysis**:** It is 'a method for systematically describing the meaning of qualitative material' (Schreier 2012, 1). A researcher follows a systematic classification process of coding and identifying themes or patterns to interpret the content of text data (Hsieh and Shannon 2005, 1278). Themes, words and phrases are tracked and analysed across transcripts. The focus is on the way of treatment of the theme, its presentation and the frequency of its occurrence. The interpretation is subjective. This analysis is subsequently linked to 'outside variables' such as gender (Berelson 1952; Robson 2002).

Any object, be it a landscape, or a photograph can be subjected to content analysis. Through this technique one can recognise the way in which words, images and practices reflect a part of reality (Neuendorf 2002). Classic novels, media reports and interview transcripts are examined in this manner. Lutz and Collins (1993) argue that it is important to understand the meanings that the photographs and narratives in the *National Geographic* magazine convey because these significantly determine the way ordinary Americans think about and respond to the rest of the world. Likewise Krishan (2016) carried out a content analysis of all the 98 articles on diverse aspects of India published in the *National Geographic* during 1947–2015. The effort was to capture the elements of the country's vitality or vulnerability.

Evidently content analysis provides us with a window onto the world (Adams 2009). Even the human body itself has been likened to a 'text' in that it can be 'read' and we have research writings under the title 'geography of human bodies'. Ratios between the width and length of nose have been used to infer the racial background of an individual.

Linked to content analysis is the interpretivist analysis. Here the documents are not considered as objective source of information or neutral resource but as a social construction. These represent the worldview of the persons who wrote them. Therefore, in addition to decoding the literal meaning of a document we try to infer the hidden meaning of the text in this case.

There are two more qualitative versions of content analysis: textual analysis and thematic analysis. These flow from semiotics, that is the scientific study of signs or codes (symbols) that underlie all forms of behaviour and language. Hence they are elements of culture. These are used in the analysis of text and visual images.

Textual analysis involves analysis of the linguistic nuances within documents to see whether they give a lead to a particular interpretation of events. The text includes printed matter, audio-visual material and websites to uncover the identity of a place and its people. Textual analysis has been applied to geography's most powerful form of representation: the map. The focus is on the relationship between identities, space and their representations (Del Casino and Hanna 2000).

Thematic analysis is a very common form of qualitative analytic research method not tied to any particular discipline. Using it, the researcher discovers, interprets and reports patterns or themes and clusters of meaning within the data. These patterns help to describe a phenomenon and address a specific research question (Boyzatis 1998; Braun and Clarke 2006; Joffe 2012).

Conversation analysis: It focuses on analysing the structure of conversation (Silverman 2000). It is based on the use of basic linguistic systems such as turn taking and an adjacency pair to classify interaction (Atkinson and Heritage 1984; Rapley 2012; Silverman 2000). Turn taking is communication mechanism for managing taking of turns in face-to-face interaction. The turns are functionally related to each other. It is a cyclical process that stops when there is nothing left to say.

An adjacency pair is a style of conversation in which the two speakers converse by taking one turn each. Such is the case with Presidential debate in the United States' elections. The sequence of two utterances produced by two different speakers takes place next (i.e. adjacent) to one another (Schegloff and Sacks 1973).

Discourse analysis: Our life is a culturally specific mode of existence comprised of thoughts, words, objects, events, actions and interactions pieced together in discourses (Gee 1999, 7). Their analysis is one of the cores of human geography (Dittmer 2010, 275). It involves analysis of the written texts along with other forms of communication, such as body language, symbolic acts, interactions, technologies and the like in a given situation and context. It is also concerned with the way knowledge is created through the use of distinctive language within a particular discourse, for example Art of living discourse, legal discourse, financial discourse, medical discourse.

Geography has silently experienced 'discursive turn' apart from 'cultural turn' in the late twentieth century. The analysis of discourses opened new avenues within human geography and research papers that drew on discourse analysis began to appear. The role of 'imaginative geographies' in composing ontological categories, such as Occident and Orient, in the work of Edward Said (1978) is an important starting point in this regard.

Fairclough (1992) has offered a three-pronged approach to discourse analysis: textual analysis that includes word choice, grammar etc; discursive practice, which is essentially a content analysis; and social practice, which includes the larger ideologies within which the social discourse is located. Making a connection between the micro-, meso- and macro-scaled discourses is one of the real methodological challenges associated with such an analysis. Increasingly, such analysis is done using computer programs (MacDonald and Headlam 2008, 71).

Ethnographic analysis: These are large, descriptive accounts detailing the 'lived experience' or way of life of particular individuals, groups or organisations (Hammersley and Atkinson 2007; Lofland *et al.* 2006; O'Reilly 2005). This kind of writing is strongly linked to the broader theoretical frameworks of phenomenology and interpretivism which argue that all social actions are intentional. Weber had called this 'verstehen', that is being able to empathise with or think like the people who are being studied.

Life history analysis: It is a framework used to interpret some of the history of people living today, for instance life history of *Jarawa* tribe, one of the *Adivasi* indigenous people of the Andaman Islands in India. Life histories can be analysed as single narratives, as collection of stories weaved around common themes such as the tales of *Panchatantra*, which perhaps are the oldest stories known in the literature of India, or unearthed to build an argument based on comparison between different accounts (Thompson 2000).

Narrative analysis: It focuses on the basic story being told, its meaning or plan, the manner of construction of account or narrative around that story, the intent of the teller and the nature of the audience (Riessman 2008). In all likelihood, the interpretations in case of interview and focus group conversations will depend on the theoretical perspective of the researcher (Secor 2010, 194–205).

118 Traversing the path: data management

Images obtained from a variety of sources such as art, photography, painting, pictures, films and advertising or texts can be geographically unpacked through a narrative that forms part of the analysis. Differences and similarities between areas can be discerned using a narrative approach to analyse images or texts. Using focus group for data collection, Singh (2012) has used narrative analysis to study preference for sons in parts of the state of Haryana.

Context, classification and connection: It is the most elementary and simplistic technique of data analysis. Context involves an understanding of the social, temporal and spatial situation of any phenomenon under study. For a meaningful appraisal, the data are arranged in some order through their classification in different categories. Having put the data into some coherent categories, the concern is to identify and measure the relationships, associations and interactions among them. An exploration into such a connectivity leads to a deep insight into the data.

You may be asked to describe agricultural practices in a hilly area. The documentation you make include note-taking, sketching and photographs.

Qualitative Data Analysis is more of an art, less rigorous and does not follow any standardised procedures or a strict prescriptive path. It is more of an inductive, open-ended process.

Robbins and Krueger (2000) have elaborated on the idea of *Q Factor Analysis*. Herein the conclusions arrived at by a researcher through analysis of interviews with the respondents are presented back to the respondents and their feedback is sought. The aim is to gain the respondent's own interpretation of the conclusions arrived at by the researcher. The research findings are brought into conversation between the researcher and the researched.

Grounded theory: It involves the 'use of an intensive, open-ended, and iterative process that simultaneously involves data collection, coding or data analysis, and memo-writing or theory building' (Groat and Wang 2002, 181). Thus, it is an inductive methodology using rigorous research procedures to arrive at conceptual categories. It generates theory from systematic research in contrast with theory generated by logical deduction from a priori assumptions (Grounded Theory Institute 2013). Grounded theory can be used with either qualitative or quantitative data. The term 'grounded theory' was introduced in *The Discovery of Grounded Theory* by Glaser and Strauss as 'the discovery of theory from data – systematically obtained and analysed in social research' (1967, 1).

Having briefly dwelt on some of the methods of qualitative data analysis, we may have a view of the conventional as well as newly developed techniques frequently used in geographic studies. The application of an advanced or sophisticated statistical technique may initially require a preview of the nature of data. At times such a procedure yields sufficient information to render a sophisticated analysis unnecessary.

Exploratory data analysis

Exploratory route stands for data visualisation as a quantity or its graphical representation. Tukey (1977, vi) introduced the term exploratory data analysis (EDA) to highlight the role of graphics prior to data analysis: to make us notice what we never expected to see. Textbooks on spatial analysis often point towards exploratory route as the first step in spatial analysis (Bailey and Gatrell 1995; Burt and Barber 1996; Fotheringham, Brunsdon, and Charlton 2000). A natural extension of EDA is exploratory spatial data analysis, ESDA (A. Unwin and D.J. Unwin 1998).

Under EDA or ESDA data are made to address some of the preliminary questions: Do observations fall into a number of distinct groups? Are there any variables having unusually high or low values? What associations exist between variables? Thus it involves exploring the distribution of data, shape of data to identify 'typical' and extreme values, the clustering or scatter of the observations, the relationships between data, whether linear or curvilinear, or the irregularities or extremities in data.

A number of graphic techniques are available to depict the shape pattern of data. Graphs are excellent as summary devices only if the intention is to communicate general features of the data, notably qualitative differences. They are poor in communicating quantitative information, in which case it is more appropriate to use the original data table. The basic principle of any EDA is to use the simplest version of any display that shows the main features of the observations.

Before analysing data it needs to be simplified and rearranged. One of the ways is to follow 'data reduction' approach, suggested by Ehrenberg (1975, 1982). It helps in identification of key features of the data to be described and interpreted, including the similarities and contrasts between the observations. This primarily involves rounding off the digits to enable quick mental calculation. For example, the exact population figures for various states and union territories since 1951 may be rounded to the nearest thousand. This will facilitate a quick view of the data.

Another way of EDA is to go by *stem-and-leaf plot*. It gives a near-graphical representation of data distribution while still containing information about each observation value. Unlike histogram, it is possible to reconstruct the original data from it. Stem-and-leaf plots and histograms indicate the variability of distribution in the population. It is used for interval or ratio data. Its purpose is to illustrate the range of values within the data; where concentrations of values occur; whether there are gaps in the values; whether there is symmetry in the batch; whether there are extreme values that differ markedly from the remaining values in the batch; and any other data peculiarities.

A stem-and-leaf display consists of a stem and leaves. To construct it, the values of the observations in a distribution are arranged in ascending order followed by separating and organising values according to their digits. The values of the data are divided into three batches: sorting digits, display digits and digits that can be ignored. The sorting digits are the leading digits. These are the stem of the observation. The display digit is referred to as the leaf.

The 'stem' is arranged vertically in ascending order. The subsequent digit which is the 'leaf' associated with each stem is arranged horizontally. Leaves of greater values are placed farther to the right.

Five-Number Summary is still another technique of EDA. The list of five numbers comprises the largest, smallest, median, and upper and lower quartile scores.

120 Traversing the path: data management

Extracting figures about the average size of household in 52 metropolitan cities of India as per Census of India 2011 data, we get the following listing:

Minimum	Lower quartile	Median	Upper quartile	Maximum
3.67	4.20	4.69	5.11	6.46

The above numbers are useful for auditing a data set and for getting a feel of the distribution of data. Listing these numbers gives a good impression of the location, spread and extreme values of a data set. These can be itemised along a vertical line drawn on a scale. Likewise, such five-summary lines can be used to depict per capita income of various states and union territories of India.

A graphical equivalent of the five-number summary is called a Box Plot, a short name for the original box-and-whisker plot. It uses interval or ratio data to depict variance around the mean. In contrast to the standard deviation, it does this by using the median and the data quartiles and plotting them. A box plot is drawn using five statistics: minimum value, second (lower) quartile, median value, third (upper) quartile and maximum value. The minimum is the smallest value and maximum the largest value in the data set. The second (lower) quartile value contains the lower 25 per cent of the data below it; median value in a range of numbers refers to the middle number; and the third (upper) quartile value comprises the upper 25 per cent of the data above it.

A box plot shows the median of each data series as a line, with a 'box' whose top edge is the third quartile and whose bottom edge is the first quartile. Often we draw 'whiskers' at the top and bottom representing the extreme values of each series. The upper and lower hinges form the box.

Lines extending away from the box to show range of data in the tails of the distribution are 'whiskers' or 'tails'. Rules governing the construction of the whiskers vary. The ends of the whiskers spell information on minimum and maximum values. However, the whiskers are not sent to the last value in case of extreme outliers in the data which are far from the mean. In such cases the outermost observations within 1.5 times the inter-quartile range of the hinge forms the limit. All other observations beyond this are considered outliers and are shown individually. The World Bank group reports make extensive use of such plots to depict a variety of data. Hydrological indicator data on the World Bank Climate Portal (http://sdwebx.worldbank.org/climateportal/) have been shown using box-and-whisker plots. By clicking on the 'Basin box plots', or 'Country box plots', researchers will access two box-and-whisker plots for the basin/country of interest: one for the 2030s and one for the 2050s (http://www.un.org/waterforlifedecade/pdf/2011_world_bank_climate_variability_change_eng.pdf).

In another case box plots have been drawn to show decadal growth rates of 28 African countries, particularly those that have GDP series from the 1960s to 1990s with World Bank, World Development Indicators 2004 as the source of data (http://www1.worldbank.org/prem/lessons1990s/chaps/Ctrynote8_AfricasGrowth.pdf).

The magnitude of earthquake that hit Nepal at different locations can be suitably shown through a box-and-whisker plot: Seismographs at various stations recorded these as 5.0, 6.3, 6.7, 6.9, 7.1, 7.3, 7.4, 7.8 and 7.9. Here minimum value=5.0, maximum value=7.9, median value=7.1, median of the lower half (Q1)=6.5, median of the upper half (Q3)=7.6. The box represents the middle half of data between the medians of the two halves. The lower and upper hinges of the box would be 6.5 and 7.6. The whiskers will extend from 6.5 to 5.0 and 7.6 to 7.9 revealing the spread of data.

Likewise Time Series Graphs can be used to identify temporal trends in behaviour of specific data. The time units are plotted on the horizontal axis, and the observations are marked on the vertical axis. It helps to understand the pattern over time. One can observe whether the change is regular, irregular or cyclic or rising and falling in regular frequency.

Scatterplot Matrix or Scatter Diagram technique is used to study relationships between variables. Two variables among whom relationship is to be observed, for example population size of a metropolitan city and average size of the household, are plotted together using x and y coordinates. This graph will reveal whether the relationship between the two is positive or negative or indifferent. Three common possibilities are clusters, outliers and patterns. Clusters are distinct groupings in the data points. Outliers are one-off cases that have unusual combinations of observed values. Spatial patterns can be discerned by writing the names of respective places or territories along with their data plotted on the graph.

Advances in the techniques of scientific visualisation through GIS have enabled researchers to explore salient patterns and relationships in geographic data. Visualisation of geographic information can be done using a variety of techniques. Masuoka *et al.* [(1996) quoted in Lo, Albert, and Yeung 2003: 235–236] identify five categories of visualisation techniques. These include two-dimensional plots [population (Y-axis) against time (X-axis) of any country, region or city]; three-dimensional plots or surface plots (relationships among three numerical variables, e.g. reflectance of land cover in a Landsat imagery); two-dimensional planimetric view (a map of vegetation laid on top of contours); three-dimensional perspective view [vegetation draped on top of a digital elevation model (DEM) or solid terrain model (STM)]; and animation (computer graphics technique of viewing the vibrancy of change over time).

The multimedia content has made the World Wide Web (WWW) as an ideal medium for producing cartographic visualisation. Its interactive and flexible nature has enabled the growth of 'mapping on demand'. Using GIS in cartography, there is an explosion of new 'spatial media' on the web (Crampton 2009, 91), known by alternate names of neogeography (Turner 2007), or the geoweb (Scharl and Tochtermann 2007).

Description of statistical data

In dealing with any data set, we often attempt to summarise it by referring to just one score which is typical or representative of all the scores. The three most

122 Traversing the path: data management

important statistical concepts that assist towards this end are measures of central tendency, measures of dispersion and coefficients of correlation. These are numerical expressions of centrality, dispersion and relationship.

Central tendency is in the nature of observations to group around one or more typical scores. There are three common measures of central tendency: the mean, considered as the most common and useful measure of central tendency; the median, defined as the score of the middle object when all objects are ranked in terms of the characteristic under consideration; and the mode, defined as the peak of the frequency distribution or the most frequent score. Average is taken as a synonym of mean though it is also meant to convey that something is not high. When the frequency distribution is symmetrical without fluctuations, the mean and median coincide with each other, otherwise not.

A complete understanding or description of a data set also requires a quantitative measure of its dispersion or scatter. This is done by using a variety of numerical summary measures: the range; inter-quartile range; percentile ranges; mean absolute deviation; variance; standard deviation and coefficient of variation (CV).

Range is the simplest measure of scatter. It describes the difference between the largest and smallest observation in the data set. It reflects the numerical limits of the observed data. Daily range of temperature is an illustration of the kind.

The inter-quartile range describes the scatter of the middle 50 per cent of the observations. Lower and upper quartiles describe its boundaries. Lower quartile is the value below which 25 per cent of the observations occur. Upper quartile is the score above which 25 per cent of the observations occur. The data are organised in ascending numerical order and counted off until 25 per cent and 75 per cent of the observations have been marked. The difference between the two is inter-quartile range.

Percentile range corresponds to the difference between the values of the bottom 1 per cent and top 1 per cent. For instance, if top 1 per cent of the population takes away 25 per cent of the national income and the bottom 1 per cent is left with only 0.5 per cent, the percentile range would be 24.5. Hence it is a measure of inequality.

The mean absolute deviation measure is the mean of all deviations from the mean of data set. It is calculated by subtracting the mean from each data item to produce an absolute deviation, summing these values together to produce a total absolute deviation and dividing this total by the number of observations in the data set. The term 'absolute' means that all negative signs are ignored and are treated as if they were positive.

The variance and standard deviation are the other measures of dispersion. Variance is defined as the average of the squared deviations from the mean, and the standard deviation as the square root of the variance. To calculate the variance we first subtract the mean from each of the data items to produce the deviations. These are then squared to remove the effect of the negative deviations. The squared deviations are then summed and the total sum is divided by the number of observations in the data set to obtain variance. The standard deviation is arrived at by calculating the square root of variance.

CV is another measure of scatter. To work it out, first calculate both the mean and standard deviation of a data set. Second, divide the standard deviation by the mean score. Finally, multiply the quotient by 100. This score is the CV in percentage. The importance of CV measure is that it permits comparisons to be made between data sets whose scatter is measured in different units or which differ significantly in magnitude. CV of rainfall for different places in a region is one good illustration. For instance if a place A has a mean rainfall of 200 cm and standard deviation of 50 cm, its CV would be 25 per cent. Another place B which has a rainfall of 40 cm and standard deviation of 20 cm has a CV of 50 per cent. The overall inference is that the variability of rainfall at place B is higher than at place A. Normally places with low rainfall are marked by high degree of variability.

The work of economist Williamson (1965) illustrates the use of CV in his analysis of regional inequalities. He postulates that the regional inequalities are small at the low level of development of the country; these tend to be high in the transitional stage of development and become low again at a high level of development.

The measures of central tendency and dispersion presented, as described above, deal with single variables. There are situations where patterns found in one variable may correspond to those found in other variables. This leads to a search for nature and degree of relationships between variables. That is how we are obliged to work out coefficients of correlation as well. Spearman's correlation technique, which deals with ranked scale data and Karl Pearson's technique, which treats interval scale data, are statistical measures of association used for working out correlation coefficients.

A geographer is typically concerned with the spatial pattern of distributions. The primary concern is with identification of spatial patterns. The techniques used for the purpose are known as geostatistics originally proposed by Hart (1954) followed by Bachi (1962, 1966), these deal with spatial data in terms of location in space.

Descriptive statistics for spatial distributions

The spatial data, as noted earlier, can be in the form of point data, line data and areal data (discrete or continuous). Some scholars also use a separate category of directional data as represented by air routes, movement of air masses and flow of ocean currents. Geographers are in search of both patterns and processes associated with these data.

Measures of centrality in spatial distributions

Central tendency in spatial distributions is referred to three measures of mean centre, median point and point of minimum aggregate travel distance. These correspond to the mean, median and mode in statistical distributions, respectively. The objective here is to identify central locations in place of calculating central statistic.

Mean centre: It can be regarded as the 'centre of gravity' of a distribution in which each item is weighted according to its location. Ebdon (1985) and Silk

124 Traversing the path: data management

(1979, 24) stress that the mean centre represents an average location and not an average of the characteristics of the phenomena to be found at that location. It is in the form of one point that enables the researcher to compare easily the shift over time of the same phenomenon or scatter of various phenomena in the same region at a given point in time. Mean centre makes real great sense when charted graphically on the map along with points of the original geographical distribution.

One simple illustration of this is the mean centre of a population distribution. Often a series of mean centres of population distribution over successive decades are located in an area to figure out the directional change in distribution of population. Mean centre thereby provides a method for tracing the areal shifts of a distribution over time. The first reported use of the mean centre was by Hilgard (1872). He observed that the westward shift of the US population can be traced through the movement of its mean centre over time. Likewise, the degree of eccentricity of various state capitals in India was worked out by Krishan and Gupta (1976). The location of a state capital was referred to the mean centre of population distribution in the state. The extent of distance between the two, corrected for difference in the area of different states, represented the degree of eccentricity of the capital. The location of the mean centre is not free from the effect of the map projection on which the area under study is represented (Aboufadel and Austin 2006, 65). Therefore, equal area projections are best suited for this purpose.

Median point: It is another measure of central tendency in spatial distributions. It is defined as the point of intersection of two perpendicular lines, each of which divides the distribution in two equal parts. It is advisable to opt for median point in study of distributions which involve area, such as territorial extent of different states of India or area under rice and sugarcane. Such phenomena do not move by themselves as people do through migration. The median point and mean centres will not differ in location if the distribution is uniform or even.

Early application of median point was made by the Russian School of Centrography. The term 'centrography' has been in use for several years for this branch of statistics (Sviatlovsky and Eells 1937). In the early twentieth century empirical research was done to aid economic planning by laws of areal distribution based on median points. The median points of production of various crops, minerals and industrial goods were worked out and were compared with each other. Recommendations were given for ensuring desired changes in their distributional pattern.

At times there may be a need to locate the median points of several interrelated spatial distributions. The classical industrial location problem of Alfred Weber is a case in point. He was interested in finding the optimal location for a factory keeping in view the spatial distribution of raw materials, labour and market. Herein is involved a search for the point which is central to the median points of the three factors of industrial location referred to above.

Point of minimum aggregate travel distance: Finally, still another measure of central tendency in spatial distributions is the point of minimum aggregate travel distance. This is the point which would require the minimum aggregate distance if all the objects in a given spatial distribution travel to it. It bears a correspondence with 'mode' in statistical distributions.

There is no mathematical solution to the location of such a point. Therefore, a 'trial and error' method is adopted for this purpose. In that sense, it is an algorithm case, or a case which is beyond a mathematical solution. The point of minimum aggregate travel distance is best suited to identification of 'optimal locations' for schools, health centres, post offices and banks. In this respect, it scores over mean centre or median point.

Population potential: Just as the mean centre, median point and point of minimum aggregate travel distance are meant to identify the central locations of given spatial distributions, the technique of population potential is meant to identify the relative proximity, nearness or accessibility of each point to the entire distribution. The population potential scores of the different points help in drawing a population potential map of an area. Such a map reveals the degree of accessibility of each part of a region in relation to the given distribution. It is a macro-spatial concept.

The concept has been borrowed from the discipline of physics where potential is defined as the 'energy in the field of a unit mass'. This energy is the product of five forces, namely gravitational, electrical, magnetic, weak nuclear (such as generation of heat in the sun by collision of atoms) and strong nuclear (which keeps the molecules of any object together). The energy of any point multiplied by its mass is its potential.

In quantitative geography, potential signifies the economic and social influence of a place on the whole distribution of which it forms a part. This influence is reflected particularly in migration flows and movement of commodities. The population potential patterns emerging on the map can be referred to those of migration, flow of commodities, levels of development, location of industries and market areas of different goods or services. The degree of correspondence or lack of it becomes a point of further research investigation.

The concept was popularised by Chauncy Harris in the mid-1950s in his attempt to specify the spatial pattern of the American domestic market. His work illustrates the essential flexibility of this measure. It is flexible in two ways. First, we can give a new meaning to population we are dealing with; the number of people, for example, to be transformed into their collective purchasing power. Second, we can replace the distances by a more meaningful substitute, for example physical distances into transport costs. Harris (1954) employed both of these modifications by specifying population as total retail sales and the distances by estimated land transport costs. He produced the population potential map of the United States on these lines. In this manner, he could determine the market potential of each and every part of the country. Population potential has been, thus, used for identifying the economic core areas of United States and United Kingdom (Neft 1966).

Measures of dispersion in spatial distributions

Dispersion refers to scattering of objects in a spatial distribution. Statistical concepts of dispersion are, on the whole, easy to transfer to spatial distributions. The degree of dispersion of any spatial distribution can be referred to three situations:

- Dispersion of objects in relation to mean centre, median point or point of minimum aggregate distance

126 Traversing the path: data management

- Dispersion of objects in relation to some specific location, such as state capitals
- Dispersion of objects in relation to each other

It is observed that in geostatistics, the efforts relating to measures of central tendency are more common than studies of spread. The two concepts, however, complement each other and such a tendency needs to be corrected in any spatial analysis. For spatial distributions, the notion of deviation is the mean distance between the central or a specific location and all the objects in the distribution. On similar lines, a measure of dispersion is arrived at also by computing the mean of distances between the nearest neighbours in any spatial distribution.

Mean distance: This is the simple average of the distances between the mean centre and various objects in a spatial distribution. The same exercise can be carried out with reference to the median point or point of minimum aggregate distance.

Standard distance: The standard distance is the spatial equivalent to the standard deviation. Distances between each observation and the mean centre are squared and summed, and this sum is divided by the number of observations and its square root is computed to find out the standard distance. Standard distances, thus, could be worked out over time for the spatial distributions in a region. A tendency towards increase in standard distance will indicate further scatter of the objects under study. Such a dispersion could be examined by calculating standard distances of population distribution of India vis-à-vis the national capital over the successive census years of 1951, 1961, 1971 . . . 2011.

Relative distance: The standard distance of a given spatial distribution is subject to the size of the region under study. For example, standard distance of a spatial distribution in Uttar Pradesh is likely to be longer than that in Punjab simply because the area of the former is four times that of the latter. This creates difficulties in comparison. Hence the concept of relative distance has been devised to overcome such situations. It is calculated by dividing the standard distance by the radius of the circle representing the area of the region. This procedure neutralises the role of the size of the region.

Quartilide dispersion: It is a simple graphical technique to obtain the idea of dispersion in a spatial distribution. This is done by drawing quartilide lines on the four sides of the region containing the spatial distribution. Quartilide line is a straight one which divides the spatial distribution in a manner that one fourth of the distribution is on one side and three-fourths on the other. The four quartilide lines will thus enclose a rectangle or square within them. If the area of this enclosed figure is small, it will indicate a high degree of concentration in the middle of the region and if large a high degree of dispersion towards the periphery is represented.

Quadrat analysis: A grid of square cells of equal size is placed on top of a map of a distribution. One then counts the number of items in each cell. A large amount of variability in the number of points from cell to cell (i.e. some cells have many points; some have none etc.) implies a tendency towards clustering. If there is very little variability in the number of points from cell to cell or the number of points per cell is about the same, this implies a tendency towards regular, uniform or spatially dispersed pattern. In a random pattern, the mean number of points per cell will be roughly equal to the standard deviation of the number of points per cell or mean and standard distance will be the same giving a mutual ratio of one.

The method was developed primarily by ecologists in the first half of the twentieth century. The statistical test used is given as

$$x^2 = \frac{(m-1)\sigma^2}{\bar{x}}$$

where m is the number of quadrats or cells, and $\bar{x}$ and σ^2 are the mean and variance of the number of points per quadrat, respectively. This score obtained is compared with a critical value from a chi-square table, with $m-1$ degrees of freedom. The choice of the quadrat size is crucial because one may find patterns at some spatial scales and not at others. Thus, it can impact the results. Curtiss and McIntosh (1950) suggest a quadrat size of 2 points per quadrat, whereas Bailey and Gatrell (1995) propose the mean number of points per quadrat should be about 1.6. In other words, if there are 100 quadrats in a spatial framework, there should be 200 or at least 160 points of distribution in it to obtain best results.

Nearest neighbour analysis: It is another objective quantitative measure for identifying the pattern of any spatial distribution, which could be viewed as a dispersion of points in reference to each other. The technique was initially developed by Clark and Evans (1954) to analyse the spatial distribution of plant species.

Herein we compute the ratio between the mean distance of all the nearest neighbours, and the mean of distances between the same points if these were randomly distributed. Hence the statistic of a random distribution will always be one. It may be added that the nearest neighbours can be reflexive, for example A may be the nearest neighbour of M and M the nearest neighbour of A.

Three limiting or extreme cases of various distribution patterns, as generated by three different processes, will emerge as follows:

Distribution pattern	Underlying process	Illustration
Clustered	Contagious spatial diffusion	Houses in an agglomerated settlement
Random	Chance spatial occurrences	Early settlements in a virgin region
Uniform	Competitive spatial situations	Central places as in Christaller's model

All distributional patterns belong either to one of the three types mentioned above or to millions of patterns lying between clustered and random or random and uniform. Nearest neighbour statistic provides a precise measure of any distribution pattern. It also indicates the possible underlying factors that were instrumental in generating a particular pattern.

128 Traversing the path: data management

In the case of competitive spatial situations, a uniform pattern of distribution will be created. Such is a case often with distribution of agricultural market towns in an area. This technique is particularly useful for identifying distortions in the distribution of public facility points, such as schools, hospitals and post offices. It is observed that in India, the facilities provided by the central government, such as post offices, are more evenly distributed, than that provided by the state governments due to greater political interference in the latter case. Guidelines for future planning can be provided by indicating the locations that could fill the gaps.

The nearest neighbour statistic summarises the spatial picture of the whole map. This can be done using geographical analysis of machine (GAM) developed by Openshaw *et al.* (1987) and refined by Fotheringham and Zhan (1996). Otherwise, the conventional method is to compute the mean of the distances, point by point, between all the objects in a spatial distribution and fix it in the formula:

$R_n = 2d\sqrt{N} / A$, where R_n is the nearest neighbour statistic, d is the mean distance between the nearest neighbours, N is the number of objects in the distribution and A is the area of the region.

The computed statistic will range from 0, if the distribution is clustered, to 2.15 if the distribution is uniform or completely ordered. If a value of 1.00 is obtained then the pattern is called 'random'. If the R_n statistic is 1.8, it means that the distribution has a tendency towards uniformity, and if is 0.8 it has a tendency towards randomness (generally speaking).

The nearest neighbour statistic is easy to calculate and comprehend. The shape of the region affects the statistic and its associated test of significance. For example, if the region's shape is long, narrow and/or rectangular, it may have relatively low values of R. Here points are by necessity close to one another. Another situation that makes a difference to the analysis is the location of points close to the boundary of the study region. Consider the case of port towns in a coastal region. The book *Quantitative Methods in Geography* by P.J. Taylor (1977) is the best for learning the technique of calculating R_n statistics.

Using the quadrat method, nearest neighbour test and the Moran statistic, the researcher obtains a single measure of net pattern for a map consisting of point locations. This single summary score is often called the 'global statistic'. The null hypothesis is: there is no underlying pattern, or deviation from randomness, among the set of points.

In other situations, the researchers may wish to know whether disease clusters around a toxic waste site, or whether crime clusters around liquor shops. There still may be situations where the interest is to detect clustering with no a priori idea of cluster location. In either of the cases 'local' or 'focused' tests – Local Moran Statistic or Getis' *Gi* statistic – are employed. These tests are useful as they uncover isolated hotspots of increased incidence, when global tests find no significant deviation from randomness. On the other hand when the global tests indicate significant degree of clustering, local statistics can help in deciding whether the area is relatively homogeneous or contains local outliers that contribute to a significant global statistic. Rogerson (2015) and Anselin (1995) have discussed such issues in detail.

Network analysis

A network is an interconnected system of nodes (vertices) and links (arcs or edges), which are lines joining nodes. Links may be of two types: directed, when they specify the direction of movement, or undirected, such as an international boundary. Directed links are known as arcs (a one-dimensional entity) and undirected links as edges. Transport system – road, rail, air, maritime networks; communication system; mobile telephone networks, or the internet; and social connections can all be represented as a network. The spatial foundation of networks varies. Some networks are defined by their links more than by their nodes, namely road, transit, rail networks. The situation is opposite for others like maritime and air networks. Links in such cases are often not clearly defined for obvious reasons. These are non-planar (three-dimensional) networks wherein the arcs of the network cross without any network node formed at this intersection. The line segments do not come into contact, implicitly or explicitly, at the point of intersections. There are still others such as telecommunication system and mobile network systems including the internet which are complex networks.

In case of transport network, a node or vertex is a point of location of any place, such as Nagpur. Route is the connecting link between two nodes (edge distance), such as railway line between Nagpur and Mumbai. Likewise, in the case of internet, servers are the core of the internet. These can be represented as nodes within a graph. The physical infrastructure between them, namely fibre optic cables, can act as links.

A network and its connectivity are symbolically represented in the form of a graph. A graph comprising a set of linked nodes is an abstraction of reality. Graph theory is a branch of mathematics that studies topological phenomena, which can be represented by network diagrams comprising the nodes and links between them (Gregory *et al.* 2009, 316). It is concerned with encoding or fixing of networks and measuring their properties (Rodrigue, Comtois, and Slack 2013; Taylor 1977, 58). In the topological approach to measurement, the networks are abstracted to simple pattern of points for intersections or stations and lines for routes or connections. It shows the connection between points and relationship between lines and points.

Graph theory does not dwell on distance, direction and all other Euclidean concepts. It identifies three types of basic structures: paths, trees and circuits. A path is a series of one or more lines connecting points such that each vertex is connected to only one other point. A tree is a branching network. A circuit graph has one or more closed loops.

The development of a railway network, as a representative of a graph, can be shown as it evolved from a simple path to a tree and then to a circuit network (Figure 8.1).

Network analysis is an expanding field, distinguished by scientific advances in methodology in recent years – be it transportation with extensive development of roads, railways, air routes, drainage system, communication system, primarily for economic reasons. The evolution of the form and extent of network is strongly linked with political economy. In controlled or feudal economy, virtually all major

130 Traversing the path: data management

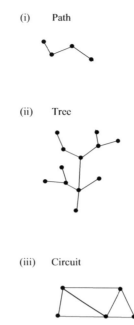

FIGURE 8.1 Basic types of graphs

lines of transport will converge on the capital city. One can also make a comparison between one country's network and another. This variation may then be related to variation in, for example, mean income per head, and thereby used as a possible indicator of economic development. Certainly the variation in the characteristics of networks is considered a reflection of certain spatial aspects of the socio-economic system. Besides, network analysis also focuses on the nature of boundaries that are barriers to movements. There are other facets of network analysis such as social network analysis, with its own body of theory, methodology and practice.

Ever since the quantitative revolution of the 1960s, the research focus using topological concepts has been on planar (two-dimensional) wide range of 'linear feature' networks such as rivers, road and rail systems. The picture somewhat has changed since the 1990s when geographers started to represent and analyse non-planar networks, that included air routes, underground railway systems and road systems with flyovers and subterranean flow channels like ocean currents. These networks need more advanced tools for analysis and representation. Several tools in the form of GIS, R-packages are available which can be useful to test measures and methods on networks.

Here we shall focus on planar examples of network analysis using topological concepts. The ensuing discussion is based on four different cases of networks.

1 Transport network
2 Boundary network

3   Drainage network
4   Spatial–social networks

Transport network

An important part of geographical studies, a transport network is a flow network. It signifies the movement of people, vehicles or goods (Bell and Iida 1997). It is represented by a set of nodes and links. The nodes represent points in space and time, and the links match with specific pieces of transport infrastructure, like a section of road or railway. Transport networks carry anything that moves from place to place – flows of goods, people, information – and give rise to regional transport systems (Bamford and Robinson 1978). A regional transport system is a combination of movements from point-to-point that occur between origins and destinations.

There are a range of topological measures developed for the description of networks:

i   Accessibility of individual nodes
ii   Centrality of a node within network
iii Spread and diameter of a network
iv   General characteristics of a route network
v   Overall characteristics of traffic flow

(i) ***Accessibility of individual nodes***: It is a relative concept, measured in relation to specified locations and modes of transport. The index of accessibility helps to describe the relative positions of individual points and the pattern of accessibility within the network. Accessibility of a node is computed by the number of links converging on it or traffic flow by which it is connected with the rest of the network. For example, nodality of a town can be measured and compared by counting the number of roads or the frequency of trains converging upon each. Accessibility of several places in a region could be computed and compared to identify the most accessible place for locating a new central facility. Places which are marked as meeting points of several links or transport lines are known as nodal centres.
The index of accessibility (A_i) is given by

$$A_i = \sum d_{ij}$$

where, d_{ij} is the shortest path from point i to point j.
When the graphs are large, computer is used to find the shortest path and then to compute accessibilities.

(ii) ***Centrality of a node within network***: It measures the relative importance of a node within a network. Centrality of a node within network is found out by counting the number of links from a given node to a node which is located farthest from it, by the shortest route. Each node will have its own number,

132 Traversing the path: data management

called König number. The node with the smallest number is the one with the highest degree of centrality.

(iii) ***Spread and diameter of a network***: Kansky (1963, 12) examined the diameter (δ) of networks. It is taken as number of arcs on the shortest route between the two farthest points on the network. Another concept to describe the whole graph is diameter (δ). The diameter is the maximum number of edges in the shortest path between the farthest pair of vertices, and is thus an index measuring the topological 'extent' of the graph. Two useful indices were derived from diameter to measure the spread of the network.

    i.   The Pi (π) index

        where

$$\pi = \frac{\text{total mileage of network}}{\text{mileage of diameter}}$$

    ii.   The Eta (η) index

        where

$$\eta = \frac{\text{total mileage of network}}{\text{number of arcs}}$$

(iv) ***General characteristics of a route network***: The general characteristics of a route network can be statistically measured using (i) measures of density; and (ii) a measure of route sinuosity.

Route density is expressed as kilometres of routeway per hundred square kilometres of territory or per 10,000 people. Instead of measuring the roads we may count the number of road junctions in relation to area.

Route sinuosity is measured by detour index. The deflection of routes by physical and other barriers is an important geographical phenomenon. The detour index (D.I) of a link or route between nodes or places is calculated by dividing the actual distance between two places by the crow flight distance between them.

$$\text{D.I} = \frac{\text{actual distance between A and B}}{\text{straight line distance between A and B}} \times 100$$

In fact, the actual route distance is almost always longer than the desired line distance or crow flight distance between places. It is obvious that lower the detour index, the more direct is a given route. Alternately, the higher the value of the detour index, the greater will be the sinuosity of the route. Such indices have high value for analysis of distance between central places in hilly or mountainous areas. The distance between them on a topographical sheet is the crow flight distance. Since the paths or roads in a hilly or mountainous area are tortuous, the actual distance between these two very points on the surface could be around 1.5 times of it. This gives a detour index of 1.5. This distinction must be kept in mind while doing a research exercise in transport geography of a hilly or mountainous region. The detour index is used for assessing the effects which the rerouting of links produce in a given network. It indicates the efficiency of a transport network.

(v) *Overall characteristics of traffic flow*: A transport network can be considered as a system of routeways, or as a system of traffic flow that is either as channels of movement, or as the movement itself. The commonly used measures of traffic flow are the (i) traffic density expressed by the amount of traffic divided by either the population or area served by the network, or the length of the routeway. The amount of traffic is generally expressed in one of the two ways: the mean of a series of traffic counts taken at selected points in the network; and the number of vehicle-kilometres travelled on the network in a given time period; and (ii) connectivity of a network (Hammond and McCullagh 1986, 66).

Connectivity of a network is defined by the degree to which the nodes of a network are directly connected to each other. This is to find out how well connected are the points in the network. It can be used to compare connectivity of two or more networks. Connectivity is measured in several ways using the three properties of network:

e = the number of lines or edges
v = the number of points or vertices
p = the number of separate subgraphs

Taylor (1977, 63) has described these concepts as follows:

Cyclomatic number: absolute circuit connectivity
Alpha index: relative circuit connectivity
Beta index: simple linkage connectivity
Gamma index: relative linkage connectivity

The simplest way of measuring connectivity is to compute the *cyclomatic number* (μ), which tells us how many basic circuits there are in the network. It is defined by:

$$\mu = e - v + p$$

Paths and trees score 0. Cyclomatic number is an absolute measure of connectivity.
A more useful measure of connectivity that makes allowance for size and is a relative measure is the Alpha index (α). It is the ratio of the number of circuits (μ) to the maximum number of circuits that could occur given the number of points

134 Traversing the path: data management

(Garrison and Marble 1962, 24). The alpha index ranges from 0 to 1. The 0 value indicates no circuits and the value of 1 means complete interconnected network.

For planar graphs it is given by the formula:

$$\alpha = \mu/2v - 5 \qquad \text{or} \qquad \alpha = e - v + p/2v - 5$$

Garrison and Marble observe that multiplying the α-index by 100 gives it a range of 0 to 100 (instead of 0 to1). This allows an interpretation of the value as 'per cent redundancy'. A tree would clearly have zero redundancy and a completely connected planar network (i.e. a polygonal graph) 100 per cent redundancy.

Kansky (1963) developed a number of descriptive indices measuring the connectivity of networks. The beta index (β) is the number of edges or links in a network (e) divided by the number of nodes or vertices (v): It is given as: $\beta = e/v$ in units of points per line. In this case the non-connected graph continues to score 0 but the paths and trees are ranged between 0 and 1. All circuit networks have score of 1 or more. Thus, beta differentiates between pre-circuit situations as well as circuit graphs. The higher the value of β, the greater is the connectivity. Hence, the value of β should rise as transport networks develop and become more efficient. The simple beta ratio is used in comparative studies of networks in different countries. The only problem with this index is that its range of possible values depends on the number of nodes or vertices or points. Therefore, a beta index should only be used to compare networks with the same number of nodes, which limits its utility as a measure.

Another useful measure of connectivity is the gamma (γ) index. It is the ratio of the number of links to the maximum number of links possible given the number of nodes. The equation for gamma is $\gamma = e/3(v-2)$ or in which $v > 2$ or $\gamma = arcs/3(nodes - 2)$. This index will always lie between 0.00 and 1.00 (for a completely connected network), as is the case with alpha index. It is different from alpha in that it enables us to differentiate between paths and trees, because it is based on lines rather than circuits.

Still another measure is the connectivity index wherein we divide the number of existing links in a network by the maximum possible links. The connectivity indices help in comparing the degree of ease in mobility in different regions. The maximum number of possible links is $1/2 \times n(n-1)$, where n is the number of nodes in the network. Therefore, the connectivity index, $C = e/1/2 \times n(n-1)$, where e is the number of links or edges in the network, and the denominator is the maximum number of links possible.

With advent of GIS-T software problems like network routing or shortest path (or least cost) can be solved using algorithms. The availability of data and the ability of GPS services to reference locations accurately have made GIS-T as a core technology for transportation (Sutton and Gillingwater 1997). For instance, a researcher may be interested to find the best route for vehicles (school buses and general passenger buses) from one location to another. This query relates to arc routing. Arcs are of interest only as elements of paths that connect the nodes (Assad and Golden 1995). In contrast, the node routing problem occurs where the key service activity falls at the nodes (customers).

Boundary networks

Maps often contain boundaries to mark areas. Areas are distinguished from one another by lines on a map that form boundary networks. The boundary networks divide the map into areas of varying size and shape. The size can be measured manually or using digital planimeter.

Area can be measured directly if we place a fine grid over a specified region and count the number of cells of the grid that fall within the region. Border cells with more than half their total area in the specific region are usually counted; those with less than half are not. The final total of cells counted as being within the region represents its area.

A simple formula can also be used to measure area. Let the number of grid squares wholly within the cell be a, let the number of grid squares through which the cell boundary passes be b.

$$\text{The area of the cell} = a + \frac{b}{2} \text{ the area of one grid square}$$

Areas also differ in shapes. It need not be only physical entity but also time-space, cost-space or effort-space (Massam 1972, 2). Shape is a property difficult to define and measure (Ebdon 1985, 143). A geographer looks for a concise statistic to measure shape as a continuous variable. The most commonly measured characteristic of shape is compactness, which however is only one characteristic of shape. A compact shape for a given area has a short boundary and bears a short distance between extremities. The measure of compactness shows how far a shape deviates from the most compact possible shape, a circle. A circle is the most compact two-dimensional shape. The simplest measure of a cell's compaction is the length/breadth ratio (L/B):

$$L/B = \frac{\text{length of long axis of cell}}{\text{length of short axis of cell}}$$

Here the long axis is the line joining the two points on the boundary which are farthest from each other in a straight line. The short axis is the longest line that can be drawn perpendicular to the long axis between two other points on the boundary. The greater the value of L/B, the less compact the shape. The L/B for a circle will be 1; its minimum value. A square invariably has an L/B of 1.41, so it is

136 Traversing the path: data management

considerably less compact than a circle. Although this ratio is easy to calculate, it is a rough indicator of compaction.

Another simple measure relates properties of the area under analysis to properties of a circle of equal area. The formula is:

$$e = \frac{d}{l}$$

where l is the long axis of the shape referring to the longest line between two points on the shape's parameter and d is the diameter of a circle (its long axis) of equal area. Here d is defined as $2\sqrt{a / \pi}$, where a is the area of the shape. A circle scores 1, and all other shapes score less than 1. The more circle like or compact the shape is, the smaller will be its long axis in relation to the diameter. Thus, the ratio approaches unity. The limiting case in terms of lack of compactness is simply a line, which has no area. In this case the diameter of the circle of equal area is 0, so that e gets reduced to 0. Hence, the measure ranges from 1 for a circle (maximum compactness) to 0 for a line (minimum or no compactness). This is a simple and quite effective indirect measure of compactness on a ratio scale.

A more refined measure of compaction is listed below:

$$\text{Compaction index } (CI) = \frac{\text{area of cell being measured}}{\text{area of smallest inscribing circle}}$$

The value of compaction index varies from 1 indicating maximum compactness, exemplified by a circular cell, to a minimum value of 0. The lower value of CI shows less compact shape.

The choice of technique for the measurement of shape will be guided by the purpose of research. In the case of administrative areas, the following need consideration: already existing administrative centre, uneven pattern of population distribution and specific channels of population mobility (Yeates 1974). Kant (1988) had used the shape efficiency index method of Massam and Goodchild (1971) that satisfies most of these requirements. He discovered a gradually rising positive relationship between shape efficiency and development level at lower spatial scales of administrative areas than in the case of those at higher levels. Some of the other methods of measuring shape are that of Boyce and Clark (1964) and Bunge (1966).

Channel (fluvial) networks

A fillip to studies on quantitative analysis of fluvial networks can be traced to Horton's (1945) classic paper, which was the first to introduce stream ordering for measurement of various attributes to discover holistic stream properties. Horton's law of stream numbers was later improved by Strahler (1957) to give the present technique of Horton–Strahler. The stream ordering is a topological characterisation of a network.

Hierarchy of stream segments in a drainage system is one of the first attributes to be quantified in an ordering classification system. Horton (1945, 291) had enunciated law of stream numbers, which states an inverse geometric sequence of the numbers of stream segments of each order with their order number. This was done on the basis of analysis of data that revealed a consistent relationship among the number of stream segments of one order and those of the next higher order in a drainage network, called the bifurcation ratio which was always around 3.

To arrive at this relationship the channel segments were assigned numbers in an order beginning from a stream's headwaters to a point somewhere down stream. The tributaries at the stream's headwaters were given the value 1. Two first-order segments join to form a stream which is given an order of 2. Two second-order streams form a third-order stream and so on. Following this bifurcation ratio is computed. Such studies may be a useful measure of areas' proneness to flooding. Higher bifurcation ratio leads to greater probability of flooding.

The stream ordering approach, particularly the Horton ordering, has been shown to be a suitable basis for the objective generalisation of river networks where density reduction through feature elimination is required (Rusak and Castner 1990). The ordering techniques have been used to support automated generalisation of river networks (Richardson 1993) using GIS.

Stream ordering is the idea behind the River Continuum Concept, a model used to find out the number and types of organisms present in a stream of a given size (Vannote et al. 1980). The concept stems from the notion that a river can only actually be understood as a continuum since it changes constantly as it moves downstream. Diverse biological communities inhabit a stretch of stream. Stream order helps in describing the structure and function of communities along a river system. In fact it can be applied to any field where branching, hierarchical networks are important.

There has been a regular flow of such studies in geography and geology journals since the mid of last century. Analysis of fluvial networks and drainage basin spatial structure was reinvigorated in the mid- to late 1980s through the application of fractal geometries and statistics. Stream networks have enabled many applications including hydrologic modelling and geomorphologic analysis of landscape.

Stream networks are now automatically extracted from DEM. This has been possible through GIS software, for example Geographic Resources Analysis Support System (GRASS), ArcGIS and specialised packages such as RiverTools and TauDEM. The idea that water flows downhill along steepest descent forms the backbone of all this. The algorithms often involve two steps although many variations exist: (i) locating the flow direction (steepest descent) for each cell in the DEM; and (ii) separating cells that represent true channels from those that do not, using a threshold criterion derived from an assumed channelisation mechanism (Luo et al. 2014).

Socio-spatial network

Network analysis also includes in its fold several network types – social, spatial or areal (such as urban), information and communication. These involve acquaintances, academic collaborations, the web, the internet, telephone lines and so on.

138 Traversing the path: data management

Some cases are discussed in the subsequent paragraphs.

Social network analysis projects relationships between individuals or groups of people (Wasserman and Faust 1994). Such individuals may be persons, nation states, organisations, groups, websites, or citations involving scholarly publications (scientometrics). Social networks generate social capital in an individual. The analysis is concerned with 'relational data' relating to contacts, ties and connections. In a topological approach, individual actors are the nodes within the networks, and relationships between the actors serve as ties also called paths, edges, links or connections.

Barnes (1954) began to use the expression social network to denote patterns of ties using concepts like bounded groups, such as tribes, families and gender, and ethnicity. Since then systematic social network analysis has been extensively used by scholars (Freeman 2006). It is an analytic approach with its own theory, methods of analysis and software for analysis. All of these can be examined in spatial perspective and hence fall in the domain of socio-spatial networks.

The techniques of social network analysis have been popularised with revolution in information and communication sector since the 1970s. With 'networking' becoming a global phenomenon and proliferation of 'social networking' micro-blogging websites such as Facebook and Twitter, research is being done on the influence of factors like geographic distance, national boundaries, frequency of air travel and language on the formation of social ties on Twitter using a large sample of publicly available Twitter data (Takhteyev, Gruzd, and Wellman 2012).

Insights into geographies of urban networks have been gained by researchers using information on corporate networks by researchers. Here the 'network structures' of firms comprises of cities as nodes (Taylor *et al.* 2009). Functional relations of varying magnitude and strength exist between cities. The bonding constitutes the link that varies with the connecting strength between cities. The urban systems are described through the analytical lens of flows between cities. Data are produced on connection between cities. The notion of 'urban networks' has increasingly become an organising paradigm within the vast literature on 'urban systems' (e.g. Camagni 1993; Yates 1997; Castells 2001).

The data are generated through questionnaires, interviews, participant observations and documentary sources. There are several things to be measured, such as centrality which identifies closeness, cohesion that gives access to basic calculations of distances and densities, regions that are organised into zones and territorial arrangements which define the network and so on.

Finally, a number of software tools like NetDraw (version 4.14, which is distributed along with UCINET), and Pajek and Mage, (look for software at the website of the International Network of Social Network Analysts [INSNA]) are available for visualising and drawing graphs. Each has certain strengths and limitations.

Network data models and GIS operations

Many GIS operations contain the network data models. The basic applications of network data models are in the field of

i   Topology
ii   Cartography
iii Geocoding
iv   Routing and traffic assignment

Topology: It concerns representations of location, direction and connectivity.

Cartography: Using cartography a transport network can be visualised for calculation and simple navigation. Different elements of the network are given symbols. For instance, road links may be accorded differentiated symbols based on their importance. A national highway link may be symbolised as a thick line and given a label (say NH1), while a state highway may be symbolised by a comparatively thinner line and labelled (SH). A district road on the other hand may be shown as a thin line but unlabelled.

Geocoding: A linear referencing system enables transportation network models to derive a precise location. For instance, a large number of addresses are marked based on a number and a street. The address information is inserted in the attributes of a network data model. This network is then used for geocoding. It then becomes possible to pinpoint the location of an address, or any location along the network, with reasonable accuracy. These are now embedded in mobile phones, cars or transport vehicles and greatly help in reaching locations through navigation.

Routing and assignment: Network data models may be used to locate most advantageous flow paths. Flows can be allocated keeping in view capacity constraints in a network. This requires drawing of a topology to show the relationship of each link with other intersecting segments. The factors operating in opposition to the flow, such as traffic lights and congestion, are also attributed to each link. These will determine the impedance of a route and have an impact on the chosen path or on how flows are assigned in the network. Routing and traffic assignment is a complex task in urban areas but relatively simple at the continental level since small variations in impedance are of limited consequences.

It follows that network analysis is pertinent to not only transport system but also to boundary geometrics, drainage patterns and socio-spatial interactions.

Morphometric analysis

In morphometric analysis a researcher is engaged in measuring and analysing mathematically the use of shape, dimensions and configuration of the earth's surface and

140 Traversing the path: data management

its landforms through various cartographical and diagrammatic techniques. The statistical information about the earth's surface is provided by topographical maps, or actually measured in the field.

Morphometry has been a significant instrument of structural geomorphology since the 1950s (Strahler 1952). The works of Dury (1952) and Christian, Jennings, and Twidale (1957) provide an elaboration of the methods.

As part of quantitative geomorphology, morphometric analysis is mainly related to analysis of varied characteristics of rivers and drainage basins. There are various indices that are worked out based on channel network like stream ordering, length of overland flow, basin form, circulatory index etc. A drainage basin may contain a number of terrain units and for each terrain unit morphometric indices like slope, drainage density, drainage texture, relative relief etc. may be computed.

Slope zone and slope aspect maps are useful products of morphometric analysis. Morphometry from maps results in drawing of hypsometric, clinometric and altimetric frequency curves.

Morphometric analysis based on GIS technique is a proficient tool for geo-hydrological studies, namely identification and planning of the ground water potential zones and watershed management.

Terrain analysis

The term 'terrain' refers to the surface and near surface attributes of an area of significance to the human beings. Terrain analysis is a process of classifying earth surface based on a host of factors like relief, lithology, soil, hydrological conditions, geological/geomorphological processes and vegetation/land cover types (FAO 1976, 79; Meijerink 1988; Van Zuidam 1985). Widely used classification scheme are that of MEXE in UK, CSIRO in Australia and ITC, the Netherlands. Advent of modern mapping technologies like remote sensing, GIS, GPS and an analytical tool like DEM have strengthened terrain research further and many geographers now use computer models for terrain analysis (Lindsay 2005; Wilson and Gallant 2000; Zhou, Lees, and Tang 2008).

Terrain classification is based on any of the commonly followed three approaches: genetic, parametric or landscape. These approaches differ in mapping methods, format for display of map information and their usability.

Mabbutt (1968) has defined and explained these approaches. Genetic approach aims at finding distinctive land units by repeated subdivision on the basis of causal environmental factors. This is typical in the case of normal geologic and geomorphic features.

Parametric approach follows the division and classification of land on the basis of selected attribute values, for example a slope map, depth-to-water-table map or lithologic map. Individual parametric maps are generally prepared for a specific purpose of land development and management. These can only be correlated with other parametric maps by means of map overlays. The parametric is an objective approach which provides a numerical terrain measurement, is calibratable and repeatable. It is, of course, expensive and time consuming.

The landscape approach classifies land particularly at the reconnaissance level, on the basis of complex of factors and attributes. The land complex as a whole is the object of study, even where a particular attribute may be of prime interest to a land classification. The approach makes use of integrated mapping units that combine geomorphic features, soils and vegetation as the basis for mapping. The landscape maps and land description is the result of working together of specialists in several disciplines. It is a subjective approach; however, the boundaries of landscape units are real and well identifiable in the field.

Remote sensing by providing numerical measurements for very large areas, economically and efficiently, acts as a bridge between the parametric and landscape approaches.

Terrain analysis has assumed significant importance in applied and basic research in geography, particularly in the fields of land and water management, soil survey, land evaluation, biogeography and environmental impact assessment. Its importance in engineering and military sciences has long been recognised. Geographers continue to get involved in terrain analyses under the aegis of Defence Terrain Research Laboratory, Government of India. S. Chattopadhyay and M. Chattopadhyay (1995) had attempted terrain analysis for the State of Kerala following landscape approach to delineate basic units. IRS-1A and TM data products were used to identify the terrain units and attribute data were extracted from the topographic maps, other thematic maps and field investigation. Altogether 24 units emerged through this exercise for the entire state of Kerala.

Fractal analysis

Fractal is defined as a non-regular geometric shape that has the same degree of non-regularity at all scales. Fractal geometry concerns rough and irregular forms found in the nature and society. It is a pattern for which fractal dimension (D) has a fractional value (Mandelbrot 1967, 1982).

Fractal analysis allied with GIS, remote sensing, spatial modelling is a technique to study fractal dimensions. It is used to measure, describe, characterise the dimension (D) of fragmented, irregular, wiggly and rough linear and areal features or surfaces – coast line, shoreline of lakes, river networks, plateau scarps, contour crenulations, landslide scars, geological fractures, oil-bearing strata; to delineate landform regions statistically; and to simulate fractal terrain (Gao and Xia 1996) and urban form/structure (McAdams 2009). Landscapes developed under different climate and geology can be compared by computing fractal values.

It is a mathematical formulation that can be conveniently used in modelling structures in which similar patterns persist at increasingly smaller scales and helps in describing somewhat random and chaotic phenomena such as crystal growth and galaxy formation. Due to scale-independent properties, it helps in comparing features irrespective of their scale of occurrence.

Fractals do not provide empirically verifiable models to study spatial forms and as such mark a considerable change in norms and standards of viewing the

142 Traversing the path: data management

spatial phenomena, which is different from the conventional ways of thinking about spatial forms (Goodchild and Mark 1987).

Fractals have been widely used as a tool in different disciplines, including physics, biology, medicine, architecture earth science, economics and geography. John A. Wheeler, the American physicist who coined the term 'blackhole' used in astronomy, wrote in a review of Mandelbrot's (1982) book *The Fractal Geometry of Nature* that the scope of fractals is growing so much that as new ideas lead to applications and applications lead to new ideas, the familiarity with the knowledge of fractals will become 'a must have' to be considered scientifically literate in the times to come. Likewise, James Gleick in his book *Chaos* (2008) says that twentieth-century science will be remembered for chaos and this includes the geometry of chaos that is fractals.

Fractal dimension for both linear and areal features can conveniently be worked out through several of mathematical algorithms now available on the shelf. Lam and De Cola (1993) and Dauphine (2012) have authored books on fractals for use in geography and a number of other contributions by geographers are emerging.

Chattopadhyay and Kumar (2007) have computed numerical value of fractal dimension (D) of selected water bodies in Kerala engaging different methods to suggest that these values can be used to characterise water bodies irrespective of their size and classify them according to the roughness of their perimeters/shorelines and finally link these observations to their geomorphic evolution.

Cities yield some of the best examples of fractals. There is a growing realisation that the naturally or organically growing city is optimal in countless ways and that social and economic order belies the physical form of cities. Moreover the irregularity and messiness about the shape and form of cities is simply being seen as a superficial manifestation of a deeper order (Batty and Longley 1994; Shen 2002).

Jiang and Yin (2014) have proposed 'ht-index' to quantify the fractal structure of geographic features. It is based on the idea of 'far more small things than large ones', which is true for geographic features. In the context of cities all over the world we observe that the number of small cities is larger in comparison to the large ones (Zipf 1949); short streets are more than that of long ones (Carvalho and Penn 2004; Jiang 2009); less-connected streets are higher in number than well-connected ones (Jiang 2007, 2009); low-rise buildings exceed in number than high-rise ones (Batty *et al.* 2008); and there are numerous small city blocks than large ones (Jiang and Liu 2012; Lämmer, Gehlsen, and Helbing 2006). This idea is equally applicable to natural and human features such as mountains, rivers, lakes, parks and forests.

Ht-index just like fractal dimension quantitatively analyses the complexity of fractals or that of geographic features. A higher ht-index of geographic features represents their non-linear, heterogeneous, mature or natural characteristic. Thus, ht-index is a useful tool for measuring heterogeneity, particularly spatial heterogeneity.

Spatial analysis of areal distributions

More often, a research student is concerned with analysis of secondary data pertaining to areal or spatial units, such as states, districts, development blocks etc. Thus an understanding of techniques to treat such data becomes all the more essential for a student of geography. These techniques could be arranged into four groups as pertinent to:

a measurement of relative concentration of a spatial distribution, such as location quotient, localisation coefficient, index of diversification/specialisation and determination of hierarchical order;
b collective treatment of spatial units in a region, such as index of areal association, disparity, segregation, auto – correlation and trend surface analysis;
c selection of indicators, such as indicators of regional development or human development; and
d data reduction techniques – factor analysis and cluster analysis. These can be applied in any branch of geography where the concern is classification of objects, or areas, on the basis of many measured attributes.

(a) Measurement of relative concentration

Location quotient: It is a measure of the relative share of a spatial unit in the total of any distribution. One ready example is the share of different states and union territories in total population of India. This gives an idea about relative concentration of population in different parts of the country. If such an exercise is repeated for a number of successive census years, we get informed about the change in or continuity of the relative concentration of population.

If we are to determine the areal concentration of individual crops, the two units of measurement used for determining the concentration of crops are (i) area under the crop and (ii) net sown area. The above expression will be elaborated as:

$$\frac{\text{Index}}{\text{of crop concentration}} = \frac{\dfrac{\text{area under crop } x \text{ in a component areal unit}}{\text{area under all crops in the component areal unit}}}{\dfrac{\text{area under crop } x \text{ in entire state}}{\text{area under all crops in the entire state}}}$$

Using absolute data, the location quotient (Q) for any activity in any area is given by the following expression:

$$Q = \frac{X_i / X}{Y_i / Y}$$

where
X_i is area under a crop (wheat) in the unit area (district)
X is area of all crops in the unit area (district)
Y_i is area under crop (wheat) in the state
Y is area of the entire crops in the state.

144 Traversing the path: data management

If the base data are percentages instead of absolute number, the location quotient (Q_i) can be written simply as follows for any area i:

$$Q_i = \frac{X_i}{\gamma}$$

where X_i is the (variable) area percentage in the district, and γ is the percentage in the state.

A location of 1.0 means the activity is represented in the area in exactly the same proportion as in the state. Less than 1.0 shows the activity to be under-represented against the average, while over 1.0 shows that the area has more than its 'fair share'. The higher the Q statistic, the greater is the degree of concentration of the activity in the area in question. Bhatia (1965) determined the regional concentration of crops, using location quotient index. The percentages of the net sown area corresponding to the high, medium and low degree of concentration of different crops were calculated and their regional patterns identified.

The concept of concentration allows us to associate and compare different crop distributions on a uniform base. This is helpful in arriving at meaningful generalisations in the crop geography of a region under study. The technique for measurement of crop concentration described is comparable to the methods used by industrial geographers for measuring the location of manufacturing (Alexander 1958), and by some urban geographers for determining the functional character of urban places (Pownall 1953; Webb 1959).

Localisation coefficient: In this technique, we examine the relative concentration of a distribution in various spatial units vis-à-vis the average for the whole region of which they are a part. As an illustration here, we may take data for per capita income of different states and union territories and also the national average. If we divide the per capita income of individual states by the national average, we get the localisation coefficients in each case. These coefficients can be mapped in the form of a choropleth map. This would reveal the spatial pattern of relative status of various states vis-à-vis the national income.

Index of specialisation: A researcher may want to make a comparison of data for a single town or a district against some national or regional benchmark. One typical measure is the index of specialisation, given by the formula:

$$s_i = \left(k_i - k_j \right) / k_j$$

where
s_i is the index of specialisation for the ith city in industry k
k_i is the percentage of the workforce of the ith city in that industry
k_j is the percentage in the nation or region as a whole.

For example, the city of Panipat with 36.73 per cent of its workforce in textile industry, compared to the state (Haryana) average of only 10.31 per cent, has a specialisation index of 36.73/10.31 = 3.56 for that industry. This approach, however, is sensitive to changes in the definition of benchmark, that is whether a national, regional or state comparison is made.

More refined method of computing specialisation was proposed in which the size of a centre was taken into account. This technique was a derivative of the basic/non-basic approach and was developed by Klaasen, Torman, and Koyck (1949) for a Netherlands study, and taken up by Ullman and Dacey (1962) in the United States. The workforces of sets of cities in the same size range are compared. The lowest proportion found for an industry in any of the towns can be judged to represent the minimum requirements, that is the lowest level for that industry that a city of a given size must support. Let us say it is 8 per cent. This is the non-basic element meant to serve the local population. If a town has 15 per cent of its work force in that industry, the extra 7 per cent (15 − 8) is its basic element, representing the degree of its specialisation.

This technique is used in classification of cities. In this case, the data regarding functional composition of working force of each city are taken into account. Find out the lowest percentage figure for each function in different cities. This figure is the minimum requirement for a city. This will vary for different functions.

Compute the percent workforce for each of the ten industries for cities in each size class. The lowest for each industry among the cities in each size class is noted. This is assumed to be the minimum requirement for a city of that size class. Similar lows are calculated for each industry and each population size of city. In case of six class sizes of cities chosen there would be six low values for each industry. The two parameters of city size population and minimum proportion of workforce (in per cent) are plotted against each other, and regression lines fitted to show the average relationships. The regression lines for the various industry groups are used to compute the 'expected' minimum for a city of a given size. The deviations between the expected and the observed values for each industry may be combined to give a single index of specialisation, S, for a city.

$$S = \Sigma\{(\Sigma_i\, P_i - M_i)\}/M_i\}/\{(\Sigma_i\, P_i - \Sigma\, M_i)^2\}/\Sigma_i\, M_i\}$$

Here, i refers to each of the n industrial sectors, P_i is the percentage of the workforce employed in each of the i sectors and M_i the minimum percentage expected for the size of the city (Ullman and Dacey 1962, 137). It reveals the relationship between size of city and specialisation. The larger the city, the larger the number of specialities it can support in the 'ecological niches' of its population structure, and thus it would be more self-contained. This finding is logically consistent in that at the lowest extreme, the family can sell virtually nothing to itself, while at the upper extreme, the total world population (about 7.3×10^9) can only sell to itself (Haggett, Cliff, and Frey 1977, 169).

Determination of hierarchical order: Krishan and Chandna (1977) devised a technique for determining the hierarchical order of 243 service centres identified in

146 Traversing the path: data management

Sirmaur district of Himachal Pradesh in India. Simplifying the procedure suggested by Hagget and Gunawardena (1964), they laid out the various steps as follows:

  i The 243 service centres were arranged in descending order of their population.
 ii The number of service centres with a specific function, say a high/higher secondary school, was noted. This happened to be 25.
iii The information cards of 25 service centres with this function were taken out and their median population was noted. This came out as 868.
 iv The same procedure was repeated for all the 15 services taken into account. The median population in each case was noted. This was, for example, 443 for post office, 520 for dispensary, 863 for agricultural market, 1917 for tahsil headquarters and so on.
  v The population figures, thus obtained, were rounded to the nearest hundred to fix scores to be assigned to different services. The post office, thus, got a score of 4; dispensary of 5; agricultural market of 9; and tahsil headquarters of 19.
 vi Applying these scores to existing services at various service centres, the functional score of each service centre was worked out. For example, a service centre providing the services of a primary school, dispensary and agricultural market carried a functional score of $4 + 5 + 9 = 18$.
vii All the service centres were arranged in descending order of their functional scores. Critical breaks were marked in distribution of the scores. These yielded six orders of hierarchy among service centres in the present case.

(b) Collective treatment of spatial units

Index of areal association: There are a number of ways to arrive at the indices of areal association between two or more spatial distributions. These could be visual, graphical or statistical. The visual technique involves overlaying of two spatial distributions upon each other. By placing the maps depicting the rates of female literacy rate and infant mortality in India upon each other, we can mark areas where both the rates are above or below the national average. These are the areas which carry a positive relationship with each other in respect of these two variables. In other cases, where one is above the national average and the other below it, a negative relationship is suggested.

Another technique to assess areal association is to prepare a map of a causative factor, such as major rivers of India, and to overlay a map of the resultant factor, such as distribution of cities. An association or disassociation between the two can be observed from the map itself. One can also calculate the percentage of cities which are located on a river and others which are not.

Still another visual graphical approach for understanding areal associations involves the use of scatter diagram. It is a useful preliminary tool to perceive whether the relationship between two distributions is positive or negative or indifferent or curvilinear. A curvilinear form is obtained when middle range scores of both X and

Y are either high or low. This is said to be the case with the female participation in the working force. It tends to be high at the low level of development, *low in the transitional stage* and again high at an advanced stage of development.

The techniques for statistically analysing relationships are broadly divided into bivariate and multivariate procedures. The relationships are examined using correlation and regression. Bivariate linear relationships are obtained by using Pearson's Product Moment Correlation technique for interval/ratio scaled variables, Spearman's Rank Correlation and Kendall's Tau Rank Correlation that deal with pairs of ranked or ordinal data, and the Phi Coefficient, Cramer's V and the Kappa index of measurement used when nominal attributes are to be correlated.

One of the most widely used technique of map comparison and areal association is the correlation analysis. An investigation of the direction and strength of the association between two variables is called simple (or bivariate) correlation analysis. The measure of relationship between two variables is termed as coefficient of correlation. The details of these techniques can be obtained from any standard book on statistical methods.

Using data for agricultural productivity and population density of each state/union territory of India, we can calculate coefficient of correlation between the two separately for every state or union territory by using districtwise data. These correlation coefficients can be mapped in the form of a choropleth map. Such a map will reveal where the relationship between agricultural productivity and population density is strong and where it is otherwise.

Residuals from regression: Here we go beyond measuring the mere strength of association between two variables through a correlation coefficient. Our interest in this case is to define the precise mathematical form of linkage of variable *X* to variable *Y* or to take it further to predict the value of variable *Y* from our knowledge of variable *X*. This is technically known as regression analysis.

The regression analysis designates each variable as having different role in the relationship. Of the two variables, one is independent (*X*) and the other is dependent (*Y*). It means that the variable *X* to some extent determines the value of *Y*. It also implies that if we know the value of *X* then we can estimate or predict the value of *Y* with a certain level of confidence. Regression analysis is often used to explore relationship where there is a cause and an effect, one thing resulting in another. For example, the total fertility rate, that is the number of children a woman is expected to bear during her productive span, may be considered as related to the female literacy rate in different states and union territories of India. Here we have two sets of data: female literacy rate as independent variable and total fertility rate as dependent variable. Regression analysis can help us in finding out the expected total fertility rate at a given level of female literacy. Here we already have the actual figures for the total fertility rate for different states and union territories. The expected total fertility rate can be worked out by regressing it with already available data on female literacy rate. The difference between the actual and expected values is known as residual from regression. These residuals for each state/union territory

148 Traversing the path: data management

can be plotted on a map. These will reveal where the actual rates of total fertility rate are higher or lower than the expected ones. This will divulge the role of factors other than female literacy rate in influencing the total fertility rate.

Chi-square test is meant to verify the significance of the relationship or co-variance between two distributions. The chi-square statistic is calculated by sub-tracting the expected frequency from the observed in each class, squaring them and summing up and dividing it by the summation of expected frequencies. The formula for the test is given below:

$$\chi^2 = \frac{(O - E)^2}{E}$$

where
χ^2 is the value of chi-square
O refers to the frequencies actually observed
E refers to the frequencies expected under the hypothesis of independence
Σ is symbol for summation.

The significance of the result is found by referring to a table of the sampling dis-tribution of the statistic. It contains critical χ^2 value given at different confidence values and degrees of freedom. If there were perfect agreement between the two data sets, χ^2 would be 0.

***Index of dissimilarity*:** It is employed to measure the difference between any two sets of paired percentages representing a spatial distribution. The formula for index of dissimilarity is:

either Σ $(p - q)$ where p is greater than q
or Σ $(q - p)$ where q is greater than p

where p and q are sets of percentages to be compared and negative signs are ignored. The index will range from 100 (maximum dissimilarity) to 0 (complete similarity).

Using this formula one can compute the index of dissimilarity in distribution of national income and number of cars in different states and union territories of India. Here at the first level, the percentage share of each state/union territory in both income and cars will be calculated. At the second level, the index of dissimilar-ity will be arrived at by using the formula listed above.

The index of dissimilarity can also be used to arrive at the index of spatial concen-tration. One can compute the percentage of population in each state/union territory of India vis-à-vis the percentage share of each in land area. The difference between the two sets of figures can be computed and summed up, wherein negative signs are ignored. A large sum will represent a high degree of spatial concentration.

The same technique can be a useful measure of inequality. The annual World Development Reports brought out by the World Bank Group often give data relat-ing to percentage distribution of the aggregate income of different countries into five quintile groups of population. The ratio between the share of the top quintile group and that of the bottom group gives a fair idea of the inequality in income distribution in a country. For example, in 2004–05, top 20 per cent of the population in India partook 45.5 per cent of the national income while the bottom 20 per cent shared only 8.1 per cent. The index of inequality works out as 45.5/8.1 = 5.6.

Index of disparity: Very often geographers are concerned with the spatial pattern and change in disparity among different regions in a country. Per capita income of different states and union territories is one such case. The disparity index in respect of different states/union territories is calculated by dividing the standard deviation of their per capita income by the national average. An increase in this index over time will represent widening of disparity and a decrease will stand for narrowing of it.

Disparity or differentials can be absolute or relative. In an absolute sense, it may be calculated by simply subtracting the lesser values from the higher values. For instance, if literacy rate for urban population in a region is 60 per cent, for rural population it is 30 per cent, then absolute disparity will be equal to 30 per cent points. Relative disparity may be worked out as ratio between the ratio between the two rates, U(urban):R(rural) = 60:30 = 2:1. For India, the absolute differential would be $84.1-67.8 = 16.3$ percentage points. The relative differential may be found by working out the ratio between the two rates, that is U:R = 84.1: $67.8 = 1.2:1$. Though the two differentials view the disparity from different angles, both suffer from a common vagary of grouping dissimilar areas into the same type. An area with an urban literacy rate of 70 per cent and a rural literacy rate of 50 per cent would have the same absolute differential as an area with 40 (urban) and 20 (rural) per cent literacy rates. Similarly, the relative differential in an area with 60 per cent (urban) and 30 per cent (rural) literacy rates would be the same as in an area with 40 (urban) and 20 (rural) per cent literacy rates. Hence, a more sophisticated technique is required to measure the differential.

A simple measure of differential was devised by Krishan and Shyam (1978):

$$ID = \frac{U - R}{T}$$

where
ID = index of urban–rural differential in literacy
U = percentage of literates in urban population
R = percentage of literates in rural population
T = percentage of literates in total population.

Using the formula indices can be calculated for all different areal units. For India based on Census 2011 data, this index would be $84.1-67.8/73.0 = 0.22$.

A sophisticated technique was used by Sopher (1974, 1980) to compute a disparity index:

$$D_s = \log (X_2/X_1) + \log (100 - X_1)/(100 - X_2)$$

150 Traversing the path: data management

In computing the disparity in literacy rate between alphas (e.g. male literacy) and non-alphas (e.g. female literacy), one would take the literacy of the former as X_2 and that of the latter as X_1.

This measure has a number of useful properties: (i) the range spread from minus infinity to plus infinity. Two possible situations can occur: one of the groups does not possess the property at all while in the other case, all members of one group hold the same property; (ii) a value of zero indicates parity or no disparity; (iii) a reversal of sign occurs with measurement of disparity in the reverse direction, such as female/male disparity in literacy is the negative of male/female disparity; (iv) there is a reversal of sign when the absence of a property is measured, for instance, male/female disparity in illiteracy is the negative of male/female disparity in literacy and (v) the measure is additive such as the sum of the disparity between groups P and Q and the disparity between Q and R is equal to the disparity between P and R.

Let us compute the disparity in literacy rate between males X_2 and females X_1 in India in 2011 using Sopher's disparity index:

male literacy $= 80.88$ per cent
female literacy $= 64.63$ per cent
$D_s = \log (80.88/64.63) + \log (100 - 64.63)/(100 - 80.88) = 0.36$.

Likewise, the literacy disparity between non-alphas and alphas is:

$D_s = \log (64.6/80.88) + \log (100 - 80.88)/(100 - 64.63) = (-) 0.36$.
The illiteracy index between males and females works out to $(-) 0.36$.

Here log has been taken to reduce effect of level of attainment on the disparity. This is to take care of the fact that even though the gender gap is the same for both states, the states with the high levels of attainments may show a lower level of disparity than states with low levels of attainments (Sopher 1980).

Kundu and Rao (1986) have shown that the above index fails to satisfy the additive monotonocity axiom. The additive monotonocity axiom specifies that if a constant is added to all observations in a non-negative series, ceteris paribus, the inequality index must report a decline. Therefore in measuring the disparity, they have used an index that satisfies all the four axioms of additive monotonicity, multiplicative monotonicity, redistribution and repetitive transfers. As such the Sopher's index was further modified by Kundu and Rao (1986) on the following lines:

$$D_s = \log (X_2/X_1) + \log (200 - X_1)/(200 - X_2)$$

where $X_2 \geq X_1$ and X_1 and X_2 are various demographic attributes of alphas and non-alphas respectively.

Index of productivity: Several scholars – geographers and regional economists – have put forward measures of agricultural productivity or efficiency which could be used to measure regional disparity in this attribute. Measures for India or some part of it have been proposed by Kendall (1939), Stamp (1952), Shafi (1960, 1972), Enyedi (1964), Khusro (1965), Bhatia (1965, 1967), Sinha (1968), Singh (1972, 1976), Hussain (1976), Dayal (1984). Some of these are illustrated below.

Index of productivity: Kendall (1939) adopted ranking coefficient method for measuring disparity in agricultural productivity among regions. In this technique the component areal units are ranked according to per hectare yield of different crops. An arithmetical average rank, called the ranking coefficient for each of the component areal units, is obtained. The assignment of ranks eliminates the scale effect or difference in area under different crops. Each crop is given equal weight or is not differentiated in terms of its value per hectare. Area with relatively high yields will show low coefficient, indicating high agricultural productivity.

The ranking coefficient method can be illustrated with the help of an example. Suppose in a region, there are 21 component areal units or districts. In a district x, on the basis of average yields, wheat ranks 4th, rice 6th, gram 8th, cotton 12th, barley 16th and sugarcane 20th. The average rank, called the ranking coefficient, of district x would be:

$$\text{Agricultural productivity} = \frac{4+6+8+12+16+20}{6 \text{ crops}} = \frac{66}{6} = 11$$

The average ranked position of all the units of the region is, thus, calculated and arranged in an ascending order or descending array. The array is divided into three equal parts to ascertain the low, medium and high agricultural productivity. With the help of the index scale, the agricultural productivity of each unit can be ascertained and plotted.

Enyedi (1964) determined an index of productivity coefficient, which was later used by Shafi in 1972 and 1974.

$$\text{Productivity index} = \frac{Y}{Y_n} \div \frac{T}{T_n}$$

where
Y is the total production of the selected crop in unit area
Y_n is the total production of the same crop at regional (national) scale
T is the total cropped area of the unit area
T_n is the total cropped area at regional (national) scale.

For example, wheat productivity index of Haryana for any year will be computed as:

$$\frac{\text{Total production of wheat in Haryana} \left(\text{in kgs}\right)}{\text{Total production of wheat in India} \left(\text{in kgs}\right)}$$

$$\div \frac{\text{Total cropped area in Haryana} \left(\text{in hectares}\right)}{\text{Total cropped area in India} \left(\text{in hectares}\right)}$$

152 Traversing the path: data management

Indices for crops in different states could be computed and compared. Shafi (1972) had modified the technique to provide an overall yield index as below:

$$\sum \frac{y_1}{t_1} + \frac{y_2}{t_2} \ldots n \div \frac{Y_1}{T_1} + \frac{Y_2}{T_2} \ldots n$$

$$\sum \frac{y_n}{t_n} \div \frac{Y_n}{T_n}$$

where
$y_1, y_2 \ldots y_n$ is the total production of the selected crops in the unit area
$t_1, t_2 \ldots n$ is the total cropped area under those crops in unit area
$Y_1, Y_2 \ldots n$ is the total production of the selected crops at national level
$T_1, T_2 \ldots n$ is the total cropped area under those crops at national level and
n refers to crops selected.

Singh (1976) introduced the relative crop yield and concentration index arranged in ranking order to measure level of agricultural productivity:

$$\text{Crop yield index } Y_i = \frac{Y_{a_e}}{Y_{a_r}} \times 100$$

where
Y_{a_e} is the average yield per hectare of crop a in the component enumeration unit and
Y_{a_r} is the average yield of the crop a in the entire region or country.

$$\text{Crop concentration index } C_i = P_{a_e} / P_{a_r}$$

where
P_{a_e} is the percentage strength of crop a in the total harvested area in the component enumeration unit and
P_{a_r} is the percentage strength of crop a in the total harvested area in the entire region or country.
The crop yield and concentration indices derived for all the units and the crops are ranked separately. The crop yield and concentration indices ranking coefficient is obtained by adding the yield and concentration ranks for individual crops and then dividing by 2. It is shown as below:

$$\text{Crop yield and concentration indices ranking coefficient for crop } a = (X + Y)/2$$

where
X is the crop yield ranking of crop a
Y is the crop concentration index ranking of crop a.

The lower the ranking coefficient, the higher is the level of agricultural productivity and vice versa.

Bhatia (1965) suggested a composite index of agricultural productivity. The measure is the weighted mean of the ratio of the yield of different crops in a district to the yields of the respective crops in the region. The proportions of the area under each crop to the cropped area are the weights. The formula is:

$$I_j = \frac{\sum Y_{ij} C_{ij}}{\sum C_{ij}}$$

where I_j is the composite index of districts j, C_{ij} is the proportion of area under ith crop to the total cropped area in the jth district and

$$Y_{ij} = \frac{E_{ij}}{E_i}$$

where E_{ij} is the yield of the j_{th} district and E_i is the yield of the ith crop in the region as a whole.

The division of the yield of each crop in the districts by the yield of the same crop in the region eliminates the bias of scale but retains its absolute difference. Data are required on the following attributes in Bhatia's method:

i   Districtwise production of different crops and their acreage. The districtwise yield of each crop (E) can be obtained by dividing the production of each crop in the district by its area

ii   The proportion of area under each crop (C_{ij}).

This can be obtained by dividing the area under each crop to the total cropped area in the district. The yield of each crop in the region is obtained by dividing the total production of each crop in the region by the total area under that crop in the region.

Dayal (1984) has depicted spatial pattern of agricultural productivity in India using three indexes of agricultural productivity: land productivity, labour productivity and aggregate productivity. He proposed a productivity measurement on reviewing the methods in practice.

The index of land productivity (P_L) computed as agricultural productivity per hectare can be defined as the market value of output of say ten crops per unit of area occupied by the crops, and is given by the formula:

$$P_L = \sum_{i=1}^{n} \left(\frac{O_i P_i}{A_i} \right)$$

where
n = number of crops
O_i = output of crop i in a district

154 Traversing the path: data management

P_i = regional average harvest price of crop i per unit weight
A_i = area occupied by crop i in the district.

The index of labour productivity (P_b) (agricultural productivity per worker) was similarly obtained and is given by the formula:

$$P_b = \sum_{i=1}^{n} \left(\frac{O_i P_i}{W_i} \right)$$

where W_i is the labour input in agriculture in a district, in terms of worker years (number of agricultural workers per year).

The land productivity is a neutral expression, that is free from the actual gains accruing to farmers, whereas the labour productivity will represent the relative prosperity or otherwise in different areas. This can be illustrated by the fact that in a high-density area like Bihar land productivity may be high but labour productivity low.

Finally, adding of the ranking coefficient of P_L and P_b gives the index of aggregate agricultural productivity. For this, the districts would be ranked first according to the value of land productivity and then according to labour productivity. Hence, each district would have two ranks ranging between 1 and 640. The two ranks would be averaged to get the composite index of aggregate productivity. Each of the three indexes could be then mapped in order to identify the agricultural productivity patterns in India at the district level.

Trend surface analysis: Any spatial data is unevenly distributed. Hence we usually prepare a choropleth map by classifying area into a specific number of categories. At times we are interested in identifying the gradient in their distribution but find the values distributed in a manner that isopleth technique is of no avail. In such cases we opt for trend surface analysis. In this technique, we start with one spatial unit and average its value and that of all its neighbours into one figure and write it inside the specific spatial unit. The same procedure is repeated for all other spatial units. Now we have a new set of figures in various spatial units. The earlier procedure is repeated on these new set of figures and a fresh set of figures is generated in various spatial units. This procedure is repeated again and again till the specific figures worked out for various spatial units brook no change. By following this process, we generate a smoothened surface of the spatial distribution under study. It easily lends itself to isoplething and identification of gradient. This technique is applied in situations where the distribution of a spatial distribution, such as rainfall in the valley and hill top settlements or percentage of irrigated area, is highly uneven in neighbouring spatial units.

(c) Selection of indicators

This technique is pertinent to measurement of regional disparities. We may be interested in identification of regional disparities in India based on data for all the

640 districts in 2011. The possible selected indicators could be per capita income to represent economic development, rate of female literacy to represent social development, percentage of urban population to represent degree of modernisation, percentage of non-agricultural workers in rural areas to represent rural transformation and inverse of infant mortality to represent life survival chance at birth. In this case we shall first prepare a master table listing the raw data, district-wise on all the five indicators. As the second step, standardised score on each indicator for all the districts will be computed. This is done by dividing the value of each score by the national average of the same variable. This will give us a new table in which the standardised scores for every district on five separate variables will be listed. As the third step, we prepare a correlation matrix with the help of this fresh table. Fourth step would be to sum up the correlation coefficients of each variable, listed row-wise. The summations thus obtained will be added up vertically down. Each summation in a row will be divided by this addition. Here we get the relative weight of each indicator. As the fifth step, we multiply the weight of each indicator with the standardised score of each district. Thereby we get a third table in series which provides the results of standardised score of each district multiplied by its weight. As the next step we add up the scores of each district thus obtained. This is the relative index of development of every district. Finally, we prepare a choropleth map with the help of computed development scores of various districts. Such a map will display regional disparities in development level of different parts of India. The same technique can be employed for identification of regional disparities in human development or quality of living space and so on.

Development levels by regions or districts can also be measured by taking recourse to the method adopted by UNDP in its Human Development Report (1990, 109). The indicators selected in this case include infant mortality rate to represent survival chance, adult literacy rate to represent economic opportunity and per capita income to represent socio-economic well-being. The first step is to measure the degree of deprivation that a district suffers on the chosen indicators. The deprivation score of a district in respect of an indicator, for instance per capita income, would be arrived at as follows:

$$
\begin{array}{l}
\text{Deprivation score of} \\
\text{the specific district} \\
\text{on per capita income}
\end{array}
=
\frac{
\begin{array}{l}
\text{Maximum per capita} \\
\text{income of any district in} \\
\text{the country}
\end{array}
-
\begin{array}{l}
\text{Per capita income of the} \\
\text{specific district}
\end{array}
}{
\begin{array}{l}
\text{Maximum per capita} \\
\text{income of any district} \\
\text{in the country}
\end{array}
-
\begin{array}{l}
\text{Minimum per capita} \\
\text{income of any district in} \\
\text{the country}
\end{array}
}
$$

In the above equation, the numerator carries the difference between the richest and the specific district in terms of per capita income and the denominator carries the difference between the richest and poorest district in the country.

The same process will be followed in case of other indicators. As a next step, the average of all the deprivation scores of the district will be worked out. Intention

156 Traversing the path: data management

here is to figure out as to how much a district is lagging behind the most developed district. Finally, the development score of the district is arrived at as follows:

Development score = 1 − Deprivation score

The human development score, thus obtained, can be standardised with 100 as the national average. Taking this as the basis, we can work out the development score of every district individually. Assuming that the average human development index (HDI) is 2.5 and that of district A is 4.0, in that case the standardised index of district A will work out as 160. The results thus obtained are mapped using the choropleth mapping technique. Resultant map will display regional disparities in human development.

The method has since been modified in 2010 (UNDP, 216–217). It measures the average attainments in a country on the same three basic dimensions of human development: a long and healthy life, access to knowledge and a decent standard of living. Sub-indices are created for each dimension. Indicators are transformed into indices by setting the goalposts from 0 to 1. For aggregation purposes, geometric mean is used.

The formula used is also the same:

$$\text{Dimension index} = \frac{\text{actual value} - \text{minimum value}}{\text{maximum value} - \text{minimum value}}$$

The HDI is calculated as follows:

$$\text{Human development index (HDI)} = \sqrt[3]{x * y * z}$$

The HDI is, thus, the geometric mean of normalised indices measuring achievements in each dimension. In addition, this method was made gender sensitive by given weight to the attributes of female population. See the reference listed above.

(d) Data reduction techniques

There are two commonly used techniques by geographers, which reduce data to make it more interpretable – factor analysis and cluster analysis.

Factor analysis: A common method of comparing spatial distributions used by geographers is the map overlay. If there are eight variables representing regional backwardness in different parts of India they would result in eight maps. The maps may be compared visually. The question is: to what extent do these eight maps together tell the story of reality? What is the story? Will the map overlay help in this case? Though it may be easy to compare two or three maps visually, it is extremely difficult to compare more than that number, particularly if the degree of variation within each map is large. It is here principal component analysis and factor analysis come handy. These provide a set of procedures that enable the researcher to find out quantitatively the basic patterns or 'stories' hidden in the structure of data. These are of particular value in division of a vast area into regions, classification of cities and social area analysis in urban setting.

Principal component analysis and factor analysis: Principal component analysis and the associated, more powerful technique of factor analysis are a common research tool, including in geography (Thompson and Hall 1969). Both are concerned with finding basic dimensions of variations in an original set of data and are linear combinations of the original variables.

The basic dimensions are the components that summarise or synthesise many general sources of variation in the original data matrix. For example, processing of data set for the year 2011 for all the states and union territories of India comprising of per cent urban population, per cent female literacy rate, per cent main non-agricultural workers in rural areas, infant mortality rate in-reverse, and per capita income yields one principal component that explains nearly 63 per cent of the total variance.

Principal component analysis and factor analysis techniques today are largely used with the help of computer software. Therefore, the focus in the subsequent discussion will be briefly on the concepts of the two techniques, computation of factor analysis, interpretation of the output, mapping of factors and the choice of the two modes of analysis.

Principal component analysis replaces the original variables by a new set of the same number of uncorrelated (orthogonal) components. That is, the variation in the set of m variables is transformed into m components. It is thus basically a descriptive method used as a prelude to factor analysis. In most analyses, only the first few components that account for relatively large share of the original variance are retained (Jolliffe 2002). These are further interpreted and used in subsequent analysis, such as in multiple regression analysis. The remaining components that account for only minor amount of variance are ignored. The new structures are usually identified by the cluster of original constructs.

Factor analysis, a term first introduced by Thurstone (1931), operates on the premise of reducing dimensionality (Bartholomew, Knott, and Moustaki 2011). It is thus a data reduction technique. When many of the original variables are highly correlated, it reduces or collapses a large number of original variables to a smaller number of new underlying factors. The resultant factors are less than the number of variables.

The new variable or factor derived captures as much of the variability in the data set as possible. There can be three situations: (i) a single factor explains almost all of the variability in the data set; (ii) there can be two factors in which case both will be uncorrelated with one another and will represent separate and independent aspects of the underlying data; (iii) at the other extreme can be a situation with no dominant factors and many factors explain an equal amount of variability in the data set.

The underlying or new factors are not measured directly. Rather these are essentially hypothetical constructs that are used to represent variables (Cattell 1973). For example, scores on per cent of households living in pucca houses, per cent of households with separate kitchen and per cent of households with separate

158 Traversing the path: data management

bathroom facility could be placed under a factor called 'quality of living space'; in this case, the latter can be inferred from the former but is not directly measured itself. In a similar vein, Yong and Pearce (2013, 80) had suggested that scores on an oral or written presentation and an interview exam could be placed under a factor called 'communication ability'; in this case, the latter can be inferred from the former but is not measured directly itself.

Computation of factors: Census is a rich source of data for geographers. It provides data on socio-economic, demographic, housing and amenities on a large number of variables. In your research work very often you select many variables, some of which measure the same phenomenon. The question to ponder is: Do these variables represent separate dimensions of socio-economic, demographic and housing structure? If not, you need to reduce them to a smaller number of underlying or new factors. Here the factor analysis technique comes into play. It helps to reduce the number of original variables into a smaller number of uncorrelated factors. Each factor captures as much of the variability in the data set as possible. The second factor is uncorrelated with the first one. It means they represent separate and independent aspects of the underlying data.

This is illustrated through an analysis of regional backwardness in India at a disaggregated (640 districts) level based on select variables pertaining to the Census 2011 data. The entire exercise has been worked out using SPSS (Statistical Package for Social Sciences) and the tables have been derived from the output generated.

The variables (X1......X8) selected are:

(X1) Percentage of households living in kutcha houses
(X2) Percent female illiterates
(X3) Percent of population never attended educational institutions (excluding 0–4 age group)
(X4) Percentage of rural main agricultural workers
(X5) Percentage of households without access to treated drinking water
(X6) Percentage of households without electricity as primary source of lighting
(X7) Percentage of households using unclean fuel for cooking
(X8) Percentage of households defecating in the open.

The first step is to work out a correlation coefficient matrix using Pearson's method (Table 8.1). This will indicate the degree of intercorrelation between all the variables.

The correlation coefficient matrix is constructed on the standardised variables. All

correlations with absolute value greater $\dfrac{2}{\sqrt{\text{No. of observations}}} = 2 / \sqrt{640} = 0.079$

are significant (Rogerson 2015, 336).

This leads us to find eigenvalues using principal component method. The eigenvalues are known as 'extraction sum of squared loadings' in SPSS.

Data analysis 159

TABLE 8.1 Correlation coefficient of regional backwardness variables*

	X1	X2	X3	X4	X5	X6	X7	X8
Kutcha houses X1	1.000	0.489	0.481	0.402	0.567	0.527	0.589	0.596
Female illiterates X2	0.489	1.000	0.981	0.499	0.464	0.573	0.608	0.703
Never attended ed. inst. X3	0.481	0.981	1.000	0.488	0.480	0.614	0.603	0.661
Rural main agri. workers X4	0.402	0.499	0.488	1.000	0.408	0.368	0.575	0.581
Untreated drinking water X5	0.567	0.464	0.480	0.408	1.000	0.689	0.803	0.510
Without electricity X6	0.527	0.573	0.614	0.368	0.689	1.000	0.691	0.588
Unclean fuel for cooking X7	0.589	0.608	0.603	0.575	0.803	0.691	1.000	0.676
Open defecation X8	0.596	0.703	0.661	0.581	0.510	0.588	0.676	1.000

* Computed using SPSS.

A 'loading' is the correlation between a component or factor and the original variable. If one were to sum the squared correlations between a factor and all of the original variables, this would be equal to the eigenvalue. When correlations are used, the sum of all the eigenvalues is equal to the number of variables. An eigenvalue (characteristic or latent roots) is the explanatory power of the respective component. It represents the amount of variance that is accounted for by a given component. In an introductory treatment of principal component analysis, however, simply consider a loading to be 'large' if its absolute value exceeds (0.40) (Stevens 1986).

From Table 8.2 it is clear that the highest eigenvalue is 5.085 followed by 0.912, which after rotation comes to 3.011 and 2.986. With eight variables in the example of regional backwardness in India, the sum of eigenvalues will be eight. Its value seen in proportion to the total variation will show the percent variation explained by the first component in the original data matrix, which is 63.568 per cent.

You can also know from Table 8.2 how many factors are essential to adequately describe the data. The number of factors is decided on the basis of two 'rules of thumb': (i) retain components with eigenvalue greater than one. But if the second eigenvalue is close to one like in the present example, you should follow the second rule; (ii) draw a scree plot (eigenvalues on the vertical axis and component on the horizontal axis) and locate a point just before the graph flattens out. All other factors or components are insignificant and hence are ignored.

Following the above logic, two factors have been extracted or retained in this analysis.

TABLE 8.2 Total variance★

Component	Initial eigenvalues			Eigenvalues/extraction sums of squared loadings			Rotation sums of squared loadings		
	Total	% of Variance	Cumulative %	Total	% of Variance	Cumulative %	Total	% of Variance	Cumulative %
1	5.085	63.568	63.568	5.085	63.568	63.568	3.011	37.639	37.639
2	0.912	11.395	74.963	.912	11.395	74.963	2.986	37.324	74.963
3	0.685	8.564	83.527						
4	0.529	6.618	90.144						
5	0.333	4.169	94.313						
6	0.287	3.589	97.902						
7	0.154	1.920	99.822						
8	0.014	0.178	100.000						

Extraction Method: Principal Component Analysis.

★ Computed using SPSS.

Further on, we will examine the loadings or correlations between the factors and the original variables. This is an important step in the analysis, as we begin to derive meaning or interpret each factor.

The factor loadings in general are fairly similar and you will need to rotate the initial factor-loading matrix to obtain a more realistic pattern regardless of the extraction technique of principal component, principal axis factor and maximum likelihood and so on (Tabachnick and Fidell 2007). A further reason of rotating the initial factor-loading matrix is to produce a transformed factor-loading matrix in which the number of high loadings on each factor is small in comparison with the number of low or zero loadings.

There are many variations of factor or component analysis, useful in specific research situations. A popular application in areal classification is the varimax rotation, whereby the axes are rotated about the origin in such a way that each of the original variables tends to load high on only one factor. This creates a relatively simple factor structure. Some name or identity is given to the dimension. This can be at the cost of some explanatory power because eigenvalues on leading factors can be reduced. An alternative to the usual orthogonal solution is an oblique rotation, in which the second and subsequent axes can be at angles other than 90° to the principal axis. This has the advantage of avoid forcing the data into an orthogonal structure if oblique axis would provide a better fit. There are many other rotations and these are discussed in greater detail in Rummel (1970, 368–422).

Table 8.3 shows the loadings of eight variables on the two components through rotated component matrix.

TABLE 8.3 Loadings of different variables on the two components

	*Rotated component matrix**	
	Component	
	1	*2*
Kutcha houses X1	0.691	0.332
Female illiterates X2	0.267	0.929
Never attended ed. inst. X3	0.283	0.910
Rural main agri. workers X4	0.362	0.580
Untreated drinking water X5	0.902	0.189
Without electricity X6	0.736	0.390
Unclean fuel for cooking X7	0.809	0.425
Open defecation X8	0.493	0.692

Extraction Method: Principal Component Analysis.
Rotation Method: Varimax with Kaiser Normalisation.
* Rotation converged in three iterations.

Note: The total of the squared loadings of all the variables on the two components will give the communality value. See also Table 8.4.

162 Traversing the path: data management

As can be seen, the variables of kutcha houses, without access to treated drinking water, without electricity as primary source of lighting and using unclean fuel for cooking 'load highly' on the first factor. These four variables have combined to form a single factor. This factor or index describes in a single column of numbers what the four variables represent. It focuses on housing and amenities. The second factor is associated with other four variables that largely represent demographics. These are illiterate female, population who never attended educational institutions (excluding zero to four age group), rural main agricultural workers and those defecating in the open. The results are interpreted within the research context. The interpretation is essentially subjective and requires naming or labelling of the factors. Here Factor_1 is considered as representing housing and amenities and Factor_2 depicting demographics. The labels are a succinct description of the factors, having been derived from the inspection of the loadings and correlation matrix.

Factor analysis thus unravels the linear relationships of interrelated data into their distinct patterns. Each pattern will appear as a factor having a distinct cluster of interrelated data. It reduces a mass of information to an economical description.

An important aspect of factor analysis is the communality. It is the total variance to be factored in and helps you decide the number of factors. In this analysis it works out to 5.997 (refer to Table 8.2: 3.011 + 2.986) as it is the sum of the squared loadings of all the variables on the two factors/components.

Table 8.3 gives information on communality for all the variables individually. It is the proportion of the variance of the variable that is held in common with all the other variables. It excludes variance unique to each variable and error variance. Once the communalities have been estimated and inserted in place of the unities in a correlation coefficient matrix, the factoring procedure continues as in the case of principal components.

You may note that while 'communality' is part of the variability in an original variable that is captured by factor analysis, the part of variability which is not captured by the factors is termed the 'uniqueness'.

Mathematically the difference between principal component analysis and factor analysis is found in the values put in the diagonal of the correlation matrix. In principal component analysis, the diagonal contains unities (1.00s). The idea is to account for all of the variance in the matrix. In contrast, in factor analysis, the communalities are put in the diagonal, meaning thereby that only the variance shared with other variables is to be accounted for.

Table 8.4 shows communalities of the variables for the two-factor solution.

From Tables 8.3 and 8.4 the reader will see that the communality for a variable, say female illiterates (X2), is equal to its squared correlation with factor_1 $(0.267)^2$, plus its squared correlation with factor_2 $(0.929)^2$, which is equal to 0.934. This variable has the maximum communality and minimum uniqueness. By contrast, the variable rural main agricultural workers (X4) with lowest communality (0.468) has the highest uniqueness. This is because it is not highly correlated with the two factors. This however does not mean that it is a less important variable of regional backwardness.

Data analysis **163**

TABLE 8.4 Communalities of individual variables★

	Initial	Extraction
Kutcha houses X1	1.000	0.587
Female illiterates X2	1.000	0.934
Never attended ed. inst. X3	1.000	0.909
Rural main agri. workers X4	1.000	0.468
Untreated drinking water X5	1.000	0.849
Without electricity X6	1.000	0.694
Unclean fuel for cooking X7	1.000	0.835
Open defecation X8	1.000	0.722

Extraction Method: Principal Component Analysis.
★ Computed using SPSS.

An important point to note here is that the factors that emerge from the factor analysis are not necessarily the 'most important ones' but are the ones that capture the nature of the data set. A factor emerges as a major one if several variables are highly correlated and are alternative measures of it (Rogerson 2015, 338).

An important output of factor analysis used by geographers, besides factor loadings, is the factor scores. The loadings are best represented simply as tables from the output such as in Table 8.3. When large numbers of variables are used, only those loading high on a factor may be presented. The table is essential in all presentations if readers are to satisfy themselves concerning the factor interpretation.

The factor scores lend themselves to graphic presentation. Geographers are particularly interested in this part of the analysis because it relates the results to the observations as areal units and, hence, the spatial patterns of the factors. You need not make eight maps to depict the spatial pattern of each variable; instead make maps that equal the number of underlying factors. Figures 8.2 and 8.3 exemplify maps drawn to depict spatial distribution as revealed by factor scores on each of the two factors on regional backwardness in India. One can see that the eight variables have been reduced to two dimensions named as housing and amenities and demographics with each dimension grouping four variables.

The question of choice: Principal component analysis is preferred as a method for data reduction, while factor analysis is given preference when the goal of the analysis is to detect underlying structure. Choice of the technique should be made in terms of the research purpose. If the role of the factor analysis is simply to convert a set of data into orthogonal dimensions, principal component analysis is adequate. When variables are highly intercorrelated, either of the two could be used.

Factor analysis is more properly used as a test procedure, when there is some a priori expectation as to the number of underlying factors and their composition, while principal component analysis is used more often as an empirical procedure seeking related group of variables and as a method of data reduction or compression. In practice, both methods often give substantially the same results (Smith 1975, 319).

164 Traversing the path: data management

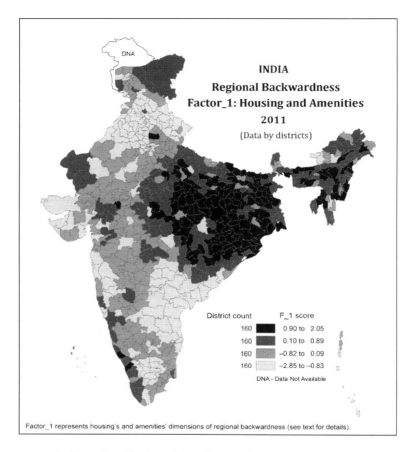

FIGURE 8.2 India: regional backwardness: factor_1 housing and amenities, 2011

The character of the correlation matrix gives a fair idea of the choice of methods. Taylor (1977, 242–243) has elaborated on this point most assiduously.

If all the correlations are large, the communalities are large and the value of one will be a reasonable estimate of the common factor analysis communality. Both models give similar results.

Any variable that has low correlations with other variables, however, tends to have a small common variance and large unique variance. In such a situation to insert unity in the communality cell is to use a poor estimate of the true communality. The influence of this variable in the subsequent principal component analysis will be overweighted. If there are many such variables in an analysis, so that the correlation matrix includes a large number of small correlations, the results of factor analysis and a principal component analysis will be quite dissimilar. In a situation in which correlations are not high and unique variances are large, the factor model is to be preferred.

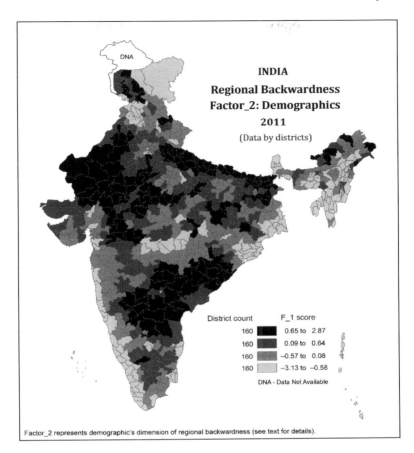

FIGURE 8.3 India: regional backwardness: factor_2 demographics, 2011

We can use similar logic concerning the size of the correlation matrix. If there are few variables, the number of correlations is relatively small, so that the communality estimates are relatively more important. Distortions resulting from the use of communalities of unity are enhanced with a small data set, and the principal component and factor analysis solutions can be expected to differ.

When the results from the two techniques are very similar, the choice of the technique is not important. When the two solutions are expected to differ the choice of technique will depend on purpose of research.

Each model has pertinent characteristics that determine its choice. Principal component analysis is a closed technique and so forms a poor basis for structuring reality. The assumption that all the variance is self-contained in the variables is unlikely to ever occur in reality.

The factor or component analysis leads to the process of areal classification. Finally, areas are allocated to classes done with some objective such as minimising

166 Traversing the path: data management

within-group variance and maximising between-group variance. If a regional system is required rather than an areal classification only adjoining areas are grouped together following contiguity principle.

Cluster analysis: Cluster analysis in geography works by grouping together similar areal units. It is based on the concept of contiguity and proximity between points distributed in space. The proximity between the spatial units is a measure of an overall similarity between them. A proto-cluster is initially formed by the most similar pair of spatial units, and the point half-way between them becomes the 'centroid' of this cluster. All these proto-clusters become a base for forming the next higher order of clusters. The process is repeated till we reach a meaningful structure of clusters. This procedure has its limitations in that no additional information can be incorporated without recalculating the entire set of data (Mather and Doornkamp 1970).

In that sense it is a classificatory technique. It gives indication of the relationships between the clusters and between the members of the clusters. It is one of the methods of data-mining, in which algorithms are used to discover and organise the structure of data. Since algorithms are a repetitive process, it is better to attempt cluster analysis with the help of computer operations. The use of SPSS package serves a real good purpose.

Cluster analysis may be approached through agglomerative or hierarchical methods and non-agglomerative or non-hierarchical methods. In case of both methods, standardisation of data is a necessary step.

The agglomerative or hierarchical process, as described above, is forward moving in which observations or enumeration units once grouped into a cluster cannot be reverted. They remain together for the entire grouping process. Here we may move from n clusters to a purposeful number of higher order clusters containing all the observations. In contrast, the number of groups or clusters to be arrived at is pre-decided in non-agglomerative or non-hierarchical methods. This is an iterative process. It is the preferred method when there are large numbers of observations.

An exercise in cluster analysis was carried out by taking standardised scores on eight indicators of 'quality of living space' for all the 640 districts of India as per the 2011 Census of India (Wadhera 2008). The indicators were percentage of households: living in permanent houses; living in two or more rooms; with bathroom within the house; percentage of households with toilet within the house; with tap within the house; with electricity within the house; percentage of households using LPG (liquid petroleum gas) for cooking; with separate kitchen within the house (Figure 8.4).

The cluster map used the 'two step' technique employing SPSS. In this method the number of clusters obtained are decided by the software and not specified by the experimenter.

Steps: Analyze > Classify > Two-Step Clusters > send your values to Continuous Variables > click Plots and select Cluster pie-chart and then click Continue > click Output and select Cluster Frequencies, Create Cluster Membership Variable and

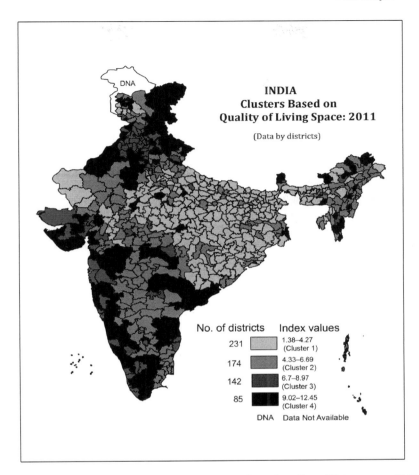

FIGURE 8.4 India: clusters based on composite index of quality of living space, 2011

click Continue > click Ok. A new column will be added in your spreadsheet (TSC) specifying as to which cluster your observation belongs.

The results obtained are in the form of regions of similar characteristics. Thus, cluster analysis is an objective way of regionalising an area into similar spatial units or of grouping spatial units bearing similarity into regions.

Cluster analysis in geography has a widespread application in the area of geodemographics, where analysts seek to reduce a large number of subregions by classifying them into a small number of types. Cluster analysis has also been used as a method of regionalisation, where the objective is to divide a region into a smaller number of contiguous subregions. In this case, it is necessary to modify traditional approaches to cluster analysis slightly to ensure that the created groups are comprised of contiguous subregions. Small exceptions may be ignored, as is done in dasymetric maps.

168 Traversing the path: data management

Models as quantitative techniques

To this point we have described some of the commonly used statistical techniques. Now we have a look at models as quantitative expressions. These are essentially meant to structure reality. In a restrictive sense, these are 'formal presentation of a theory' (Harvey 1967). They offer some kind of explanation, prediction or prescription. Gravity model is a simple example of a predictive model. It states that, for example, the interaction between a city and its region decreases with distance. Based upon this idea we can delimit the umlands of competing cities in a region. The cut-off point of umland between two cities can be determined by apportioning the distance between the two in the ratio of their population size. If the distance between a city with a population of 1 million and another with a population of 0.6 million is 80 km, then following the gravity model, the umland of the million city will extend up to 50 km and that of the other up to 30 km. Following the same technique, Krishan and Gupta (1975) regionalised India on the basis of population size of the cities and the railway/road distance between them.

Spatial data analysis and new quantitative geography

In this era of 'information explosion', a geographer needs to have knowledge of both 'descriptive statistics' and 'inferential statistics'. The former enables the geographer to summarise large sets of statistical or spatial data so that concise measurements of their attributes are obtained. This is the common practice. That is how mean annual rainfall of a place is calculated or given. The latter enables the geographer to infer or make statements about the characteristics of a universe based on data collected from a sample. Electoral exit polls depend very much on inferential statistical techniques as applied to sample information or data collected over extensive areas.

Data analysis, thus, can be geared to a variety of purposes. It helps in the identification of patterns, such as median points of area and the population of India; it confirms nature and degree of relationship, as between birth rate and infant mortality rate; it serves as a tool for evaluating the performance of some government schemes, such as the impact of the National Rural Employment Guarantee Scheme on out-migration from a backward region; it offers a clue to the optimal location of new projects, such as sighting the capital for a newly formed state, and so on.

What type of spatial analysis tool we will use depends on the specific purpose of our research project and the questions we wish to answer. Geographers are often interested in spatial patterns and processes. Spatial pattern defines the way a spatial distribution is organised. Urban sprawl is often radial along the roads radiating out from a city. Spatial processes refer to the ways the space gets transformed over time. The transformation of agricultural land into urban over time is one such example. Hence it is common to combine spatial analysis with mapping in geography. This can be conveniently done with the help of GIS packages.

Computing activity goes beyond routine analysis of spatial data with standard statistical packages – for instance, running a regression program in SAS or SPSS.

It involves computational methods and techniques to represent spatial properties, to explain geographical phenomena and to solve geographical problems (Couclelis 1998). Three broad areas of emphasis in new quantitative geography include exploratory spatial data analysis, visualisation and modelling and prediction.

The techniques and approach of exploratory spatial data analysis give the feel of the data by either graphical methods or descriptive statistics. This type of analysis looks for unusually high and low values of the variables, their distribution, associations and the distinct groups which observations may form, among other things.

Availability of data for each location has spurred interest in 'local spatial analysis' or 'local modelling'. Techniques focused on spatial variations and spatial differences in the location of points are employed so as to produce information on spatial point patterns. When mapped, these variations can be visualised. Emphasis on difference across space and the search for exceptions rather than the general trend are the norm.

Visualisation of the data prior to putting it through some formal analysis gives a synoptic sense of the database.

GIS software can be used in modelling applications using data integration and management. An example is to assess the effects of proximity to the national highway on land prices in Gurugram city of India. The hydrological cycle is another example of a dynamic natural system that can be modelled with the help of GIS.

Likewise, we can predict global weather patterns, which can directly impact agriculture and fishing industries around the world.

Geography focuses on the analysis of spatial data. Spatial analysis is defined as the 'quantitative procedures employed in locational analysis' and the focus of locational analysis is 'the spatial arrangement of phenomena' (Johnston 1994). It includes a wide variety of operations and concepts, such as simple measurement, classification, surfaces, arrangement, geometrical overlay and cartographic modelling. Clarke (1997, 184) identifies a number of 'geographic properties' of phenomena, including size, distribution, pattern, contiguity, neighbourhood, shape, scale or orientation and asks the question how can variations in these properties be described and analysed? To this, some scholars have added the element of direction (Burt and Barber 1996). These require specialised software for handling spatial data. The analyst has to write a program in a language to handle it.

Spatial data and Geographic Information Systems (GIS)

Spatial data refers to locational information about all the features on the earth, along with their attributes. Such data can be stored digitally in two formats: raster (or gridded) and vector (or graphic). The graphic form is represented by points, lines and polygons.

Raster data format is actually a spatial data model consisting of a network of rows and columns of cells or pixels. This network takes the shape of a grid, where each grid, generally a square, contains a number that represents the value of the data within it. Almost every kind of spatial data can be represented effectively by

170 Traversing the path: data management

rasters. Satellite images are the best example of data collected in raster format. Hence it is always essential to specify the resolution of the raster – that is, the spacing between the grid points and the extent or size of their domain (Dadson 2017, 6).

Vector data format is the second type of spatial data model which is used to represent geographic features in points lines, and polygons. It consists of information stored as a set of points showing known locations in space, such as towns, sampled sites or places of interest. The points may be connected to form lines to represent linear features, such as roads, rivers and railways. The lines may be connected to form polygons, so as to represent areas of different land cover, geological strata or administrative jurisdictions (Dadson 2017, 5).

Spatial data is an essential component of GIS. This provides a base for spatial analysis, with its tremendous stimulus to quantification in geography. Spatial data lends itself to identification of geographical patterns: clustered/dispersed, autocorrelation in the set of areal data, spatial outliers and spatial trends. At the simplest level are exercises, such as 'nearest neighbour analysis' of the hospitals in a city, 'connectivity index' of its road network and size and shape parameters of its vacant lands. Such and many other kinds of spatial analysis can be performed precisely with the help of GIS software. With the passage of time, as the amount and size of the data increase from high to higher resolution images, the handling capabilities of GIS software will grow in tandem.

GIS is more of an umbrella term for software, hardware, databases, professionals and procedures, all linked by computer networks. As a technological tool, it captures, processes, stores, analyses and manipulates any spatial information. The attribute or non-spatial information is also captured along with it.

Some other technologies related to GIS, but that do not go by the name of GIS, are computer-assisted drawing and drafting (CADD), automated mapping (AM), facilities management (FM), database management system (DBMS) and land information system (LIS), among others. With regular advancements of the system, various other technologies, such as Global Positioning System (GPS), digitised image processing for remote sensing operations and drone surveying, have also become a part of the GIS. This has led to a formation of a bigger hub of geographical information science, abbreviated as GIScience in place of GIS.

GIS technology was preceded by an upsurge of remote sensing technology. The two may be distinguished from each other. While 'remote sensing is predominantly a data generation or collection technology, GIS is principally dedicated to data handling' (Mesev and Walrath, 2007). Also referred to as earth observation, remote sensing provides vital information about the physical, chemical and biological properties and processes of the earth's surface without recourse to direct physical contact. Spatial data generated through earth observation and provided by different sources are used in a GIS environment to generate models of environmental and social processes. The product or information becomes a handy tool for planning and prediction, which are core to the 'business' of geography (Longley and Barnsley 2004, 68–69).

GIS and remote sensing are interdependent. While remote sensing serves as a database for GIS, the GIS provides an additional base to remote sensing, such as defining boundaries on an unmarked surface. Google Maps, which was launched in 2005, is the best example of a GIS product based on remote sensing. Research which focuses on landscape changes or land cover transformation depends heavily on Landsat, IRS LISS-V and Cartosat imageries as the base and GIS for the mapping and analysis of earth information.

GIS, in particular, has entered into every sphere of human activity and concern. It is often used in research pertaining to terrain analysis, land cover transformation, disaster damage estimation, tourism promotion, public utilities provision and what not. Highly significant has been its role in urban planning, environmental engineering, resource management and documentation of qualitative information.

Spatial queries are at the core of GIS. The purpose of these queries is to find answers to specific questions through spatial analysis. For instance, from a map showing all varieties of educational institutions, GIS can help you in sieving out all the high schools and quantify their distributional patterns in terms of Rn value. It can also lay out the shortest path connecting all the schools, especially for an inspection assignment. The optimal locations for a given number of new high schools can also be worked out. Likewise, in other situations, one can sift out and locate anomalous districts where urbanisation level is lower than the national level but per capita income higher, where rainfall is lower than 100 cm but the percentage of cropped area under rice is higher and where the density of the rail network is low but the development level is high. Likewise, one can filter out wards in a city where fires were relatively frequent but had no fire services, and so on. For all such queries, the GIS software uses SQL (structural query language) to obtain the intended results.

Montello and Sutton (2006) enunciate the ways in which GIS can help in the manipulation of data. First, it is capable of transforming a map on a given scale or projection to any other scale or projection, as per requirement. Second, it helps in computing the spatial attributes of areas, such as the shape of administrative areas or centrality of their headquarters. Third, it is handy in laying out the shortest path on a network, which is so essential for people involved in touring from one place to another. Fourth, it enables the aggregation of data to successively higher spatial levels and their mapping. A population density map prepared on the basis of 1 sq km spatial units can be converted into a map based on 4 sq km spatial units and further on to 16 sq km spatial units. Such a series of maps can demonstrate how the same distribution assumes a rather varying spatial disposition on different scales. Fifth, it is a useful technique for interpolation of data, as on temperature, rainfall or topographical maps. Sixth, it can be used for building spatial models. An illustration can be cited in respect to a weather forecasting model based on information pertaining to atmospheric pressure, cloud movements and temperature conditions. Finally, overlaying and analysing maps belonging to different points in time to discern spatial change are important functions of GIS. This is pertinent to studies relating to urban sprawl and transformation of land cover on the periphery of the metropolitan cities.

A practical exercise in GIS

For research on the transformation of land cover, such as in the peripheral zone of a metropolitan city, the use of GIS software starts with the procurement of spatial data. These may come from topographical sheets, satellite images or already available shape files (vector data). A shape file is a format for storing the location, shape and other attributes of a geographical feature.

While procuring data layers, as it is termed in the GIS environment, from various base sources such as geographical maps and satellite images, a uniform coordinate system is assigned to them. In such analysis, topographical maps are geo-referenced or assigned coordinates with a UTM WGS 1984 projection system. UTM is the Universal Transverse Mercator Projection System, WGS is a datum and refers to the World Geodetic System, and 84, or 1984, is the year of its first establishment.

After managing vector data, there's a need to process raster data – that is, satellite images – of two different points in time, representing the benchmark one and the present. For this, geometric and radiometric corrections are carried out with the help of image processing software. The inbuilt functions in this software are meant to remove geometric and radiometric errors from the procured images. The next step is to delineate the area under research focus. This can be mapped or marked on the topographical sheet and digitised. The same area can be clipped out of a satellite image, say a scene of LANDSAT 8 series. Once such an image is in hand, the land cover depicted by it is to be classified into a desired number of categories, say seven to ten.

For finalisation of the classification, chunks of various categories of land cover are randomly selected, processed through software and applied to the entire image. Thus a complete land cover picture distinguishing different categories of the area under research is obtained. The same is done in respect to the other scene or image, say from the LANDSAT 5 series representing the benchmark year over which the land cover transformation is to be analysed. This is to be followed by a reconnaissance survey to assess the accuracy of the classification adopted. The images of both points in time are taken to the field. Another way is to use processing software on each image by selecting 40 to 50 reference points per category of land cover. The land cover of each point can be verified by using Google Earth software.

In this manner, the land cover of the study area is obtained for two points in time. Using the change detection algorithm, available in the image processing software, a single image representing the transformation of one land cover category to another, or persistence of the same, becomes available. This can be subjected to further statistical treatment, such as the calculation of the percentage of transformation in respect to each category of land cover. The final steps would be to describe the entire process followed and prepare the report based on the results obtained.

Finally, it must be ensured that any data analysis is directly relevant to the research question, objective and hypothesis. This should be done using an appropriate technique, and the researcher should be in a position to justify its choice. For this, a thorough understanding of the theory and mechanism of the technique is a must. Second, the researcher should prefer to go for simple techniques and not the more complex ones. They are handy to use and easy to understand. Experience confirms that simple techniques give almost the same results as do the more sophisticated ones. Third, it will be appreciated if the research student demonstrates the calculations of the technique by taking some hypothetical example. These calculations can be included as a footnote at the relevant place in the text. A simple mention or listing of the technique will not do. If possible, try to invent a new technique. Above all, it is not enough to just obtain the result by using a technique. The results obtained should be critically reviewed for any mistake or inconsistency. It is equally important to interpret the result. In the end, one must understand that data analysis is not an end in itself but the beginning of the interpretation of the results obtained.

The very act of analysing quantitative and qualitative data is a discriminating and rigorous phase of research. We choose what to observe, what to record and what to render invisible. Thereafter, we start the analysis. We sift and sort, select and discard, compare and contrast for the sake of identifying the pattern and figuring out the process. Interpretation has to follow. This demands an insightful journey into the soul of what has been discovered through analysis.

References

Aboufadel, Edward, and David Austin. 2006. "A New Method for Computing the Mean Center of Population of the United States." *The Professional Geographer* 58 (1): 65–69.

Adams, P. 2009. *Geographies of Media and Communication*. Oxford: Wiley-Blackwell.

Alexander, John W. 1958. "Location of Manufacturing: Methods of Measurement." *Annals Association of American Geographers* 48 (1): 20–26.

Anselin, L. 1995. "Local Indicators of Spatial Association-LISA." *Geographical Analysis* 27: 93–115.

Assad, A.A., and B.L. Golden. 1995. "Arc Routing Methods and Applications." In *Handbooks in Operations Research and Management Science* (Volume 8), edited by M.O. Ball, T.L. Magnanti, C.L. Monma, and G.L. Nemhauser, 375–483. Amsterdam: Elsevier.

Atkinson, J.M., and J. Heritage, eds. 1984. *Structures of Social Action: Studies in Conversation Analysis*. Cambridge: Cambridge University Press.

Bachi, R. 1962. "Standard Distance Measures and Related Methods for Spatial Analysis." *Papers and Proceedings of the Regional Science Association* 10: 83–132.

―――. 1966. *An Introduction to Geostatistics* (Hebrew text). Compiled by J. Yam. Jerusalem: Academon.

Bailey, T.C., and A.C. Gatrell. 1995. *Interactive Spatial Data Analysis*. Harlow: Longman.

Bamford, C.G., and H. Robinson. 1978. *Geography of Transport*. Plymouth, UK: MacDonald and Evans.

Barnes, J.A. 1954. "Class and Committees in a Norwegian Island Parish." *Human Relations* 7: 39–58.

Bartholomew, D., M. Knott, and I. Moustaki. 2011. *Latent Variable Models and Factor Analysis: A Unified Approach*. 3rd ed. West Sussex, UK: John Wiley & Sons.

Batty, M., R. Carvalho, A. Hudson-Smith, R. Milton, D. Smith, and P. Steadman. 2008. "Scaling and Allometry in the Building Geometries of Greater London." *The European Physical Journal B* 63: 303–314.

Batty, M., and Paul A. Longley. 1994. *Fractal Cities: A Geometry of Form and Function*. London, UK: Academic Press.

174 Traversing the path: data management

Bell, M., and Y. Iida. 1997. *Transportation Network Analysis*. Chichester, UK: John Wiley & Sons.

Berelson, B. 1952. *Content Analysis in Communication Research*. Glencoe, IL: Free Press.

Bhatia, Shyam S. 1965. "Patterns of Crop Concentration and Diversification in India." *Economic Geography* 41 (1): 39–56.

———.1967. "Spatial Variations, Changes and Trends in Agricultural Efficiency in Uttar Pradesh, 1953–63." *Indian Journal of Agricultural Economics* 22 (1): 66–80.

Boyce, R.B., and W.A.V. Clark. 1964. "The Concept of Shape in Geography." *Geographical Review* 54: 561–572.

Boyzatis, R. 1998. *Transforming Qualitative Information: Thematic Analysis and Code Development*. London: Sage.

Braun, V., and Clarke Victoria. 2006. "Using Thematic Analysis in Psychology." *Qualitative Research in Psychology* 3 (2): 77–101.

Bunge, W. 1966. "Theoretical Geography." *Lund Studies in Geography Series C, No. 1*. 2nd ed. Lund, Sweden: Gleerup.

Burt, James E., and Gerald M. Barber. 1996. *Elementary Statistics for Geographers*. 2nd ed. New York: The Guilford Press.

Camagni, R. 1993. "From City Hierarchy to City Network: Reflections about an Emerging Paradigm." In *Structural and Change in the Space Economy*, edited by T.R. Lakshmanan and P. Nijkamp, 66–87. Berlin: Springer-Verlag.

Carvalho, R., and A. Penn. 2004. "Scaling and Universality in the Micro-Structure of Urban Space." *Physica A* 332: 539–547.

Castells, M. 2001. *The Rise of Network Society*. 2nd ed. Oxford: Blackwell.

Cattell, R.B. 1973. *Factor Analysis*. Westport, CT: Greenwood Press.

Chattopadhyay, S., and Mahamaya Chattopadhyay. 1995. *Terrain Analysis of Kerala*. Technical Monograph 1/95. STED, Government of Kerala, 44p + 36 fig.

Chattopadhyay, S., and S. Suresh Kumar. 2007. "Fractal Dimensions of Selected Coastal Water Bodies in Kerala, SW Coast of India – A Case Study." *Indian Journal of Marine Sciences* 36 (2): 162–166.

Christian, C.S., J.N. Jennings, and C.R. Twidale. 1957. "Geomorphology." In *Guidebook to Research Data for Arid Zone Development* (Volume IX), edited by B.T. Dickson, 51–65. Paris: UNESCO.

Clark, P., and F.C. Evans. 1954. "Distance to Nearest Neighbour as a Measure of Spatial Relationships in Populations." *Ecology* 35: 445–453.

Clarke, K.C. 1997. *Getting Started with Geographic Information Systems*. Englewood Cliffs, NJ: Prentice Hall.

Coffey, A., and P. Atkinson. 1996. *Making Sense of Qualitative Data: Complementary, Research Strategies*. London: Sage.

Couclelis, H. 1998. "Geocomputation in Context." In *Geocomputation: A Primer*, edited by Paul A. Longley, S.M. Brooks, R.A. McDonnell, and B. MacMillan, 17–29. Chichester, UK: Wiley.

Crampton, J.W. 2009. "Cartography: Maps 2.0." *Progress in Human Geography* 33 (1): 91–100.

Cressey, Donald Ray. 1953. *Other People's Money: A Study in the Social Psychology of Embezzlement*. Michigan: The University of Michigan.

Curtiss, J., and R. McIntosh. 1950. "The Interrelations of Certain Analytic and Synthetic Phytosociological Characters." *Ecology* 31: 434–455.

Dadson, Simon J. 2017. *Statistical Analysis of Geographical Data: An Introduction*. Oxford, UK: Wiley.

Dauphine, Andre. 2012. *Fractal Geography*. Croydon: Wiley-ISTE.

Dayal, Edison. 1984. "Agricultural Productivity in India – A Spatial Analysis." *Annals of the Association of American Geographers* 74 (1): 98–123.

Del Casino, V. Jr., and S.P. Hanna. 2000. "Reorientations and Identities in Tourism Map Spaces." *Progress in Human Geography* 24 (1): 23–46.

Dittmer, Jason. 2010. "Textual and Discourse Analysis." In *The Sage Handbook of Qualitative Geography*, edited by Dydia DeLyser, Steve Herbert, Stuart Aitken, Mike Crang, and Linda McDowell, 274–286. London: Sage.

Dury, G.H. 1952. *Map Interpretation*, 167–79. London: Pitman.

Ebdon, D. 1985. *Statistics in Geography*. 2nd ed. Oxford: Basil Blackwell.

Ehrenberg, A.S.C. 1975. *Data Reduction*. Chichester, UK: Wiley.

———. 1982. *A Primer in Data Reduction*. Chichester, UK: Wiley.

Enyedi, Gy. 1964. "Geographical Types of Agriculture in Hungary." In *Applied Geography in Hungary*, edited by M. Pécsi, 58–105. Budapest: Hungarian Academy of Sciences.

Fairclough, N. 1992. *Discourse and Social Change*. Cambridge: Polity.

FAO. 1976. "A Framework for Land Evaluation." *Soils Bulletin* 3, Rome.

Flick, U. 2009. *An Introduction to Qualitative Research*. 4th ed. London: Sage.

Fotheringham, A.S., Chris Brunsdon, and Martin Charlton. 2000. *Quantitative Geography: Perspectives on Spatial Data Analysis*. London: Sage.

Fotheringham, A.S., and F. Zhan. 1996. "A Comparison of Three Exploratory Methods for Cluster Detection in Spatial Point Patterns." *Geographical Analysis* 28 (3): 200–218.

Freeman, Linton. 2006. *The Development of Social Network Analysis*. Vancouver: Empirical Press.

Gao, Jay, and Zong-guo Xia. 1996. "Fractals in Physical Geography." *Progress in Physical Geography* 20 (2): 178–191.

Garrison, W.L., and D.F. Marble. 1962. "The Structure of Transportation Networks." *U.S. Army Transportation Command, Technical Report*, 11–62.

Gee, J.P. 1999. *An Introduction to Discourse Analysis*. London and New York: Routledge.

Glaser, B.G., and A.L. Strauss. 1967. *The Discovery of Grounded Theory: Strategies for Qualitative Research*. Chicago, IL: Aldine de Gruyter.

Gleick, James. (1988) 2008. *Chaos: Making a New Science*. Rev. ed. New York: Penguin (Non-Classics).

Goodchild, Michael F., and David M. Mark. 1987. "The Fractal Nature of Geographic Phenomena." *Annals of the Association of American Geographers* 77 (2): 265–278.

Gregory, Derek, Ron Johnston, Geraldine Pratt, Michael Watts, and Sarah Whatmore. 2009. *The Dictionary of Human Geography*. 5th ed. Oxford: Wiley-Blackwell.

Groat, L., and D. Wang. 2002. *Architectural Research Methods*. New York: John Wiley & Sons.

Grounded Theory Institute. 2013. *What Is Grounded Theory?* http://www.groundedtheory.com/what-is-gt.aspx.

Haggett, P., Andrew D. Cliff, and Allan Frey. 1977. *Locational Models*. London: Edward Arnold.

Haggett, P., and K.A. Gunawardena. 1964. "Determination of Population Thresholds for Settlement Functions by the Reed-Muench Method." *Professional Geographer* 16 (4): 6–9.

Hammersley, M., and P. Atkinson. 2007. *Ethnography: Principles in Practice Paperback*. 3rd ed. London: Routledge.

Hammond, R., and P.S. McCullagh. 1986. *Quantitative Techniques in Geography: An Introduction*. 2nd ed. Oxford: Oxford University Press.

Harris, Chauncy D. 1954. "The Market as a Factor in the Localization of Industry in the United States." *Annals of the Association of American Geographers* 44 (4): 315–348.

Hart, J.F. 1954. "Central Tendency in Areal Distributions." *Economic Geography* 30 (1): 48–59.

Harvey, D. 1967. "Models of the Evolution of Spatial Patterns in Human Geography." In *Models in Geography*, edited by R.J. Chorley and P. Haggett, 549–608. London: Methuen.

Hilgard, J.E. 1872. "The Advance of Population in the United States." *Scribner's Monthly* 4 (2): 214–218.

176 Traversing the path: data management

Horton, R.E. 1945. "Erosional Development of Streams and Their Drainage Basins." *Bulletin of the Geological Society of America* 56 (3): 275–370.

Hsieh, H.F., and S.E. Shannon. 2005. "Three Approaches to Qualitative Content Analysis." *Qualitative Health Research* 15 (9): 1277–1288.

Hussain M. 1976. "A New Approach to the Agricultural Productivity Regions of the Sutlej-Ganga Plains of India." *Geographical Review of India* 38 (3): 230–236.

Jiang, B. 2007. "A Topological Pattern of Urban Street Networks: Universality and Peculiarity." *Physica A* 384: 647–655.

———. 2009. "Street Hierarchies: A Minority of Streets Account for a Majority of Traffic Flow." *International Journal of Geographical Information Science* 23 (8): 1033–1048.

Jiang, B., and Junjun Yin. 2014. "Ht-Index for Quantifying the Fractal or Scaling Structure of Geographic Features." *Annals of the Association of American Geographers* 104 (3): 530–540.

Jiang, B., and X. Liu. 2012. "Scaling of Geographic Space from the Perspective of City and Field Blocks and Using Volunteered Geographic Information." *International Journal of Geographical Information Science* 26 (2): 215–229.

Joffe, H. 2012. "Thematic Analysis." In *Qualitative Research Methods in Mental Health and Psychotherapy: An Introduction for Students and Practitioners*, edited by D. Harper and A. Thompson, 209–224. Chichester, UK: Wiley-Blackwell.

Johnston, R.J. 1994. "Spatial Analysis." In *The Dictionary of Human Geography*, edited by R.J. Johnston, D. Gregory, and D.M. Smith, 577. Oxford: Blackwell.

Jolliffe, I.T. 2002. *Principal Component Analysis*. 2nd ed. New York: Springer-Verlag.

Kansky, K.J. 1963. *Structure of Transportation Networks: Relationship between Network Geometry and Regional Characteristics*. Chicago: University of Chicago Press. Department of Geography, Research Papers, 84.

Kant, Surya. 1988. *Administrative Geography of India*. Jaipur: Rawat Publications.

Katz, Jack. 2001. "Analytic Induction." In *International Encyclopaedia of the Social and Behavioral Sciences*, edited by Neil J. Smelser and Paul B. Baltes, 84. Amsterdam, The Netherlands: Elsevier.

Kendall, M.G. 1939. "The Geographical Distribution of Crop Productivity in England." *Journal of the Royal Statistical Society* 102: 21–32.

Khusro, A.M. 1965. "Measurement of Productivity at Macro and Micro Level." *Journal of the Indian Society of Agricultural Statistics* 17 (2): 278–283.

Klaasen, L.H., D.H. van Dongen Torman and L.M. Koyck. 1949. *Hoodfliinen van de sociaal-economische anfwikkeling der gemeente Amerstoort van 1900–1970*. Leiden: Stenfert Kroese.

Krishan, Gopal. 2016. "India in the National Geographic: 1947–2015." *Regional Vitality of India*. Unpublished. A Research Study submitted to ICSSR, New Delhi.

Krishan, Gopal, and M.M. Chandna. 1977. "The System of Service Centres in the Outer Himalayas: A Case Study of District Sirmaur, Himachal Pradesh, India." In *Man, Culture and Settlement*, edited by Robert C. Eidt, Kashi Nath Singh, and P.B.S. Rana, 277–286. New Delhi: Kalyani Publishers.

Krishan, Gopal, and S.C. Gupta. 1975. "The Regionalisation of India on the Basis of Population Potential of Cities." *Area* 7: 115–119.

———. 1976. "The Locational Eccentricity of State Capitals in India." *Asian Profile* 4: 139–143.

Krishan, Gopal, and Madhav Shyam. 1978. "Regional Aspects of Urban-Rural Differential in Literacy in India: 1971." *Journal of Developing Areas* 13 (1): 11–21.

Kundu, A., and J.M. Rao. 1986. "Inequity in Educational Development: Issues in Measurement, Changing Structure and Its Socio-Economic Correlates with Special Reference to India." In *Educational Planning – A Long Term Perspective*, edited by Moonis Raza, 435–466. New Delhi: NIEPA.

Lam, Nina Siu-Ngan, and Lee De Cola. 1993. *Fractals in Geography*. Caldwell, NJ: The Black Burn Press.

Lämmer, S., B. Gehlsen, and D. Helbing. 2006. "Scaling Laws in the Spatial Structure of Urban Road Networks." *Physica A* 363 (1): 89–95.

Lindsay, J.B. 2005. "The Terrain Analysis System: A Tool for Hydro-Geomorphic Applications." *Hydrological Processes* 19: 1123–1130.

Lo, C.P., K. Albert, and W. Yeung. 2003. *Concepts and Techniques of Geographic Information Systems*. The Indian Reprint. New Delhi: Prentice Hall.

Lofland, J., D.A. Snow, L. Anderson, and L. Lofland. 2006. *Analysing Social Settings: A Guide to Qualitative Observation and Analysis*. 4th ed. Belmont, CA: Wadsworth.

Longley, Paul A., and Michael J. Barnsley. 2004. "The Potential of Geographical Information Systems and Earth Observation." In *Unifying Geography: Common Heritage, Shared Future*, edited by John A. Matthews and David T. Herbert, 62–80. London: Routledge.

Luo, Wei, Xiaoyan Li, Ian Molloy, Liping Di, and Tomasz Stepinski. 2014. "Web Service for Extracting Stream Networks from DEM Data." *GeoJournal* 79 (2): 183–193. doi: 10.1007/s10708–013–9502–1

Lutz, C., and J. Collins. 1993. *Reading National Geographic*. Chicago: University of Chicago Press.

Mabbutt, J.A. 1968. "Review of Concepts of Land Classification." In *Land Evaluation*, edited by G.A. Stewart, 11–28. Melbourne: Macmillan.

MacDonald, Stuart, and Nicola Headlam. 2008. *Research Methods Handbook: Introductory Guide to Research Methods for Social Research*. Manchester, UK: Centre for Local Economic Strategies.

Malterud, K. 2012. "Systematic Text Condensation: A Strategy for Qualitative Analysis." *Scandinavian Journal of Public Health* 40 (8): 795–805. doi:10.1177/1403494812465030

Mandelbrot, B. 1967. "How Long Is the Coast of Britain? Statistical Self-Similarity and Fractional Dimension." *Science* 156 (3775): 636–638.

Mandelbrot, B. 1982. *The Fractal Geometry of Nature*. New York: W.H. Freeman and Company.

Massam, B.H. 1972. "The Spatial Structure of Administrative Systems." *Resource Paper No. 12. Association of American Geographers*. Commission on College Geography.

Massam, B.H., and M.F. Goodchild. 1971. "Temporal Trends in the Spatial Organisation of a Service Agency." *Canadian Geographer* 15: 192–206.

Masuoka, P., W. Acevedo, S. Fifer, T. Foresman, and M.J. Tuttle. 1996. "Techniques for Visualising Urban Growth Using a Temporal GIS Database." *Proceedings ASPRS/ACSM Annual Convention and Exhibition*, Baltimore, MD 3: 89–100.

Mather, P.M., and J.C. Doornkamp. 1970. "Multivariate Analysis in Geography with Particular Reference to Drainage-Basin Morphometry." *Transactions of the Institute of British Geographers* 51: 163–187.

McAdams, Michael A. 2009. "The Application of Fractal Analysis and Spatial Technologies for Urban Analysis." *Journal of Applied Functional Analysis* 4 (4): 569–579.

Meijerink, A.M.J. 1988. "Data Acquisition and Data Capture Through Terrain Mapping Units." *ITC Journal* 1: 23–44.

Mesev, Victor, and Alexandra Walrath. 2007. "GIS and Remote Sensing Integration: In Search of a Definition." In *Integration of GIS and Remote Sensing*, edited by Victor Mesev, 1–16. West Sussex, England: John Wiley & Sons Ltd.

Montello, Daniel R., and Paul C. Sutton. 2006. *An Introduction to Scientific Research Methods in Geography*. Thousand Oaks, CA: Sage Publications.

Neft, David S. 1966. *Statistical Analysis for Areal Distributions*. Monograph Series No. 2. Philadelphia: Regional Science Research Institute.

Neuendorf, K.A. 2002. *The Content Analysis Guidebook*. London: Sage.

178 Traversing the path: data management

Nkwi, P., I. Nyamongo, and G. Ryan. 2001. *Field Research into Socio-Cultural Issues: Methodological Guidelines.* Yaounde, Cameroon, Africa: International Center for Applied Social Sciences, Research, and Training/UNFPA.

Openshaw, S., M.E. Charlton, C. Wymer, and A.W. Craft. 1987. "A Mark I Geographical Analysis Machine for the Automated Analysis of Point Data Sets." *International Journal of Geographical Information Systems* 1: 359–377.

O'Reilly, K. 2005. *Ethnographic Methods.* Abingdon: Routledge.

Pownall, L.L. 1953. "Functions of New Zealand Towns." *Annals Association of American Geographers* 43 (4): 332–350.

Rapley, M. 2012. "Ethnomethodology/Conversation Analysis." In *Qualitative Research Methods in Mental Health and Psychotherapy: An Introduction for Students and Practitioners,* edited by D. Harper and A. Thompson, 177–192. Chichester, UK: Wiley-Blackwell.

Richardson, D.E. 1993. *Automatic Spatial and Thematic Generalization Using a Context Transformation Model.* Doctoral Dissertation, Wageningen Agricultural University, N1.

Riessman, C. 2008. *Narrative Methods for the Human Sciences.* London: Sage.

Ritchie, Jane, Jane Lewis, Carol McNaughton Nicholls, eds. 2014. *Qualitative Research Practice: A Guide for Social Science Students and Researchers.* 2nd ed. New Delhi: Sage.

Robbins, Paul, and Rob Krueger. 2000. "Beyond Bias? The Promise and Limits of Q Method in Human Geography." *The Professional Geographer* 52 (4): 636–648.

Robson, C. 2002. *Real World Research.* 2nd ed. Oxford: Blackwell.

Rodrigue, Jean-Paul, Claude Comtois, and Brian Slack. 2013. *The Geography of Transport Systems.* 3rd ed. London: Routledge.

Rogerson, Peter A. 2015. *Statistical Methods for Geography: A Student's Guide.* 4th ed. Thousand Oaks, CA: Sage.

Rummel, R.J. 1970. *Applied Factor Analysis.* Evanston, IL: Northwestern University Press.

Rusak Mazur, E., and H.W. Castner, 1990. "Horton's Ordering Scheme and the Generalisation of River Networks." *The Cartographic Journal* 27: 104–112.

Said, E. 1978. *Orientalism.* Harmondsworth: Penguin.

Scharl, A., and K. Tochtermann. 2007. *The Geospatial Web: How Geobrowsers, Social Software and the Web 2.0 Are Shaping the Network Society.* London: Springer.

Schegloff, E.A., and H. Sacks. 1973. "Opening Up Closings." *Semiotica* 8 (4): 289–327.

Schreier, M. 2012. *Qualitative Content Analysis in Practice.* Thousand Oaks, CA: Sage.

Secor, Anna J. 2010. "Social Surveys, Interviews, and Focus Groups." In *Research Methods in Geography: A Critical Introduction,* edited by Basil Gomez and John Paul Jones III, 194–205. West Sussex, UK: Wiley-Blackwell.

Shafi, M. 1960. "Measurement of Agricultural Productivity in Uttar Pradesh." *Economic Geography* 36 (4): 296–305.

———. 1972. "Measurement of Agricultural Productivity of the Great Indian Plains." *The Geographer* 19 (1): 4–13.

———. 1974. "Perspectives on the Measurement of Agricultural Productivity." *The Geographer* 21 (1): 1–10.

Shen, G. 2002. "Fractal Dimension and Fractal Growth of Urbanized Areas." *International Journal of Geographical Information Science* 16: 419–437.

Silk, J. 1979. *Statistical Concepts in Geography.* London: Allen and Unwin.

Silverman, D. 2000. "Analysing Conversation." In *Researching Society and Culture,* edited by C. Seale, 261–274. London: Sage.

Singh, Jasbir. 1972. "A New Technique for Measuring Agricultural Efficiency in Haryana, India." *The Geographer* 19 (1): 14–27.

———. 1976. *Agricultural Geography of Haryana.* Kurukshetra: Vishal Publications.

Singh, Nina. 2012. "Son Preference in a Patriarchal Setting in North-West India: Some Observations from Rural Haryana." *Population Geography* 34 (1 & 2): 1–18.

Sinha, B.N. 1968. "Agricultural Efficiency in India." *The Geographer* 21 (special number): 101–127.

Smith, David M. 1975. *Patterns in Human Geography*. Harmondsworth, UK: Penguin Books.

Sopher, David E. 1974. "A Measure of Disparity." *The Professional Geographer* 26 (4): 389–392.

———. 1980. "Sex Disparity in India Literacy." In *An Exploration of India: Geographical Perspectives on Society and Culture*, edited by David E. Sopher, 130–188. London: Longman.

Stamp, L.D. 1952. "The Measurement of Agricultural Efficiency with Special Reference to India." *Silver Jubilee Souvenir Volume*. Indian Geographical Society: 177–178.

Stevens, J. 1986. *Applied Multivariate Statistics for the Social Sciences*. Hillsdale, NJ: Lawrence Erlbaum Associates.

Strahler, A.N. 1952. "Hypsometric (Area–Altitude) Analysis of Erosional Topography." *Geological Society of America Bulletin* 63: 1117–1142.

———. 1957. "Quantitative Analysis of Watershed Geomorphology." *Eos, Transactions American Geophysical Union* 38 (6): 913–920.

Sutton, J., and D. Gillingwater. 1997. "Geographic Information Systems and Transportation." *Overview Transportation Planning and Technology* 21: 1–4.

Sviatlovsky, E.E., and W.C. Eells. 1937. "The Centrographical Method and Regional Analysis." *Geographical Review* 27 (2): 240–254.

Tabachnick, B.G., and L.S. Fidell. 2007. *Using Multivariate Statistics*. 5th ed. Boston, MA: Allyn & Bacon.

Takhteyev, Yuri, Anatoliy Gruzd, and Barry Wellman. 2012. "Geography of Twitter Networks." *Social Networks* 34 (1): 73–81.

Taylor, P.J. 1977. *Quantitative Methods in Geography: An Introduction to Spatial Analysis*. Boston, MA: Houghton Mifflin Company.

Taylor, P., D. Evans, M. Hoyler, B. Derudder, and K. Pain. 2009. "The UK Space Economy as Practised by Advanced Producer Service Firms: Identifying Two Distinctive Polycentric City-Regional Processes in Contemporary Britain." *International Journal of Urban and Regional Research* 33: 700–718.

Thompson, D., and R. Hall. 1969. *A Bibliographic Guide to Factor Analysis Methods and Applications*. Maryland: University of Maryland, Department of Geography.

Thompson, P. 2000. *The Voice of the Past: Oral History*. 2nd ed. Oxford: Oxford University Press.

Thurstone, L.L. 1931. "The Measurement of Social Attitudes." *The Journal of Abnormal and Social Psychology* 26 (3): 249–269. http://dx.doi.org/10.1037/h0070363

Tukey, John W. 1977. *Exploratory Data Analysis*. Reading, MA: Addison-Wesley.

Turner, A. 2007. *An Introduction to Neogeography*. Santa Clara, CA: O'Reilly Media.

Ullman, E.L., and M.F. Dacey. 1962. "The Minimum Requirements Approach to the Urban Economic Base." *Lund Studies in Geography, Series B, Human Geography* 24: 121–143.

UNDP. 1990. *Human Development Report*. New York: Oxford University Press.

———. 2010. *Human Development Report – The Real Wealth of Nations: Pathways to Human Development*. New York: Oxford University Press.

Unwin, A., and David, J. Unwin. 1998. "Exploratory Spatial Data Analysis with Local Statistics." *The Statistician* 47: 415–423.

Van, Zuidam R.A. 1985. *Aerial Photo Interpretation in Terrain Analysis and Geomorphological Mapping*. The Hague: Smits Publishers.

Vannote, R.L., G.W. Minshall, K.W. Cummins, J.R. Sedell, and E. Gushing. 1980. "The River Continuum Concept." *Canadian Journal of Fisheries and Aquatic Sciences* 37: 130–137.

Wadhera, Bharti. 2008. *Regional Variations in the Quality of Living Space in India*. Unpublished PhD Thesis, Department of Geography, Panjab University, Chandigarh.

Wasserman, Stanley, and Katherine Faust. 1994. *Social Network Analysis: Methods and Applications*. Cambridge: Cambridge University Press.

Webb, John W. 1959. "Basic Concepts in the Analysis of Small Urban Centers of Minnesota." *Annals Association of American Geographers* 49 (1): 55–72.

Williamson, J.G. 1965. "Regional Inequalities and the Process of National Development: A Description of the Patterns." *Economic Development and Cultural Change* 13 (4, part 2): 3–45.

Wilson, J.P., and J.C. Gallant eds. 2000. *Terrain Analysis – Principle and Application*. New York: John Wiley & Sons.

Yates, R. 1997. "The City-State in Ancient China." In *The Archaeology of City-States: Cross-Cultural Approach*, edited by D. Nichols and T. Charlton, 71–90. Washington, DC: Smithsonian Institution Press.

Yeates, M.H. 1974. *An Introduction to Quantitative Analysis in Human Geography*. New York: McGraw-Hill.

Yong, An Gie, and Sean Pearce. 2013. "A Beginner's Guide to Factor Analysis: Focusing on Exploratory Factor Analysis." *Tutorials in Quantitative Methods for Psychology* 9 (2): 79–94.

Zipf, G.K. 1949. *Human Behavior and the Principles of Least Effort*. Cambridge, MA: Addison Wesley.

Zhou, Q., B. Lees, and G. Tang, eds. 2008. *Advances in Digital Terrain Analysis*. Berlin: Springer.

Znaniecki, F. 1934. *The Method of Sociology*. New York: Farrar and Rinehart.

9

DATA REPRESENTATION

For conveying a message, graphicacy (visual presentation) together with literacy (in written form), oracy (through articulation) and numeracy (with the help of numbers) are 'the four aces' in the 'pack of education' (Balchin and Coleman 1966, 85). Graphicacy as a form of communication brings into play some form of symbolic language or arrangement of numerals to convey information about spatial relationships that cannot be adequately or effectively conveyed by verbal means (Balchin 1972). It is synonymous with visuals, maps, diagrams, photographs, sketches, charts, cartoons, posters and tables. Graphics serve the purpose of giving a visual shape to data for illustrating and strengthening the text for a deeper and better understanding. These render simplicity to complexity and communicate difficult ideas with clarity, precision and efficiency. This requires an ability to conceptualise a spatial form of the information and represent it (Butt 2002, 83).

Conventionally, graphics are differentiated as tables and figures. A table comprises of a grid with columns and rows. A figure embraces all other graphic forms, including maps, graphs, diagrams, charts, photographs and drawings, each one very differently created. All of these are summary devices, each of which has a distinctive role. These are extremely useful for sharing information, helping to highlight the main points raised in the text. To a great extent, they are meant to serve as a substitute to text. It is rightly said that a graph is a thousand times more powerful than words in communicating a message.

Graphics have to be placed at appropriate places in the text. Ideally these are adjusted within the body of the text. If there is insufficient space, a table or map can be placed at the top of the next page. The researcher may refrain from lumping them at the end of the chapter or the report, unless specifically required. In such cases, they get diminished in their relevance.

For a research student, it is essential to know the essence and underlying idea of each method of graphicacy, in addition to cultivating a skill to conceptualise and

182 Traversing the path: data management

draw it. The choice of a particular method to represent specific data has to be judicious and the researcher should be in a position to justify it. If you wish to adapt in place of adopting someone else's table/diagram/map, you should redraw it and acknowledge the original source. If some material is to be copied in its original form, especially for inclusion in a book, permission will have to be obtained from the copyright holder (usually the publisher).

Let us now move to a discussion on components of a table; map and its varied aspects; use of diagram, chart and graph; GIS in cartography and visualisation of geographic information and terrain representation.

Tables

The representation of data in the shape of a table is known as 'tabular presentation'. Tables are commonly used for organising collected raw data and also for representing final data to be included in a thesis/dissertation, research, paper or report. Once recorded, data need to be sorted, reorganised, summarised and reshaped into a final table or graph. A table has to be illustrative of your text and not simply reproduce it. Draw a table that can stand alone without any explanation. At the same time, a table does require a spotlight on its core message.

Types of tables: The commonest types of tabular matter employed in a research work are inventory tables, statistical tables, and numerical tables. Inventory tables are in the form of an inventory of information pertaining to any item, such as names of the states and union territories of India or the capitals of different countries of the world. Statistical tables portray descriptive or inferential statistics or both. Descriptive statistical tables present the derived results such as frequency distribution, mean, mode, and standard deviation. These display results of processed data. Inferential statistical tables represent statistical test values of sample populations such as the level of confidence in respect of a statistical result obtained, or randomness in spatial distribution. These are based on a processing of sample data. Numerical tables display general information, quantitative or qualitative. The tables prepared by Census of India or those listing National Sample Survey Regions by states/union territories of India would fall under this category. An illustration of a model numerical table is given in Table 9.1.

Still another way to categorise tables is by number of variables about which information is displayed. These would be univariate, also known as frequency tables; bivariate, depicting cross-tabulations; and multivariate.

There are many other kinds of tables as well: for example, Geological time-scale tables which provide sequential listing of eons, eras and periods of geological time; and Hierarchy tables such as one showing macro, meso and micro regions of India. The basic objective of a table is to render simplicity to complexity. In its own turn, it is meant to be purposeful, properly architectured, and effective in conveying the intended message.

Basic components of a table

Numbering: The word 'Table' and the table number set in Arabic numerals (Table 1 or Table 1.1) are typed on a line above the table. It must find a place in the text by

Data representation **183**

TABLE 9.1 India: literacy by states/union territories, 2011

States/Union territory*	Percentage of literates in		
	All areas	Urban areas	Rural areas
States			
. . . .			
. . . .			
. . . .			
Union territories			
Delhi			
Chandigarh			
. . . . .			
INDIA			

Source: Census of India 2011.

States and union territories are listed in descending order of their literacy rates.

that number, either directly or in a bracket. In the example given above, Table 9.1 represents the literacy rates of different states and union territories of India; or else Indian states and union territories differ widely in their literacy rates (Table 9.1). Numeration of tables may be done in one of these ways: the table number, for example Table 1, may be placed on a line by itself, either flush left before the title or centred above the title, depending on the style followed. They may be numbered continuously straight through the entire text, as in the case of a project report. A doctoral thesis may adopt separate numbering for each chapter. This leaves a scope for addition or omission of a table without disturbing the entire system. Likewise, in a book consisting of individual contributions by different authors, the numeration starts afresh with each chapter or paper. In case of textbooks also the tables may be given double numbers, such as Tables in chapter 2 will be listed as 2.1, 2.2, 2.3 and so on. Tables in an appendix are usually numbered differently in the form A.1, A.2, A.3.

Title: The caption or label of a table is called the title, set flush left above the table frame. It should be a concise but complete statement on what the table intends to convey. It must refer to the area it concerns and the year or period it refers to. Do give units of measurement, such as km² or percentage, in table headings, if required. Table titles should not be in full capitals. The first word and other words, barring conjunctions, prepositions and articles, can be capitalised. A subheading in the table title is usually enclosed in a bracket. *See* India: Number of Households below the Poverty Line, 1973–74 to 2013–14 (in million).

Stubs and column headings: Stub is the left-hand column of a table. It lists the categories or items about which information is given in other columns. The listing is vertical. It may or may not carry a heading as many a times the table title makes

184 Traversing the path: data management

clear what is in the stub. Items in the stub may form a straight sequential list (as all the states/union territories listed alphabetically) or a classified one (states/union territories listed in descending order of their population size). Listing of spatial units by rank on a given variable adds to the analytical value of the table.

Columns in a table must be precisely aligned and labelled. Horizontal rules may be used above and below the column headings and to show totals at the foot of a table. If the number of spatial units is large, say 100, a thin horizontal line may be drawn or space be left blank to separate every 10th spatial unit. Vertical rules should not be used as divider of columns.

Column headings may carry sub-headings particularly when it is required to indicate the unit of measurement used in the column below. Sub-headings are usually put within parentheses and abbreviations such as (#), (%), (mi.), (*100 km) and so on.

The body: The vertical columns to the right of the stub and below the column headings, typically consisting of figures, constitute the body of the table. These columns represent the real substance of the table. Their arrangement should be clear and orderly to the extent possible.

Tables should not be used if the number of columns and rows is two or fewer. A textual description is enough in such cases. On the contrary, it may become difficult for the reader to make any sense of the data if there are too many rows or columns. In such situations it may be more prudent to condense the data, or separate the data into supplementary tables. If two or more tables contain identical columns or rows of data, you may have to combine those tables. Provide space for column/ row totals or other numeric summaries to make it easier to understand the data.

The design: The table number and the title are set in the same font size as the body of the table, normally 8 to 9 point. Sub-heading, if there is any, may be set in a smaller size or different style. Footnotes are also normally set one size smaller than the body of the table. Round off the numbers as much as feasible. It is normal to round the figures to at least two decimal places unless it is required to retain more decimals. Align decimal places.

An important aspect of the design is to craft the key elements of your table in such a way that every element stands out from another. This can be achieved with typography, line thickness, size, colour, space. We may elaborate here on elements of typography: typeface or theme fonts, font size and font weight. The unique design or style of the alphabet by which we identify the name, say Times New Roman or Georgia, would be considered as the typeface. Letters are cast at a particular size or weight (12 point bold, for example). 12 point Times New Roman bold and 16 point Times New Roman italic would be two different fonts and weights but carry the same type face or font theme.

You can try several combinations for your table. For instance make headlines bigger than body matter, bring about changes in font weight (bold/italic/underlined) which is more effective than typeface. Use **bold for emphasis,** which may work better than ALL UPPERCASE. Ensure that the contrast between background and text is strong. The aim should be to create visual difference between elements. Contrast guides our eyes where to look first or what is significant.

Regardless of however you create contrast, remember that there should not be anything like 'too much contrast'. Also, 'less is more' when it comes to creating an effective table.

For missing data insert n.a. (an abbreviation of not available). Use the figure zero when the variable under representation is absent in an area. You may place − (en dash) when data is of negligible quantity. As far as possible, a table should be kept upright and not rotated in any direction. Make it as elegant and not much packed.

One firm rule is that a table should not spill over to the next page.

Footnotes: Footnotes to a table are of four general kinds and should appear in this order: source notes; other general notes; notes on specific parts of the table; and notes on level of probability. Source note is introduced by the word 'Source(s)', generally set in italics. All other notes be referred to by the word 'Note(s)'. Footnotes are typed below the body of the table. They are not numbered. These could be distinguished from each other by a symbol, such as a small dot or bar or a star.

It is most desired that the main message of the table is conveyed in one representative sentence. The purpose of the table is greatly served if this practice is always followed. This may be placed just below the table, that is, above the source.

Maps

Maps are reckoned as geographers' most distinctive and essential tools for visual communication (L. Pulsipher, A. Pulsipher, and Goodwin 2008, 4). Ullman's comments cited in Muehrcke (1981, 1) capture the quintessence of maps in geography: 'Geographic thought is inevitably linked to maps . . . if you cannot map a thought you do not have a geographic thought'. These essentially serve to depict the spatial distributions, patterns, relations, interactions, flows, exchanges of any nature, scaled to an observable scale and isolated for study and interpretation (Fellmann, A. Getis, and J. Getis 2005, 20).

As the core element of cartography, a map provides the geographer with a method to portray, classify, represent and communicate spatial patterns and relationships for a convenient understanding of complex reality. It makes generalisation possible. Map brings the vast world around or its parts into the laboratory for a microscopic analysis.

Map making has now entered a digital era. The computer technology has made it more interactive and virtual on screen. A dissertation or thesis in geography must have maps and diagrams. These should be scattered all over, every chapter having some maps.

The introductory chapter should carry a map detailing the location of the study area and the base map needs to be placed appropriately in the dissertation. Any place or geographic feature or region/country whose name appears in the text must find a place on some map. The basic principle is that all such mapping should be uncluttered, reactive to the purpose and effective in communicating the intended message at an appropriate scale which allows easy visual appeal and appreciation.

Types of maps: Maps can be just illustrative, showing locations of geographic features or thematic, representing a segment of spatial reality. These are a source of

186 Traversing the path: data management

information on the location, shape and size of key features of the landscape, distributional pattern of various phenomena and of relationship among them. In the process of geographic research, maps may have *avatars* in three forms:

(i) Experimental maps for preparing the draft of the dissertation. A series of maps, using different techniques or varying set of categories, may be prepared for the final selection of the best. Here maps are used as a tool. A variety of maps representing different attributes of agriculture, and marking agricultural regions is one such case.

(ii) Selected maps for inclusion in the text. Here maps are used as evidence to the text. These maps are drawn to perfection.

(iii) Derived maps from the final maps. Here maps are used for summarising a message emerging from the analysis in the dissertation. A map listing strategy for development in each agricultural region is one illustration of the kind. It is constructed by overlaying of various maps depicting different aspects of agriculture.

The above three kinds of maps take form at successive stages of preparing the doctoral thesis. In the first phase these are experimental, in the second phase a representation and in the final phase a net product. For a research student, maps are geared to perform the above listed triple functions.

Special features: An effort should be made to make maps as purposeful as possible. Some instances can be cited below:

- Maps representing two mutually related variables superimposed upon each other should be preferred. The idea is to capture cause and effect on the map. A map showing rice-producing areas in India may be overlain over the isohyet map. One can discern here a critical isohyet which divides the rice and other cereal-producing areas.

- For this reason, colour maps should be given a priority. These facilitate overlaying of two spatial patterns over each other. A rural population density map of India in black and white can be easily overlain by a rural population growth rate map in colour. This may bring forth a negative relationship between the two, by and large.

- It is always desirable to depict background features on a map while showing some geographical distribution. A map showing location of cities in India may have a background depiction of major transport routes and rivers. This will reveal the role of related factors.

- Names of administrative areas may be given even on a choropleth map, if necessary. A map showing per capita income by states/union territories of India may provide the names of these administrative units over the choropleth shading. This ensures completion to information.

The impression conveyed by a map is a function not only of what is being depicted but also of data quality, definition of variables mapped and class intervals or grouping of data. Equally important are map scale, graphic design and map perception by the reader. A map should ensure desired visual impact, a vivid understanding of the spatial distribution and a ready grasp of synthesised information of two or more spatial distributions on the same map. Such situations can be either mixture or compound.

Maps also display mixtures of information wherein different symbols and colours are used on the same map to show different items, such as dots for cities, brown lines for contours, red solid cross for hospital, black lines for rail tracks and so on. Several maps present 'compounds' rather than mixtures. Compounds represent two varieties, one in which a spatial distribution is overlain by another distribution to show the relationship between the two; and the other when a variety of related maps are placed on the same sheet. A map showing an overlay of infant mortality rate and birth rate is an illustration of the first kind. Population density maps of India for the years 1951, 1971, 1991 and 2011 on a single sheet are an illustration of the second kind.

We may focus here in some detail on issues relating to elements, symbolisation, class interval, and spatial contiguity and geographical clustering on thematic maps.

Map elements

Theme along with the name of the study area occupies the first space within the map frame. The title is adjunct to this as a map element. It should be descriptive but concise. The name of the study area and the theme under reference are usually split and centred over two lines. The font size will differ for each level of emphasis. The theme usually contains reference to a specific time/period; include the year or range of period, as the case may be, in the title. This is followed by reference to the type of enumeration/observation unit. Thus a map should, if possible, indicate: what – the theme or characteristic of the map; where – the geographic area; and when – temporal information and spatial scale of the enumeration unit.

All this may be illustrated as follows:

India (Name of the study area)
Urbanisation (Theme being displayed)
2011 (Year; pertains to the theme)
Data by districts (enumeration unit)

The legend is a crucial element of any map. It is set at an appropriate place within the map frame. In a thematic map do not mark the legend 'Legend' or 'Key'. Rather, it should supplement the theme by describing it in the shortest possible expression. In the above case, the legend may carry the word 'Percentage' above the series of categories represented by different colours or shades of the same colour or in different textures of black and white. All the non–self–explanatory symbols on the map must be represented exactly as they appear on the map. For example DNA representing 'Data Not Available' must find a mention in the legend.

All maps must indicate the scale of the area mapped. Scale bar or line scale is most appropriate for thematic maps. However, for reproduction in books, scale should be indicated only if permission for production of map with approved boundaries has

188 Traversing the path: data management

been sought from the nodal agency. For example, if a map for India is to be drawn permission needs to be sought from Survey of India. Such a map is not to get distorted when it is enlarged or reduced. Most maps provide some indication of their orientation. If not, north is assumed to be at the top of the map.

An appropriate frame will make the map more compact in its design as it separates the map and its elements from the rest of the page. The anchoring of the map to the page fixes the eye movement of the reader and confines reader's attention to the map area. Maps which employ secondary data must mention the source. For maps based on primary data, personal fieldwork may be listed as the source. Above all, the map frame must conform to the requirements of the journal or book in which the text is going to be published.

Inset maps are drawn sometimes either to gain a full understanding of scale or to enlarge a portion of the map. These should be placed in conformity with other map elements. These may require their own scale, legends or titles depending on the nature of detailing required.

All the elements discussed above should comply with considerations of balance, unity and harmony of the map (Tyner 1992, 44–51). The map in Figure 9.1 is meant to represent map elements and the next map in Figure 9.2 is an illustration of a choropleth map.

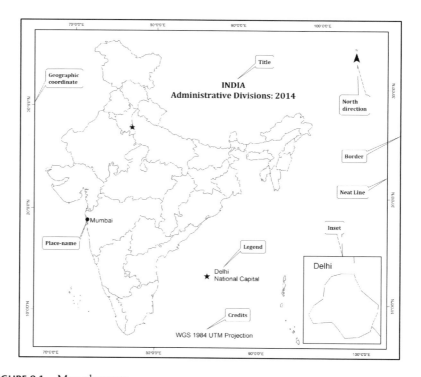

FIGURE 9.1   Map elements

Data representation 189

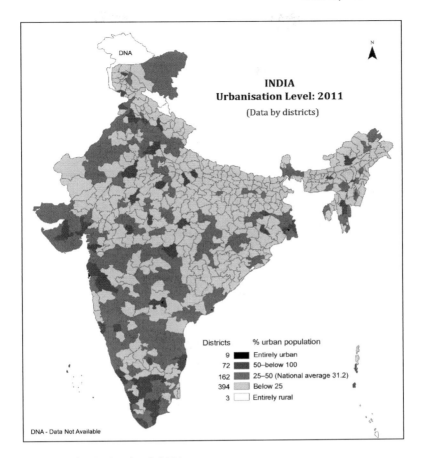

FIGURE 9.2 Urbanisation level: 2011

Symbolisation

Nature of mappable data and symbolisation: A map is an integrated assemblage or synthesis of four categories of information: points, lines, areas and names. These are presented in terms of different patterns, shapes, sizes, thicknesses, characters, symbols, forms and hues.

Mappable data vary immensely. The characteristics of data are to be considered for mapping. It may be at points (zero dimension), lines (one dimension) or in areas (two dimensions). Also, data in volume can occur at points (population in cities), along lines (flow of migrants from Bangladesh) or over areas (amount of precipitation) and can be symbolised by point, line or area marks. Data for attributes are collected by some geographic area, places, administrative units or regions. It may also be quantitative (population of each slum locality in Lucknow), qualitative (Lucknow slum localities classified in three categories of notified, recognised and

190 Traversing the path: data management

identified) or a mix of the two (notified slums in Lucknow with a population of more than 5000). All information is shown with symbols.

The mapped quantities are simplification or generalisation of the source quantities. For instance, a point symbol on a map may show a city of 108,756 people as per the Census, falling in the population range between 100,000 and 250,000. Likewise, isopleths drawn with an interval of 20 m might indicate a point of 48 m altitude benchmark recording, in the range between 40 and 60 m above sea level. A population density map may cover all the districts with a density of below 100 under one category.

Map symbols may have different shape, size, colour, pattern and texture. Each attribute is used for a specific purpose. The nature of data, whether qualitative or quantitative, determines the type of symbol used. Data on a nominal (qualitative) scale are represented by using differentiating symbols, colours and pattern. Data on an ordinal, interval or ratio scales are depicted by using differentiating ordered variables with size, colour and texture variables. A brief note on different visual symbols for differentiating or ordering of attributes would be appropriate here.

Visual symbols used for differentiating or ordering of attributes: Map symbols with different shapes imply differences in quality. Distribution of colleges, primary health centres and agricultural markets, for example can be shown by adopting symbols of different shapes for the three items. The shapes can be pictorial or geometrical or alphabetical. Different shapes suggest qualitatively different items (Krygier and Wood 2011).

Map symbols with different sizes imply differences in quantity. A larger circle or square implies greater quantity than a smaller one. Different sizes of the same symbol represent quantitative rather than qualitative variations.

Colours are used on maps in a number of ways. These are distinguished by their hue, value, intensity or chroma/saturation. Hue is the characteristic that enables colours to be classed as green, brown, blue and so on. A distinction between hue and colour needs to be understood. Colour is a holistic term covering not only hue but also value, intensity and chroma. In fact, variations of a single hue produce different colours (Wong 1987, 43). For example, a green hue can be lawn green, pastel green, camouflage green, dark olive green, which are colour variations within the same hue. In normal parlance the word 'hue' tends to be used as a synonym for colour (Chilvers, Osborne, and Farr 1988).

Symbols with different hues readily imply differences in quality. For example, an administrative map of India depicts various states and union territories by different hues. There is a convention to use certain hues for land-related features, such as blue for water bodies, green for vegetated areas, brown for contours and so on.

Value refers to different shades of one hue, such as dark and light green. Map symbols with different values readily imply differences in quantity. Dark green is more than light green. Values suggest an ordered difference, which is appropriate for showing quantitative data.

Chroma connotes the intensity or purity of a colour. Colours with strong chroma are the most luminous, most bright. Colours with weak chroma are dull as they contain a large proportion of grey. Colour chroma or intensity (or saturation) is a subtle visual variable that is best used to show specific data variations, such as states of India with higher or lower than national average of per capita income. Such data are qualitative or quantitative. Intensity may suggest order, but due to distinctness in variation of value the sense of order is weak.

Pattern is the systematic repetition of dots and lines, broken or smooth, on the map. The variations in pattern are attributed to shape and texture (spacing). This is best illustrated by international, state and district boundaries on an administrative map. The respective symbols for this purpose can differ by thickness and continuity or discontinuity of lines or by difference in colour or both. Likewise varying patterns of lines and dots can be used on choropleth maps. Texture refers to spacing of symbols. Dots placed with varying texture or spacing can depict variations in population density. One can select appropriate texture to create varying visual impressions through graphic representation of data (Robinson *et al.* 1995).

The point, line and spatial symbols used for mapping of data are discussed in the sections to follow.

Data representation with point symbols: The data may be qualitative or quantitative in nature. Qualitative data are nominal and therefore point symbols of different shapes and colours are used to visually differentiate items and their attributes. Take the example of pilgrimage centres in India. These can be symbolised using differentiating visual symbols; an orange temple for Hindu, green mosque for Muslim and blue gurudwara for Sikh pilgrimage centres. Qualitative differences get best reflected using pictorial symbols in colour.

Quantitative point data are available at ordinal, interval and ratio scales. These are symbolised with graded visuals. A point symbol can be a sphere, cube, circle, dot or other geometrical figure of conventional form representing a specified quantity. These are meant to show total quantities at exact locations. In deciding what quantity a symbol is to represent, we must initially focus on the general character of the distribution we intend to map.

The dot map shows the locational character of a distribution more clearly than any other type of map. It goes by the number of dots depending upon the scatter of a distribution in a given area. The density of dots represents the degree of concentration of the phenomenon under reference.

The numerical value and size of the dot is to be decided with utmost care. In case we assign a small number of people to each 'dot', it will lead to overcrowding of dots in a densely settled region in the form of a solid black mass. Such a map does not at all reveal any picture of the distribution of people within the black mass. Similarly, if each dot is made to represent too many people, we will find a difficulty in placing the dots in sparsely settled regions, where one dot may carry a higher number of people than the population of the entire area.

Dot placement should be guided by specific knowledge of locations of a given distribution. If a dot map is being prepared to represent population in various villages of a district in which settlements are agglomerated in nature, all the dots for a given village should be located closer to each other in place of scattering them over

192 Traversing the path: data management

the whole area of the village. Likewise, if settlements in a mountainous region are located along the valley, the placement of dots representing population distribution would assume a linear pattern.

Traditionally, on topographic maps, point symbols have also been used to depict spot heights and bench marks. Here a value (elevation above mean sea level) is put against the dot on the surveyed spot. This dot is meant to confirm the exact location. Likewise, small, thin dots are also placed on the bed of seasonal streams.

Generally dot maps show only one factor attribute but several distributions can also be shown using differently coloured dots or different shaped point symbols, such as distribution of rice and wheat areas in India by green and brown dots respectively.

The graduated symbol map varies the size of a single symbol, placed within each geographic area, in tandem with the data value of various spatial units. These symbols readily imply magnitude rather than density. Such a map gives a comparative picture of the totals in different areas. The symbol design includes squares, triangles, circles, pictographic shapes and volumetric shapes.

As an illustration, we may want to depict population size of every city in India as per 2011 census. We'll do so using a point symbol, such as graduated circles at the location of cities. It could be done by representing the population size by proportionate graduated (drawn according to the scale) circles. If we were to display an additional ratio-scaled attribute, such as percentage of slum population in each city, we could fill this in each circle by graduated hues, representing varying percentage of slum population. Similarly, portrayal of distribution of rural population by dot method and of towns by graduated circles on the same map is a common practice.

For graduated symbols, the legend may be classified or unclassified: classified graduated symbol maps show data by grouping the items being represented. For example, three different size symbols could be chosen to represent three different population size categories of towns of less than 20,000; 20,000 to 100,000; and above 100,000. This facilitates easy discernment of category of towns but without detail of data. Unclassified graduate symbol maps scale each symbol to each value. This is the normal practice though not free from the problem of comparability. In any case, legend should effectively represent the shape and scale of the symbols.

A graduated symbol, such as a circle or sphere, is drawn in proportion to the quantity it is meant to represent. This would be 'area' in the case of graduated circle and volume in respect of sphere. If a graduated circle of 1 cm represents 1000 persons, in that case 25,000 persons will be represented by a circle of $\sqrt{25,000 / 1000} = 5$ cm radius. A circle with 5 cm radius covers an area which is 25 times of the circle with 1 cm radius. Likewise, in a sphere of 1 cm radius, 27,000 will be represented by a sphere of $\sqrt[3]{27,000 / 1000} = 3$ cm.

Data representation with line symbols: Symbols showing attributes of features regarded as lines are easy to observe on maps. These include rivers, coastlines, lakes, boundaries, roads, railroads and all kinds of flows (such as traffic flow) or movements (migration) between locations.

The nominal linear data are shown with shape and colour variable. The shape of line symbols of differing character will vary; roads will be in intercepts of straight lines but not rivers which may carry sinuous shape. As far as colour is concerned, it is blue for river, red for roads, black for railway lines etc. When difference in kind and importance is to be projected, for example, national highways, state highways and district roads, shape can be combined with thickness. Features like rivers, ocean currents or winds have to take into account the dimension of direction.

Quantitative data are shown through size and colour to depict line features. Size is more effective than colour in symbolising line data. We may be interested in depicting the in-migrants to the National Capital Territory of Delhi from various states and union territories of India. The flow data may be (i) range-graded, that is, lines of scaled width are used to represent a specified range of numbers of in-migrants: under 10,000, 10,000–20,000, 20,000–50,000, 50,000–100,000 and over 100,000 or (ii) ratio-scaled, that is, lines are drawn proportional in width to number of in-migrants. Size is used as the ordering visual variable in both cases. In addition, the visual variable of colour can be used also to distinguish in-migrants by blue colour and out-migrants by red colour.

Line symbols to show area attributes include hachures, profiles, oblique traces and isarithms. All of them help in visualising a surface. Hachures are short line symbols traditionally used to depict landforms. Slope steepness is expressed through their spacing and thickness. Profiles, oblique traces and isarithms are conceptually similar. Profiles are produced from the intersection of a plane perpendicular to the x, y datum. These can be constructed from an isarithmic map. Oblique traces result from the intersection of a series of planes with the base datum at some angle θ, where θ lies between $0°$ and $90°$. These traces may be portrayed graphically. Isarithms are imaginary lines connecting points of equal value.

Isarithms have two forms: isometric and isoplethic. The only difference between the two is the form of the original data used for the map. Isometric lines result from actual point data, such as elevations above or depth below sea level. Isopleths are drawn for derived values, including averages, measures of dispersion or correlation coefficients, such as mean monthly temperature or variability of rainfall or correlates of per capita income and urbanisation level. Normally we should not attempt isopleths for absolute values, such as population size of settlements in an area. Isopleths can be drawn for derived values. The examples are density of population or percentage of cultivated area to total area or mean annual rainfall.

Isometric and isopleth maps are best suited for identification of spatial trend in a given distribution. These give an idea whether a distribution over space is changing rapidly or gradually. Such maps also help in interpolating non-existing data for places of our interest. By taking into account the interval and space between two isopleths we can arrive at the data for any place which lies between them. Isometric and isopleth lines also serve as the boundaries of regions which we construct. For example, the 100 cm isohyet on the rainfall map of India broadly separates the predominantly rice-producing areas from wheat-producing ones in the Ganga plain.

Data representation with areal/spatial symbols: There can be situations when data to be represented are by spatial units and require to be mapped by area symbols. Soil maps, for example, depict areas of different soil types. When colour is available,

194 Traversing the path: data management

it is the most effective visual mode to differentiate such spatial distributions. Here the texture of the soils as sandy, clayey, loamy or silt may be depicted by the varying intensity of the same colour.

For qualitative depiction of area types, such as hill, swamp, desert and forest, we use conventional/standard symbols. These symbols have areal dimension and represent nominal data. However, with digital technology, colour in addition can be easily and effectively used.

The choropleth map is the most common mapping technique for data classified on the basis of administrative or enumeration units – countries, states, regions, districts and so on. These maps vary the shading of each area in accordance with the associated value. Generally we map ratios or percentages by choroplething technique. Examples include sex ratio map that is the ratio between female and male population and percentage of senior population, 60 years and above, in the total population. Mapping total numbers by choroplething is not recommended because mostly the spatial units on the map differ in their area size. In the legend dark shade means higher value and light shade stands for lower value. Largest values are placed at the top of the legend and smallest at the bottom.

Ratios in the context of spatial data can be worked out in different ways, each representing a different purpose. This can be best illustrated by a study of high schools in a district. If we calculate ratio between number of schools and area, it represents accessibility parameter of school; a ratio between number of schools and population will cover the adequacy dimension; and the percentage of settlements having a school will unfold the availability aspect.

The data used in the making of a simple choropleth map can also be used for a dasymetric map. In dasymetric maps, the boundaries of the spatial units are relaxed as per need. These maps enclose areas of relative homogeneity, separated by zones of abrupt change. To create these homogeneous areas, cartographers use other sources of information about related phenomena. Based on the knowledge gleaned from these sources, more homogeneous units are created by ignoring minor exceptional units which are deemed as disturbing the overall pattern.

The areas of uniformity are created by clustering or grouping contiguous similar attribute values into regions. Many different clustering techniques can be used. The pixels in raster data sets are often clustered in this manner.

When there are wide variations in data by spatial units, a cartogram is an effective technique. It is a variant of the graduated symbol map. Cartograms vary the size of geographic areas, rather than of the symbol, based on the given data. The area size of different countries of the world, for example, is drawn in proportion to their population size while retaining their shape. While difficult to create, these are visually striking.

Number of classes and class intervals

When we represent data at points, lines, or over areas, we group similar attribute values into classes. In every case we have to take a decision on the number of classes and class intervals. The number and range of class intervals greatly affect the accuracy, usability, legibility and attractiveness of maps. The class interval for distributional data is applicable to choropleth mapping, isoplethic portrayal or presentation of range-graded proportional point symbols. If these intervals are judiciously chosen the reader may gain a clearer understanding of the spatial distributions than he or she could have obtained from the original data. If the categories are poorly selected one gets only distorted or inaccurate impression of the distribution.

Number of classes: Basic to any formation of classes is the idea that the distribution is segmented and can be organised into different groups. The problem of selecting classes is an important phase of constructing a thematic map since in this step the map-maker controls map interpretation (Jenks and Coulson 1963, 119). This is generally influenced by the intended audience, the visual appeal, the technical means available and the spatial pattern of the distribution. For an amateur audience a small number of classes is advised; medium number of classes carry greater appeal, computer-assisted cartography is friendly to a large number; and spatial distributions with wide range necessitate larger number of classes. Monochromatic or black and white map lends to few distinct classes while chroma progressions on a colour map can allow more classes (Jenks and Knos 1961). A simple, precise map with four or five classes is attractive and catches the eye of an ignorant, naïve audience, raw at reading graphics. Trained eyes may appreciate visual appeal and additional information through seven or eight portray (Schultz 1961).

The number of spatial units for which data are to be represented is still another consideration in deciding the number of classes. Three to four classes may suffice if a map showing per capita income is to be prepared for 29 states and 7 union territories of India. In this case too many classes may split similar areas. Three classes would serve the purpose of representing high, medium and low values. The scope of having more of classes increases with larger number of enumeration units. On a map depicting a spatial distribution in 640 districts of India, a spatially differentiated picture will be obtained by using five to seven categories. These will stand for ranging in values 'very high, high, relatively high, average or moderate, relatively low, low, very low values'. To show extremely wide variations in world density of population, we may require up to ten classes. On the other hand, if we are keen to demonstrate a contrast, even two classes will suffice. A map showing the states/union territories of India which took form at the time of reorganisation in 1956 and others which were carved out later is one such case.

There are situations where classes are predetermined. A land use map will go by the given number of classes in the prevalent system of classification. The same is the case with a map showing climatic types.

Class intervals: The selection of the class intervals is one critical issue in isopleth and choropleth maps, although it is equally true that class intervals are required for any type of graded symbolisation, based on point, line or area symbols. Mackay (1955, 71) referred to class intervals as 'the mesh sizes of cartography', which should

196 Traversing the path: data management

filter out extraneous details and capture the essence of the quantitative spatial distribution. Robinson (1961, 58) had rightly noted that different interpretations can arise from the same data if different sets of class intervals are employed. Some examples will further clarify the matter.

Spatial symbols are often used for many phenomena that have a tendency towards extremes in their spatial distribution. One notable example is the world map of population density which ranges up to 20,000 by individual countries. This issue is managed by increasing the width of class intervals while approaching the upper end of the density scale. This can be done by either adopting geometric progression or logarithmic scores.

It follows that a choropleth map involves issues like choice of intervals – number and their breaks. The nature of intervals can vary – arithmetic, geometric, quantile (equal share), standard deviational and so on. This all depends upon the nature of data. If the distribution is normal, arithmetic intervals serve the purpose; if these have a wide range, geometric intervals become necessary (for details see Evans 1977).

Another case wherein the same principle applies is that of representation of relief on maps covering large expanse of country (Wright 1942, 537). As the lowlands and plains are far more extensive, vast stretches of land than the vertically rising mountains, it is normal to increase the size of the contour intervals with rise in elevation. This will allow for more topographic detail to be shown for the lowlands, and less clustering of contours on the highlands, than would be the case if the intervals were uniform.

The golden rule is that isopleth intervals should be chosen to avoid excessive numbers of isolated 'islands' of highs and lows, but may be made to coincide with rapid rather than gradual changes in distribution. An isopleth is usually best employed to separate regions of diversity instead of near uniformity (Mackay 1951, 8).

What is the test of a meaningful system of class intervals? It is the one which represents the spatial reality most truly. The selection of class interval should cover the full range of the data; have neither overlapping values nor vacant classes; be large enough in number to avoid losing the details of the data, but not be so numerous as to damage the reading quality of the map. Of the many possible methods of determining class intervals the cartographer should generally select the system that gives the best areal representation of the data (Jenks and Coulson 1963).

Class intervals that are expressive of distributional data are not easily determinable by visual inspection alone. Therefore one of the ways to arrive at appropriate class interval is to plot the raw data on the base map to figure out the critical breaks in its distribution. A note may also be taken of the spatial distribution of the causally linked phenomena. For example, while preparing a population density map of India, we cannot ignore the underlying role of physical regions.

This technique can be combined with the otherwise common statistical devices already in practice. In particular, frequency, cumulative and clinographic curves are three graphic aids that may be used in the selection of class intervals.

Frequency curves help in identification of breaks in statistical distribution of data. It is assumed that such breaks coincide with breaks in spatial distributions. Hence category breaks or intervals can be decided by taking such break points into consideration.

Cumulative curve enables us to determine what proportion of any map will be covered by different class intervals. Cumulative curves of different distributions can be plotted and compared on a single graph to discover interrelationships. For example, cumulative graphs (ogives) of population density, mean annual precipitation and size of farm can readily be compared for the same area and their interrelationships studied.

Clinographic curve is used in landform analysis to show the profile of the land. Since this curve shows average slopes, it is ideal for the study of changes or breaks in slope. There must be causative factors to explain why a curve flattens or steepens at a particular point. If the breaks in slope are of geographical significance, they should be considered when class intervals are chosen.

Frequency, cumulative and clinographic curves should be used to supplement each other and not employed separately, because different combinations of class intervals will usually be suggested by each graph. Graphic aids do not cease to be of value after they have served their initial purpose in the study of class intervals. These can be employed to supplement the maps to understand other facets of the distributional data.

The selection of class intervals is to be guided by maximising between-class variation and minimising within-class variation. It has to take into account the factor of spatial contiguity and relationship with causative factors. Similar contiguous areas should not be fragmented by inappropriate class intervals. Thus, class intervals are determined on the principle of spatial clustering of similar units and separation of dissimilar ones.

In considering class intervals or classes it is desirable to understand the meaning of class boundaries, class limits and class mark and class frequency.

Class boundaries separate one class from another. Suppose the classes were 100–200, 200–300, 300–400 and so on, the numbers 100, 200, 300, 400 are the class boundaries. Here it is not clear what should be done with certain values, such as 200 or 300. Where should they be placed: lower class or upper class, or into both? It can be resolved if we specify the class limits.

Class limits are the smallest and largest possible measurements in each class. These are meant to avoid any overlapping. Specified in terms of their class limits, the first three classes would be 100–199, 200–299 and 300–399. When the classes are described in terms of the class limits each boundary is understood to be half-way between the upper class limit of the lower class and the lower class limit of the upper class. For the class limits100–199, 200–299 and 300–399 the class boundaries are 99.5, 199.5, 299.5 and 399.5.

Class mark is the mid-point of a particular class interval. It is the point half-way between the class boundaries of a class. If the class boundaries are 99.5–199.5, 199.5–299.5 and 299.5–399.5, then the class marks are 149.5, 250.5 and 350.5.

Class frequency is the number of observations in any particular class.

198 Traversing the path: data management

Methods of determining class intervals

There are a variety of methods for the purpose. These may be classified as (i) based on arithmetic, geometric and logarithmic series; (ii) based on summary measures of central tendency and dispersion; and (iii) based on critical cut-off points. The intervals chosen may yield equal classes, unequal classes or irregular class limits.

Based on arithmetic, geometric and logarithmic series: In arithmetic series each class is separated from the next by a stated numerical difference. In arithmetic progression classes increase by an orderly amount in comparison to the next lower class. Consider this simple case of arithmetic progression in representation of percentage of population growth in India during 2001–11 in the categories of less than 12, 12 to 24, 24 to 36 and 36 and above. Since the average growth rate of 17 per cent falls in the second category, the districts falling in the first category can be deemed as having experienced net outmigration, those in the second category recorded a growth rate which was largely the result of natural increase, and the districts in the third and fourth category can be highlighted for net in-migration in increasing order.

Some other forms of arithmetic series can also be listed as follows:

i   Class size *decreases at a constant rate*. For instance, if we take class distribution to be 0–12; 12–22; 22–30; 30–36, class size decreases by 2 per cent points.
ii In this case the first class is 0–12. Hence $a= 12$. Applying arithmetic series $[a - (n - 1)d]$, the second class will have size 10; $[12 - (2 - 1)2]$. Therefore, the second class becomes 12–22 and so on. Class size decreases as 12, 10, 8, 6, which is an arithmetic series with $d=2$. If the class size was to increase at constant rate the formula would be $[a + (n - 1)\ d]$.
iii Class size at each level *decreases at an increasing rate*. In the distribution 0–35; 35–65; 65–85; 85–90, the class size is 35, 30, 20 and 5 and the rate of decrease is 5, 10 and 15 respectively.
iv Class size at each level *increases at an increasing rate*. In this case the categories could be as follows: 0–5, 5–20, 20–50 and 50–100; the class size is 5, 15, 30 and 50; and the rate of increase is 10,15, 20 respectively.

Geometric progression has each class separated by a stated numerical ratio. Geometric progressions of class widths are extremely useful for distributions where frequency declines continuously with increasing magnitude ('J-shaped' distributions). In such distributions the range between the lowest and the highest value is large. This is the case with country wise density of population in the world. The categories in geometric progression could be as follows: less than 50 persons per km^2; 50–100; 100–200; 200–400; 400–800; and more than 800 persons per km^2.

Arithmetic progressions are more commonly used at the lower end of the scale and geometric progressions at the higher end of the scale, since in arithmetic progression, each class only varies by common difference so it is applicable for data with low range, giving appropriate spread of classes, while in geometric progression each varies by common ratio so it is applicable for data with high range, hence limiting the number of classes.

Logarithmic progressions have to be resorted to when the difference between the lowest and highest value is extreme in a frequency distribution. This can be illustrated by the per capita income of 205 countries in the world in 2014, as listed by the World Bank. The range spreads between US$250 for Malawi and US$103,050 for Norway. For representation of such data, we often adopt log value, which for 100 would be 2; for 1000 it would be 3; for 10,000 it would be 4 and for 100,000 it would be 5. The class intervals would, thus, be less than 1000; 1000 to 10,000; 10,000 to 100,000 and over 100,000.

Based on summary measures of central tendency and dispersion: Some methods take into consideration the mean, range and standard deviation of a frequency distribution while classifying it into a desired number of classes.

In case of the mean, the class intervals are centred on the mean. The mean lies at class midpoint if the number of classes is odd (say 5) and a class boundary if the number is even (say 4). The five categories will successively represent very high, high mean, low and very low values. On the other hand, if four categories are devised, these will stand for high, relatively high, relatively low and low values. Adoption of mean as a guiding post is recommended if the frequency distribution is normal.

The mean can be combined with standard deviation to form categories or classes. These are taken as mean plus/minus 1σ (standard deviation) and 2σ and above/below. In this case, we shall get six classes. If the mean is 100 and standard deviation 25, the six classes would be above 150, 125–150, 100–125, 75–100, 50–75 and below 50. The standard deviation system is best for frequency distributions which are approximately normal, or fairly symmetrical with a pronounced concentration near the mean. It should be applied also to skewed unimodal distributions which have been transformed to symmetrical form, for example by taking logarithms, cosines or reciprocals.

In cases of a skewed distribution of data it is often preferable to use the median and two quartiles above and two below for formation of classes. This would give four classes in all. This is meant to keep the play of extreme values under control.

When presenting or analysing measurements of a continuous variable, it may be required to group subjects into several equal groups. For example, if we have worked out the development indices for all the 640 districts of India and have ranked them in descending order of their development scores, it is possible to group them into four classes having an equal number of 160 districts each. The top 160 districts will be the most developed ones and the bottom 160 districts the least developed.

While presenting country wise data pertaining to distribution of national incomes, the World Bank divides the population into five groups or quintiles in each case. Income distribution is presented as the percentage share of the national income of each of the quintile groups. In India, for example, the top 20 per cent of

200 Traversing the path: data management

the population or the top quintile partakes 45 per cent of the national income. On the other extreme, the fifth or the bottom quintile group of 20 per cent population is left with only 8 per cent of the national income. This is indicative of gross disparity in income distribution in India.

Likewise, the World Bank Group in its World Development Report 2014 has grouped the countries into quintile groups on the basis of their indices on preparation for disaster management. This approach is in line with the methodology used in the construction of the Worldwide Governance Indicators (see Kaufmann, Kraay, and Mastruzzi 2010).

One effective technique to make classes is to divide the range of a given data into equal intercepts for determining the interval for the purpose. Assuming that the highest index of quality of living space for any district in India is 80 and the lowest for any district stands at 20, the range works out as 60. If we intend to classify all the districts in the country on the parameter of quality of living space into six classes, we divide this range by 6 and thereby obtain an interval of 10 for the purpose. Accordingly, the six classes would be with the indices of 20–30, 30–40, 40–50, 50–60, 60–70 and 70–80.

Critical cut-off points: It is a purposive method of the choice of class intervals. For example, we may like to depict the districts which in 2011 lag behind India's literacy rate in 1991, 2001 and 2011. Naturally the country's literacy rates in these three census years become the cut-off points for the classes. Another example could be to highlight the districts in a state like Uttar Pradesh which are at a higher than the state average or national average of urban population. In this case, the state and national averages of the percentage of urban population become the two critical breaks.

Using graphic techniques namely the frequency graph, the clinographic curve and, the cumulative frequency curve, class limits are adopted to highlight the 'natural breaks' or characteristics in the distribution. Here the breaks in the plotted curves are taken as the class interval breaks. These may suggest randomly changing class intervals. These can be approximated to easily understandable figures. Suppose we have to show percent urban population in 640 districts of India. A frequency graph would have percent urban population on the X-axis and frequency or number of districts on the Y-axis. By marking the critical breaks on this curve, we can construct classes.

Spatial contiguity and geographical clustering

KÜnzel (quoted in Monmonier 1972, 206–207) has proposed a 'method of areal grouping'. The data for administrative units are first inscribed on a base map and then subjected to careful scrutiny and comparison. The critical spatial breaks in data are observed over the map. These break points can be taken into account for determining the class intervals.

Another helpful method is to plot the specific data for all the spatial units and attempt a quick isoplething of the same. Such an exercise will give a clue to the overall spatial distribution of data and the major critical breaks which can be discerned. These will provide a clue for determining the class intervals.

A cartographer should generally select the system that gives the best areal representation of the data (Robinson and Sale 1969, 169). Contiguity relationships thus would play a role in selection of class interval. This is possible only after several maps of the same distribution have been prepared, each based on one of the standard methods of classification.

The use of cluster analysis helps in identifying contiguous areas. In this case, class intervals emerge only after the desired number of clusters has been formed. This is the reverse of all the situations where classes take form after the interval/s has/ have been finalised.

In all geographic studies, it is better to identify critical breaks in spatial distributions rather than to depend upon critical breaks in statistical distributions.

Diagrams

A diagram is a two- or three-dimensional graphic representation of statistical data and geographical features through some visualisation technique. Excluding maps, all other graphics can be included under its broad umbrella such as graphs, drawings, charts, representation sketch, layout, illustration and so on. Monkhouse and Wilkinson (1971) have clearly differentiated by naming their illustrative textbook *Maps and Diagrams*. Besides maps, the book is a treatise on diagrams used to depict relief, climatic data, population, economic and settlement data. The diagrams can be without or with the locational element.

It has been observed that human geographers, in particular, usually do not include diagrams in their thesis/dissertation. They rely mainly on maps. This tendency is contradictory to that of economists who make use of diagrams but are indifferent to maps. This trend needs to be reformed. All relevant diagrams must find a place in the dissertation and be of high quality. One may look on India Today or World Development Report for diagrams drawn for ready attention. The message to be conveyed through a diagram should be bold and unambiguous. If possible, they should give a three-dimensional view for great impact.

Graphs: These usually represent the relationship between two (or more) variables, as shown by plotting their values as distances from a pair of axes (X and Y) usually drawn at right angles to each other. By convention, while the independent variable is charted on the X-axis (horizontal) the dependent variable is plotted on the Y-axis (vertical). The resultant graph is a collection of points, often joined by a line or represented by bars.

Graphs have a great appeal. These are effective in conveying complex relationships. We may use words when numbers are few, three to five; may opt for tables when elaborate numerical information is to be given; and go for graphs when display of relationships is involved (Van Belle 2002, 154).

When drawing a graph, a research student may reflect on the need of creating it, the pattern it is likely to reveal and the contribution it is going to make to the text

202 Traversing the path: data management

of the research document. Hence it is to be a quality product. A graph acquires an aesthetic design if it follows the principle of golden rectangle. In this case, the ratio between the x coordinate and y coordinate is to be 3:2, or if the x coordinate has a length of 12 cm, the y coordinate should be 8 cm.

Bar graphs and line graphs are two major categories of graphs. The former are used to show comparative volume of any geographic phenomenon, such as month-wise rainfall in Delhi; the latter is meant to depict the trend in occurrence of a phe-nomenon, for example mean monthly temperature in Delhi. Usually line graphs are opted for items which have continuity, such as temperature, while bar graphs may be good for items which occur with breaks, such as rainfall.

Above all, special care should be taken in selecting the scale for a graph. Scale is not to be manipulated for magnifying or reducing the effect of what is being represented. Likewise a graph is not to be unnecessarily complex or misleadingly simple. It will be helpful to a reader if the message emerging from the graph is placed below it in the form of a simple sentence.

Charts: Charts are used to display series of numeric data arranged in a graphic set-up. In this way large quantities of data and the relationship between different series of data will be easily understood. The choice of chart will depend on the intended message. Some examples of charts include pie, doughnut, line, scatter, bubble, column, bar, area, cylinder, cone, surface, contour and pyramid. Excel sup-ports many types of charts. Picking up from the wide array of designs you may display data in ways that are meaningful to your audience.

Curves: Geomorphologists recognise the importance of cartography for map-ping of landforms and landform assemblages. The process of mapping has resulted in morphological, morphometrical and spatial information which could be explored further with appropriate analytical techniques (Davis 1986). Similarly, Lorenz curve is a special kind of curve which is drawn along with the line of equal distribution to depict inequality in a given distribution. If in an Indian state, 10 per cent large cultivators, each with at least 4 ha of agricultural land, take away 50 per cent of land; 20 per cent medium cultivators, each with 2–4 ha of agricultural land, share 20 per cent of land; 30 per cent small cultivators, each with 1–2 ha of land, account for 20 per cent of land; and the remaining 40 per cent marginal cultivators, each with less than 1 ha of land, have to do with the remaining 10 per cent of the land, such an unequal distribution can be shown by a Lorenz curve. In quantitative terms, this curve can be used to work out the Gini Coefficient, as a statistical measure of unequal distribution.

Use of Geographic Information Systems in cartography

The digital age has revolutionised cartography, particularly in the preparation, display and analysis of maps through the Geographic Information Systems (GIS). With sophisticated and interactive GIS applications, maps provide the mecha-nism for the visualisation of the results of spatial analysis. Maps can now be conveniently manipulated, transformed and analysed by their users. Geographic information can also be presented as a perspective view, an animation (a dynamic sequence of maps), a fly-by or fly-through (a virtual reality representation of the real world) or simulation (a what-if scenario that is not a representation of the real world). In addition, geographic information contained in digital maps can be converted easily into other forms of presentation, such as graphs, charts and statistical tables. Different from the conventional functions of maps, comprehensive information presentation is the primary function of the map in the GIS environment (Lo, Albert, and Yeung 2003, 227).

Computer databases are now the data store and the computer network the primary data carrier. It allows you great flexibility in adjusting the number, interval and shades of categories and the scale of the map. The construction of maps at different scales from the same database is also facilitated. Queries posed for answers on the basis of maps are also resolved. Above all, preparation of a variety of diagrams and colour maps is rendered easy with the help of this technology.

Today, the technology revolution has extended beyond GIS to include new methods of visualising data. It is now possible to create three-dimensional terrain models that can be viewed from different angles. Digital terrain models are used to represent topographic surfaces and other geographic phenomena, such as climate, meteorology, pollution, landcover and distribution of socioeconomic variables. The developments in morphometry, which have been a significant instrument of structural geomorphology since the 1950s, are currently connected with digital elevation modelling and GIS. The morphometric parameters used in tectonic geomorphology include hypsometric variables, characteristics of gradient and georelief energy, valley networks and valley profiles, shapes of basins, morphology of slopes, etc. (https://web.natur.cuni.cz/ksgrrsek/ acta/2004/AUC_2004_39_Panek_The_use_of pdf accessed on 16 February 2015).

If the data are complex and require visual presentation to convey a message effectively, the most common choices are tables, charts, graphs, isopleths and maps. A table is an effective tabular presentation of a message and can be compared with précis writing in literature. It describes as objectively and precisely as possible the substance or ideas contained in the text. In it, the emphasis is on discrete numbers, and readers are required to infer relationships or trends on their own. Charts and graphs make a more visual impact but communicate information less precisely when compared to a table but definitely carry more effective visual impact. Isopleths provide the best view of spatial trends. Maps are invariably effective in displaying spatial patterns and variations. The purpose and effect quotient of each method of data representation is different. Choose the most suited form with this in mind, not the one that comes to mind first. Your computer software enables you to draw from a larger range of graphics. If you are doing advanced research, readers will expect you to portray data and information through graphics favoured in your field. Always be in search of more creative ways of representing data if you are writing a dissertation or article in a field that usually displays complex relationships in large data sets.

Meanwhile, a kind of neo-geography of production and consumption of geographical knowledge has evolved (Turner 2007). Now spatial information is being

204 Traversing the path: data management

generated and used by millions of ordinary citizens through the use of smartphones, Facebook and GPS. Google Maps fall in the same line. It has come to be known as a citizen cartography or ubiquitous cartography or volunteered geographic information. The outcome of such a development is 'everywhereness of information in our daily life' (Elwood 2010, 350). The landscape of neo-geography is uneven. It is carved differentially by the income level of the people, availability of infrastructure and nature of government policies. In any case, the use of spatial media is making every individual two-in-one: locally based and globally networked.

References

Balchin, W.G.V. 1972. "Graphicacy." *Geography* 57 (3): 185–195.

Balchin, W.G.V., and A.M. Coleman. 1966. "Graphicacy Should Be the Fourth Ace in the Pack." *The Cartographer* (5 November) 3: 22–28 (Reprinted from The Times Educational Supplement).

Butt, Graham. 2002. *The Continuum Guide to Geographic Education*. London: Continuum.

Chilvers, Ian, Harold Osborne, and Dennis Farr, eds. 1988. *Oxford Dictionary of Art*. Oxford: Oxford University Press.

Davis, J.C. 1986. *Statistical and Data Analysis in Geology* (Chapter 6: Map Analysis). Chichester, UK: Wiley.

Elwood S. 2010. "Geographic Information Science: Emerging Research on the Societal Implications of the Geospatial Web." *Progress in Human Geography* 34 (3): 349– 357.

Evans, Ian S. 1977. "The Selection of Class Intervals." *Transactions of the Institute of British Geographers* New Series 2 (1): 98–124.

Fellman, Jerome D., Arthur Getis, and Judith Getis. 2005. *Human Geography: Landscapes of Human Activities*. 8th ed. Boston, MA: McGraw-Hill.

Jenks, G.F., and M.R. Coulson. 1963. "Class Intervals for Statistical Maps." *International Yearbook Cartography* 3: 119–134.

Jenks, G.F., and Duane S. Knos. 1961. "The Use of Shading Patterns in Graded Series." *Annals of the Association of American Geographers* 51 (3): 316–334.

Kaufmann, Daniel, Aart Kraay, and Massimo Mastruzzi. 2010. "The Worldwide Governance Indicators Methodology and Analytical Issues." *The World Bank Policy Research Working Paper 5430*. http://elibrary.worldbank.org/doi/pdf/10.1596/1813–9450–5430

Krygier, John, and Denis Wood. 2011. *Making Maps: A Visual Guide to Map Design for GIS*. 2nd ed. New York: The Guilford Press.

Lo, C.P., K. Albert, and W. Yeung. 2003. *Concepts and Techniques of Geographic Information Systems*. The Indian Reprint. New Delhi: Prentice Hall.

Mackay, J. Ross. 1951. "Some Problems and Techniques in Isopleth Mapping." *Economic Geography* 27: 1–9.

———. 1955. "An Analysis of Isopleth and Choropleth Class Intervals." *Economic Geography* 31 (1): 71–81.

Monkhouse, F.J., and H.R. Wilkinson. 1971. *Maps and Diagrams*. 3rd ed. London: Methuen and Co.

Monmonier, Mark S. 1972. "Contiguity-Biased Class-Interval Selection: A Method for Simplifying Patterns on Statistical Maps." *Geographical Review* 62 (2): 203–228.

Muehrcke, P. 1981. "Maps in Geography." *Cartographica* 18 (2): 1–41.

Pulsipher, L., A. Pulsipher, and C. Goodwin. 2008. *World Regional Geography: Global Patterns, Local Lives*. 4th ed. New York: W.H. Freeman and Company.

Robinson, A.H. 1961. "The Cartographic Representation of the Statistical Surface." *International Yearbook of Cartography* 1: 53–63.

Robinson, A.H., J.L. Morrison, P.C. Muehrcke, A.J. Kimerling, and S.C. Guptill. 1995. *Elements of Cartography*. 6th ed. New York: John Wiley & Sons.

Robinson, A.H., and R.D. Sale. 1969. *Elements of Cartography*. 3rd ed. New York: John Wiley & Sons.

Schultz, G.M. 1961. "An Experiment in Selecting Value Scales for Statistical Distribution Maps." *Surveying* and *Mapping* 21: 224–230.

Turner, A. 2007. *An Introduction to Neogeography*. Santa Clara, CA: O'Reilly Media.

Tyner, Judith. 1992. *Introduction to Thematic Cartography*. Englewood Cliffs, NJ: Prentice Hall.

Van Belle, G. 2002. *Statistical Rules of Thumb*. New York: John Wiley & Sons.

Wong, Wucius. 1987. *Principles of Color Design*. New York: Van Nostrand Reinhold.

Wright, John K. 1942. "Map Makers Are Human: Comments on the Subjective in Maps." *Geographical Review* 32 (4): 527–544.

10

DATA INTERPRETATION

One typical feature of most of the doctoral theses in geography in India is the fact that they are strong on description but weak on explanation and lacking in statement of message emerging from their research. This implies that much is missing in data interpretation. A critical obligation is left unattended.

Interpretation is an intellectual construct derived out of a research finding or a descriptive detail. Critical thinking skill, familiarity with a wider field of knowledge and awareness of the perspective in which research was done are basic to any interpretation. The task involves distilling the completed research.

Here is an illustration. When the British introduced the 'stamp paper' in India in 1765, the explanation given was that it is a measure for regulating procedures. The interpretation was that it was intended to mark their authority on any transaction, such as land sales or purchases, carried out. They also ensured, thereby, their pan-India presence.

Wolcott (1994, 10–11) effectively synthesises the successive steps of data description, analysis and interpretation. He calls them the 'Way First, Second and Third', as presented in the form of a flowchart in Table 10.1. Interpretation is going beyond the first way of 'digging into data' as well as the second way of 'churning the data'. This is the third way of 'conversing with the data'. Aptly put, it amounts to reaching and exhibiting the deeper meaning of the results obtained much beyond the limits of certainty associated with data analysis.

To begin with, the establishment of the linkage between data interpretation and objectives and hypothesis of the study is essential. Sometimes it may call for an additional data analysis beyond what has been accomplished. If a study of trends in regional disparities does not conform to Williamson's model of low incidence of disparity at both the low and high levels of development and high incidences in the transitional stage, it may call for an additional analysis to test some other hypothesis for arriving at a meaningful interpretation.

Data interpretation 207

TABLE 10.1 Wolcott's ways to interpretation

	Process	*What*	*How*
First way	Description	Descriptive account of data in original form	Observations reported
		What is going on?	Data 'speaks for itself'.
Second way	Analysis	Identifies key factors and relationships	Systematic description of interrelationships
		How do things work?	Data 'talks amongst itself'.
Third way	Interpretation	Meanings and context explored	Theory and speculation
		What is to be made of it all?	We enter a 'conversation' with data.

Source: Sara MacKian. 2010. "The Art of Geographic Interpretation." In *The SAGE Handbook of Qualitative Geography*, edited by Dydia DeLyser, Steve Herbert, Stuart Aitken, Mike Crang and Linda McDowell, p. 360.

Once you wade through the stages of data analysis and discussion, you enter the next higher level stage of contemplation and assessment of the results. The findings are not an end in themselves, rather the beginning of a much more meaningful thought process. Several questions may occur to you: What do the results convey beyond figures? What is their message? What are they speaking in silence?

It calls upon the researcher to figure out and state the theoretical idea which underlies his or her findings. Such an idea can be tested through research by others. Hence research findings of a particular exercise get placed in the wider domain of knowledge. This requires an understanding of all the factors relating to a finding and awareness about already existing observations, theories and ideas. Empirical observations are hooked to theoretical formulations.

This necessitates revisiting the review of the literature. You begin to place your own findings in the larger realm of already existing literature in your subject area. Remember to relate your observations only to the research writings relevant to your theme. One of the foremost questions that should crop in your mind is how do your findings and interpretations differ from those of other acclaimed scholars or researchers? You have to look for the reasons if there is a difference between the two.

If the interpretation is corroborative or supportive, this will strengthen our understanding of the issue involved. Dissenting voices are not to be abandoned. Your interpretation will be an addition to the existing knowledge and can be reported and shared in a seminar, workshop, conference or paper or in a debate with others.

This leads you to another situation of reflecting on and building on shared understandings on a wider platform. The process of interpretation demands that you take cognisance of differing viewpoints and situate your interpretation against other writings on the theme. You should not be overly disturbed if your findings are not in line with those of other researchers. Taking it as a challenge, start looking for the reasons why this might be so. Interpretations can vary if the techniques used are different and the perspective and purpose of the research are not the same. The method of data collection can also diverge. It is every bit possible that our ideas, observations and messages are not in tandem with each other given our incomplete understanding of the complex reality of our world.

You may remember that an observation that is not in tune with your general interpretation is no less important. It can be 'an exception that proves the rule'. The results which are in the nature of anomalies should not be rejected but accepted and revealed. This is the way existing interpretations are confronted and finally confirmed or overturned in the research process.

Interpretation vis-à-vis data analysis: The process of reflectivity on the part of the researcher moves analysis into interpretation. The results obtained from analysis of both quantitative and qualitative data are interpreted. Pertinent, precise and pithy statements are abstracted from statistical analysis or qualitative details. The theoretical principle underlying the research finding is given an expression. Intention is to offer an insightful and stimulating statement on the basis of the research pursued and results obtained.

While describing the origin, development and decay of 19 civilisations in world history, Toynbee (1934–1961) propounded the thesis of 'challenge and response'. The idea is that countries constrained by a paucity of natural resources tend to accept this as a challenge and work out an effective response to overcome the situation. Japan is one such example. In a study of the spatial pattern of public amenities, the distribution of post offices was found to be more regular than that of schools. The interpretation would be that services provided by the central government are more rationally located than those by the state government. Likewise, a slowing down of migration to big cities in India could be interpreted as outpricing of such places for the poor in terms of access to land or housing. They have to seek a residence on their periphery.

It is truism that the same fact can have differing interpretations. This can again be illustrated by the interpretative narrative of the decline of once glorious empires in the history of the world. Based on an elaborate discussion on the process and underlying dynamics, Diamond (2005) attributed this phenomenon to the environmental impairment or imbalance between the population and the natural resource base, Tainter (1988) to the mismanagement of situations as they became increasingly complex over time, and Acemoglu and Robinson (2012) to exploitative institutions which sucked people dry and turned them into rebels.

An interpretation statement in geography is expected to carry a spatial flavour. To say that the rising vitality of various states of India is turning this nation–state into a state–nation is an interpretative statement. To say that emigration is stimulated more by pull factors and outmigration by push factors is an interpretation statement. To say two neighbouring states tend to acquire similar administrative practices is again an interpretation statement.

In the data analysed manually or through the GIS medium, the fundamental understanding and interpretation pertain to the structuring of events and occurrences over space (Longley *et al.* 2001, 109). Through the use of spatial autocorrelation property in conjunction with the property of temporal autocorrelation, any interpretation becomes more valid and convincing. Spatial autocorrelation relates to the 'First Law of Geography' and affirms 'everything is related to everything else, but near things are more related than distant things' (Tobler 1970). Temporal autocorrelation views events as part of the process and invokes the 'present as the key to the past'. That is how scholars such as Toynbee, Diamond and Tainter could offer stimulating interpretations of world history by scanning things in a time-space perspective.

Interpretation vis-à-vis data representation: Like data analysis, data representation has also not remained untouched from interpretation. In the case of a thesis or dissertation, map interpretation is considered an intellectual process wherein geographical features and relationships portrayed on a map are understood by decoding cartographic symbols (Monmonier 2002, 475). It requires an eye for associations, conformity, contiguity and anomalies in distributions. In the case of India, for instance, the interpretation often uses expressions such as north–south divide, east–west separation and mainland-periphery contrast in whatever it is representing.

In human geography, cartography is no longer guided by positivist tenets or seen as an objective science of spatial communication between the mapmaker and the map user. Today, maps are being used in interpretations in multiple ways and cannot be traced back to an objective mind or text (Harley 1989). Along the same lines, Brotton (2012) observes that maps are invariably ideological and subjective in nature, and represent the ecology of a particular period in history. He constructed a history of the world by interpreting 12 maps as produced from the ancient to the present time. There is no ideal map for all times (Crampton 2001). Robinson (1952, 13) rightly observed long ago that the design of any map should be guided by its purpose or use.

In ever-more exploratory environments, maps are now engaged in the construction of knowledge (Harley 1989). GIS, GPS and remote sensing are contemporary map production and interpretation tools. These tools enable us to address several real-world concerns: global environmental change, natural resource inventory, management of heritage sites and monitoring of changes in city environments, to list a few. In each case, maps are generated using software applications, and geographers are engaged in interpreting many of these outputs. Through Google, ever available on a smartphone, maps have become key factors in popularising geographic literacy amongst the masses. Geographers themselves have begun to use and interpret maps in new and innovative ways.

The post-modern turn forced academics to once more question what they knew, how they knew it and how they presented it (Tierney 2002). A case in point are the maps which came to be equated with socially constructed texts. Landscapes depicted on historic maps are interpreted as mirrors of the societies that produced them.

Interpretation of qualitative research: Such research derived from photographs and paintings of places and landscapes, and from interviews and group discussions

210 Traversing the path: data management

has made headway in geography. These depictions and details are taken as evidence of the attributes of people and their cultures. Vernacular landscapes have been under a research lens, in particular, and these were linked with the cultures that fashioned them. Some illustrations of this kind include old photographs of cities, urban graffiti (Ley and Cybriwsky 1974) and fast-food restaurants and coffee shops (Winchester, Kong, and Dunn 2003, 37). Landscape paintings have often formed a part of regional studies.

Ever since the concept of landscape was first introduced by Wimmer in 1885 and its further exposition by Schluter in 1906, the manner in which landscapes have been explained and interpreted has differed greatly over space, time, culture and belief (Bender 1993). For Blache (1903), landscape constituted an integrated web of natural and cultural attributes, and exemplified terrestrial unity. Sauer (1925) equated the study of landscape with a geographical way of thinking about culture. Hartshorne (1939, 173–174) concluded that cultural landscape represented the ultimate integration of natural and human phenomena. A renewed interest in landscape ecology could be seen with the arrival of remote sensing and GIS. Using this technology, an attempt was made to understand the interaction between people and landscapes through the interpretation of old topographical sheets.

The cultural turn in geography in the 1980s, in the form of the branching out of the discipline in several human subfields, led to an emphasis on landscape as an image or construct. The focus was not on the form but on understanding and interpreting the meaning of the processes that created landscapes. Still more, the students of designed landscape, vernacular landscape and architect landscape, to name a few, offered varied interpretations of landscape. By comparison, the physical geographers continued using their toolkits to study the form and evolution of physical landscapes, of course with greater precision and detail.

The portrayal of landscapes is usually interpreted with some ideological bias. Lewis (1979) stressed that places do not always speak to us very clearly. We may have to work hard to unfold their secrets, interrogate their silences and uncover their hidden histories if we are to get beneath the surface. Mitchell (2000, 114) followed this approach to landscape interpretation. He focused on the production of spaces and conflicts that take place within and between them. This means that the landscape photographs of ethnic neighbourhoods, monumental buildings and dilapidated structures are placed together to highlight mutual separations and visible inequity in urban living.

A common ground for various qualitative methods, ranging from traditional ethnography, interviews and focus group discussions, to archive analysis, landscape interpretation and visual methodologies, is their interpretivist tendency. The belief is that we can know the world only through interpretations of situations. Detailed narrative descriptions and holistic interpretations that capture the richness and complexity of behaviours, experiences and events in natural settings and defined locations are what count.

It is usually seen that many qualitative researchers seem to end up with an analysis of 'text' gained from interview transcripts, fieldwork diaries or participant observations. They equate analysis with interpretation. The text is lifted out of qualitative details and labelled as interpretation. This is a misrepresentation of the nature of interpretation, which seeks deeper meaning of anything beyond all that is visible on the surface.

We are also witnessing the emergence of some qualitative geographers who are treating their data more creatively (MacKian 2010, 364). They are reinventing storytelling, performing arts and popular perceptions. All this is symbolic and an expression of more aesthetic, less wordy and deeply moving experience in place. Tuan (2001) suggests that there are active and passive elements to experience, and although we can analyse the 'active' through the words the respondents speak, it is more difficult to interpret the 'passive' – what they are not telling us. The crucial issue is how to derive sense out of both.

The question of relevance: How relevant and useful are the findings of a research study? This depends on the strength of the derived interpretation. Hence every researcher is obliged to address this issue with utmost care. As an end product of a perceptive research mind, it links the work with four unified concepts of significance, generalisability, reliability and validity (Blaxter, Hughes, and Tight 2006, 221).

The concept of significance has both a technical and general connotation. The technical significance is ascertained through a proper interpretation of the correlation coefficients and regression equations, and rigorous testing of the hypothesis. A prior adoption of a relevant research technique for the purpose is taken for granted. On the other hand, the general significance refers to the importance of the research finding. This may be in terms of the addition to existing knowledge or a critique of a prevailing belief or an input to policymaking.

Generalisability refers to the extent to which the research findings are representative of other circumstances, populations, times and settings or areas. A research piece is generalisable if its findings have widespread applicability. This is observed when a finding can be fitted into an available model. Then there are anomalous situations where such a condition of generalisability is not met. Take the case of the demographic transition model, which affirmed that the fall in the death rate preceded the decline in the birth rate in different countries of the world. This, however, was not the case in France, where this process was in reverse. Such anomalies are of special interest in geography.

The idea of reliability has to do with the repeatability or consistency of a finding. Work is rated as reliable if other research on the same question, using the same method, in the same setting or by the same person at another time arrives at basically the same results. The interpretation can, however, differ. Several researchers may have confirmed that the temperature over a vast part of the world increased by $1°C$ during the last 100 years. Many may explain it as a result of global warming, while others may attribute this to a change in land cover. Likewise, interpretations are also bound to vary. Some may interpret it as good for temperate countries, while others may interpret it as problematic for tropical countries.

Rightful interpretation is subject to the validity of a research study. Validity is referred to as matters such as accuracy, dependability, legitimacy and relevance of research. An interpretation is valid only if it directly responds to the objective of the

212 Traversing the path: data management

study. This is assured by a systematic pursuit of the research process, adoption of a proper methodology and derivation of an unbiased conclusion. Physical geography offers a greater scope of validity than human geography because it is firmer on measurements.

Above all, an authentic geographic interpretation is to take into account not only 'what is present' in an area but also 'what is absent'. Only an understanding of both will lead to a reliable interpretation. Christaller could come up with his central place theory by marking not only where central places were present but also where they were absent in South Germany (Christaller 1972, 601–610). The bottom line is that geography has to be an integrated study of both 'what is present' and 'what is absent' in an area.

References

Acemoglu, Daron, and James A. Robinson. 2012. *Why Nations Fail: The Origins of Power, Prosperity and Poverty*. New York: Gown Business.

Bender, B., ed. 1993. *Landscape: Politics and Perspectives*. Oxford: Berg Publishers.

Blache, Paul Vidal de la. 1903. "La Géographie Humaine (The Human Geography)." *Revue de Synthèse Historique* 7: 219–240.

Blaxter, Loraine, Christina Hughes, and Malcolm Tight. 2006. *How to Research*. 3rd ed. Berkshire, UK: Open University Press.

Brotton, Jerry. 2012. *A History of the World in Twelve Maps*. London: Penguin.

Christaller, Walter. 1972. "How I Discovered My Theory of Central Places: A Report About the Origin of Central Places." In *Man Space and Environment*, edited by P.W. English and R.C. Mayfield, 601–610. Oxford: Oxford University Press.

Crampton, J.W. 2001. "Maps as Social Constructions: Power, Communication and Visualisation." *Progress in Human Geography* 25 (2): 235–252.

Diamond, Jared. 2005. *Collapse: How Societies Choose to Fail of Succeed*. New York: Penguin.

Harley, J.B. 1989. "Deconstructing the Map." *Cartographica* 26: 1–20.

Hartshorne, R. 1939. *The Nature of Geography: A Critical Survey of the Current Thought in the Light of the Past*. Chicago: Rand McNally.

Lewis, Pierce F. 1979. "Axioms for Reading the Landscape: Some Guides to the American Scene." In *The Interpretation of Ordinary Landscapes*, edited by D.W. Meinig, 11–32. New York: Oxford University Press.

Ley, D., and R. Cybriwsky. 1974. "Urban Graffiti as Territorial Markers." *Annals of the Association of American Geographers* 64 (4): 491–505.

Longley, Paul A., M.F. Goodchild, D.J. Maguire, and D.W. Rhind. 2001. *Geographic Information Systems and Science*. Chichester, UK: Wiley.

MacKian, Sara. 2010. "The Art of Geographic Interpretation." In *The SAGE Handbook of Qualitative Geography*, edited by Dydia DeLyser, Steve Herbert, Stuart Aitken, Mike Crang, and Linda McDowell, 359–372. London: Sage Publications Ltd.

Mitchell, D. 2000. *Cultural Geography: A Critical Introduction*. Oxford: Blackwell.

Monmonier, Mark S. 2002. "Map-Reading." In *The Dictionary of Human Geography*, edited by R. Johnston, D. Gregory, G. Pratt, and M. Watts, 475. London: Blackwell.

Robinson, A.H. 1952. *The Look of Maps*. Madison: University of Wisconsin Press.

Sauer, C.O. 1925. "The Morphology of Landscape." *University of California Publications in Geography* 2 (2): 19–54.

Tainter, Joseph, A. 1988. *The Collapse of Complex Societies*. Cambridge: Cambridge University Press.

Tierney, W.G. 2002. "Get Real: Representing Reality." *Qualitative Studies in Education* 15 (4): 385–398.

Tobler, Waldo. 1970. "A Computer Movie Simulating Urban Growth in the Detroit Region." *Economic Geography* 46 (2): 234–240.

Toynbee, Arnold J. 1934–1961. *A Study of History (12 Volumes)*. Oxford: Oxford University Press.

Tuan, Yi Fu. 2001. "Life as a Field Trip." *The Geographical Review* 91 (1/2): 41–45.

Winchester, H., L. Kong, and K. Dunn. 2003. *Landscapes: Ways of Imagining the World*. Harlow: Pearson Education.

Wolcott, Harry F. 1994. *Transforming Qualitative Data: Description, Analysis and Interpretation*. London: Sage.

PART IV

Catching up with the destination

The finale

11

RESEARCH WRITING

The purpose of all the effort gone through so far was to come out with a treatise which is worthy of being described as outstanding in research through rigorous analysis, insightful interpretations and flawless writing. Three R's of a good research remain elementary in terms of reading (of all relevant literature), arithmetic (objectification through scientific approach) and writing (as an unbiased representation). Research is not only to search but to find, which after all must culminate in a written document. Creativity and surprise are the two most critical elements in writing.

Writing is a craft. Good writing does not come naturally – it has to be cultivated. This is a way of thinking and penning notes through the entire process of research. Academic writing, including thesis writing, should be more searching, more discovery oriented, more honest and less pompous and less dependent on the ritual. These should be stories well told, with their texts and contexts made explicit. Since most of the academics are not professional writers, they have to learn the 'principles of writing' meaningfully (Wolcott 1990, 10).

Barnes and Duncan (1992, 1) declared that very little attention is paid to writing in human geography. Things have changed considerably since then. Nowadays books on research methods and methodology for geographers usually include a chapter on writing (DeLyser 2010, 342).

Depending upon the purpose, research writing assumes varying disposition. It can be in the form of a thesis/dissertation, or a technical report, a research paper/ article, a topic analysis or an assignment. The writing style differs somewhat in each case, though the general principles of presentation remain largely the same.

Thesis/dissertation

These two terms are often used interchangeably. There is, however, a need to distinguish between the two. The Cambridge International Dictionary of English (1995)

218 Catching up with the destination: the finale

is of some help on this count. On p. 398, it defines dissertation as a long piece of writing on a particular subject, especially one that is done as a part of a course at college or university. It is done as a part of a course, meant for the Master's or Master of Philosophy (MPhil) degree. Likewise, on p. 1510, it defines thesis in the same phraseology except for the fact that it is for a PhD. It is pursued as an assignment in itself and not as a part of a course.

The written presentation of a thesis/dissertation has to follow certain guidelines. Often every university lays down a specific format to conform. This must be gone through to comply with. Panjab University, for example, requires the candidate for PhD degree to submit four printed or typewritten copies of the thesis. The thesis must be a piece of original research, characterised by either the discovery of new facts or a fresh interpretation of the known facts or theories. The thesis is to be satisfactory in its literary presentation.

The Regulations Calendar of the London School of Economics specifies essential requirements in respect of a thesis submitted for the award of PhD thesis. This research product is expected to add something new to the existing base of knowledge. By that token, it has to distinguish itself by an element of originality, discovery of fresh facts and critical thinking. It ought to represent an insightful and comprehensive understanding of the theme of its research. This may be done through a purposeful survey of relevant literature not only in terms of its contents but also methodological techniques used. In essence, a doctoral thesis is essentially a test of the research skill of the candidate. Normally it should not exceed 100,000 words, inclusive of footnotes but exclusive of bibliography and appendices. Above all, it must bear a quality which is worthy of publication in the form of a book or monograph or a number of research papers in reputed journals.

Almost the same directive principles hold good for an MPhil dissertation, with a proviso that it should limit itself to 60,000 words. See Annexure 2 for precise statements and for details visit: http://www.lse.ac.uk/intranet/LSEServices/TQARO/Calendar/RegulationsFor Research Degrees.pdf.

Elements of a thesis/dissertation

The four elements in this case can be listed as follows:

i   Form: the physical attributes
ii Structure: the arrangement of chapters, sections, subsections, paragraphs and sentences
iii Content: the subject matter
iv Style: the literary presentation

Form: It refers to the physical attributes, such as the cover design, size, paper quality, print type etc. The thesis must be attractive with strong binding and a scholarly cover. The paper used should be of good quality and of standard size. For thesis/dissertation bond paper (preferably Executive Bond 80 gsm) of A-4 size (8-1/4 ×

11-3/4 inches approximately) is used. Manuscripts are now usually prepared with word processor on computers. A margin of at least 2.5 cm on all edges of the page should be left except on the left side with 4 cm to facilitate binding. Chapter opening should begin at least 8–10 cm from the top of the page.

A serif font such as Times New Roman 12 is most appropriate for the main text. Alternative fonts or typeface like Courier or Helvetica can also be used. A sans serif font like Ariel 10 is clearest for tables. Footnotes or endnotes, headings and other elements might require smaller type sizes. It is important to select readable and widely available font.

The typing must be at least 1.5-space, or double-space. The following items call for single-space: block quotations, table titles and figure captions and lists in appendixes. The following items should be single-spaced: table of contents; list of figures, tables and photographs; footnotes, endnotes, bibliography or reference list.

The front matter is to be numbered separately from the rest of the text. Every page of the front matter, that is list of contents, tables, figures etc. is usually numbered in small roman style (i, ii, iii and so on). The rest of the text, including back matter, is numbered sequentially with Arabic numerals, starting with page 1.

Structure: It refers to the sequential arrangement of the contents of the thesis/dissertation. A manuscript has three parts, in turn comprising of several subparts: (i) Front Matter/Preliminaries – including the title page design, acknowledgements/preface, list of contents/tables/maps and diagrams; (ii) Main Text – chapters in sequence, including introduction and summary/conclusions; and (iii) Back or End Matter/Miscellaneous, including references/bibliography and annexures (listing of names/techniques/questionnaires). Index is not given in a thesis/dissertation but must be provided in the case of a book. A conventional thesis/dissertation follows a formal format, as below:

   i Title page as per guidelines of the university
   ii Supervisor's certificate and declaration
   iii Acknowledgements
   iv List of contents: sections, chapter headings and page numbers
   v List of tables, maps and diagrams and other optionals like photographs
   vi Chapters in sequence, including introduction
   vii Summary and conclusions
   viii Bibliography/References
   ix Annexures
   x Abstract

Many universities require that a thesis/dissertation should include or is accompanied by an abstract. The abstract is a brief summary of the work. It is expected to be a concise but comprehensive statement on objective of research, methodology followed, research output, theoretical derivations and questions suggested for future research. If a hypothesis has been posed for testing, its validation or otherwise must be stated. If required, a CD copy of the entire dissertation/thesis should also be prepared for submission, in addition.

220 Catching up with the destination: the finale

Contents: It essentially refers to the text of the thesis/dissertation. Here the basic task pertains to division of the main theme into meaningful subthemes to be dealt within various chapters. An arrangement of this kind on conceptual lines always creates a greater stimulus. This requires rigorous reflection on all possible alternative schemes. For example, a study of urbanisation in India could be pursued by historical periods, ancient, medieval, modern and post-independence; size of towns, small, medium and cities; function of towns, industrial, service and trade and commerce; regions, the Himalayas, the Great Plains, the Peninsula and the Coastal regions and so on. Any selection made is to be justified. Likewise, a study of regional disparities could be chaptered by different parameters of development, such as economic, social, political and ecological, or by colonial, post-colonial and post-reform periods. Again this scheme has to be weighed vis-à-vis other alternatives and justified.

Style: It is the way we use the tools of language to communicate ideas. These tools might include our choice of words, punctuation marks and sentence structure (Henn, Weinstein, and Foard 2009, 289). As a research writer, address the following questions to yourself (Day 1996):

- Can I enjoy it? If so, what makes it interesting? Is it just the subject matter, or the way it is written? Does it challenge any established theory or an idea? Is it written in a stimulating manner?
- Can I understand it? Is the language simple or complicated? Is it well organised? Do paragraphs and sections flow from one to another? Or is it disjointed? Is it clear which part of the write-up deals with which element of the research?
- Can I communicate? Are the outcomes and implications of the research clear? Have the relevant historical, cultural and geographical frames of reference been made clear? Does it carry value as a possible policy input?

Basic parameters of the style

The primary essentials of research writing may be mentioned as follows: First, the entire writing must be marked by clarity, coherence and objectivity. The writer should be successful in making his communication easily understandable to the reader in fewest possible words. Sentences should be short, simple and specific and the words plain. The Fog Index of writing [0.4 (average word length of a sentence plus per cent of words with more than two syllables)] should not exceed the danger mark of 12, beyond which texts become difficult to read (Gunning 1952). Words that are capitalised, are combinations of short simple words or, for example, arise because of the use of the past tense are excluded from the calculation. The Fog Index is a measure of the 'readability', a description so used because it was felt that long words and sentences made for 'foggy' reading.

Second, the entire writing must have a geographic flavour, spatial thrust and effective use of the idiom of the discipline. As far as possible, evolve typologies as a part of the writing process. Engage description and explanation together. A discussion on in-migration areas in India, for example, could be placed under following type of areas: newly reclaimed agricultural lands, urban–industrial concentrations, plantations and mining areas, multipurpose project sites and other localities with development activities. Likewise, areas of out-migration could be grouped as those which are poverty stricken and others where income levels are high but not enough to meet the aspirations of the people. This is true of both pre- and post-colonial periods.

Third, a sense of rhythm is essential for good writing. There has to be a balance in every sentence and word. Every sentence in a paragraph, every paragraph in a section, every section in a chapter and every chapter in the book should keep the reader in a smooth flow. The sentences should be short, accurate and unambiguous. Use active voice. Each paragraph is expected to have a distinct shape. Paragraphs are to place sentences into a meaningful order. The first sentence in a paragraph expresses the main idea that the paragraph will deal with. Those in the middle should expand upon the main idea. The last sentence is meant to clinch the argument of the paragraph and indicate a transition to the next paragraph. Tables and charts are equivalent to paragraphs in that they should deal with one main idea. It is desirable to represent every chapter in the form of a chart outlining the sections and subsections. This makes things easy to understand and exposes the gaps in the structure of writing.

Fourth, the research is usually written in past tense. The present tense is used for relating what other authors say and for discussing the literature, theoretical concepts, methods etc. In his book *Spatial Organisation: The Geographer's View of the World*, Abler, Adams, and Gould (1971) stipulate that '. . . And future tense is used for describing how you will accomplish your research'. Shurter, Williamson, and Broehl (1965, 81–87) argues that writers should make effective use of verbs, be direct, use an appropriate tone and be specific. For some specifics, see Table 11.1.

Fifth, an important aspect of style is symmetry. A definite style must be adapted to print titles and subtitles of chapters. A uniform style (full capitals/capitals and lower case/italic/roman/boldface type) must be followed all over the text. Avoid footnotes. If something is important enough to mention, make it a part of the text. If it is not important enough to be in the text, put it in an appendix.

Sixth, avoid making categorical statements by use of words like always, never, must – it is being overbearing in research. There is no place for moralising in research writing. Do not mix facts with your opinions. Likewise do not accept others' viewpoints without a critical scrutiny. Avoid quoting others extensively. Do not plagiarise. The issues raised in introduction that frame the research should be referred back in the conclusions to establish whether your findings could resolve them or not. There must not be a mismatch between findings and recommendations. Any recommendation is expected to originate from your analysis.

Finally, ensure that the thesis is publishable in the form of a book, monograph or a series of research articles. The whole document should be authentic, coherent and flawless. In terms of word limit, a thesis for PhD degree may carry a length of 250–350 pages and an MPhil dissertation of 100–150 pages.

222 Catching up with the destination: the finale

TABLE 11.1 Apposite use of verb tenses in different research documents

Section	Research proposal	Thesis/dissertation/report
Introduction	The purpose of this study is . . .	The purpose of the study was . . .
	The study will . . .	The study showed . . .
	The proposal concludes with . . .	The thesis is divided into five chapters
		Chapter four presents
Review of Literature	Both documents have the same use of tense	
	Gosal (1977) concludes . . .	Use for more generalisable findings
	Gosal concluded (1977) . . .	Use for the specific findings of a particular study
Methodology	The procedure will involve . . .	The procedure involved . . .
	The study incorporates or will incorporate a framework . . .	The study incorporated a framework . . .
	The major research questions are . . .	The major research questions were . . .
	Three sources of data will be used . . .	Three sources of data were used . . .
	The limitations of the study are . . .	The limitations of the study were . . .
Conclusions	Not applicable	The average score was . . .
		The findings imply . . .

Source: Based and Modified from Gary Anderson and Nancy Arsenault. 1998 (2002 reprint). *Fundamentals of Educational Research*, p.73. London: Routledge Falmer.

Writing technique

The text of a research piece becomes interesting if a stimulus–response technique is adopted as a writing style (Monroe, Meredith, and Fisher 1977). It can acquire the following possible modes:

i   Question–answer: When you generate a question, the reader will expect you to provide the answer soon. Question must be relevant, thought provoking and pertinent to the theme under discussion. What is geographic definition of development? It is, in simple words, quality of a regional system.

ii Problem–solution: When you highlight a problem, the reader will expect a solution or an explanation to it. The problem projected should be of high value. What explains exceptionally high temperatures in north-west India during summer? One significant factor is the presence of an anticyclone in the upper atmosphere which allows intense insolation.

iii Cause–effect, effect–cause: Herein a fact and its reason are placed together. This method helps to blend description with explanation. The availability of an already developed irrigation system helped Punjab in emerging as a pioneer in the Green Revolution. Whether you mention a cause first or an effect first, the reader will expect you to reveal the other.

iv General–specific: A general statement has to be backed with specifics, which clarify, qualify or explain the general statement. An illustration or example for the sake of clarity would be in fitness of things: Land use zoning was typical of some ancient cities, such as in the case of Mohenjo-Daro.

Text of the thesis/dissertation

A purposeful introduction is most important in this case. It is the lead-in to help the reader follow the logic of the whole work. The most critical is an effective statement of the objective, research question and hypothesis of the study. The literature survey is to show how the study fits into what is already known and to locate it in relation to existing knowledge and practice. Equally the research design must be written systematically, incorporating the details of how the work was executed, which sources were tapped for data and in which manner data were processed, analysed and interpreted.

Successive chapters in the main body of the treatise are expected to follow a logical sequence. These should be linked with each other through a preparatory statement towards the end of the previous chapter. To maintain a semblance of balance, the chapters should be of nearly equal length.

Flow charts should accompany every chapter in the dissertation/thesis to provide 'a quick glance' of its contents. If done, such an effort will bring to light any gaps or lack of logical presentation in the chapter. This will also help in organising the summary part of the chapter in a more organised manner. Two illustrations of such charts are given in Figures 11.1 and 11.2.

A bigger challenge lies in writing the conclusion. The conclusion is meant to sum up the findings but without repeating the exact words we have already harnessed. The best conclusions do summarise, but they also move at least one step farther, suggesting, for example, the broader implications of the work in question and calling for research on fresh questions identified. So before you write your last words, imagine someone fascinated by your work and who wants to follow up on it.

Annexures are additional materials that cannot be accommodated within the text but are essential to its context. These are helpful to a reader seeking further clarification, such as text of documents supporting the discussion in the main document, survey questionnaires or sometimes even charts or tables. The appendix should not be a repository for raw data that the author was unable to work into the text.

When there are two or more annexures in a book, these should be numbered like chapters, Annexure 1, Annexure 2 etc. or designated by letters Annexure A, Annexure B etc. Each should be given a title as well. An annexure may be placed at

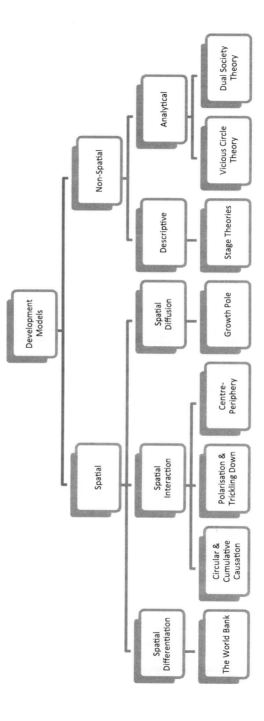

FIGURE 11.1 Typology of development models

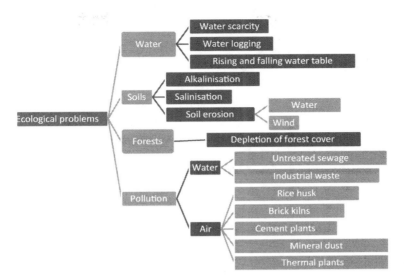

FIGURE 11.2   Major environment problems

the end of a chapter if essential. This can be a case of listing the names of districts in different National Sample Regions of India.

Often an *abstract* is a requirement of any thesis/dissertation. As a succinct representative of the whole work, it is to be printed as a separate piece from the main text and should therefore be a stand-alone document. It should report the crucial outcomes of the research work, and should not overstate or contain material that is not there. While writing it, follow your university's specific guidelines and adhere to the limits of the word count mentioned. If writing for an audience 'in the know' you can use the technical language of your discipline or profession, but otherwise it has to be simple and direct in expression.

In research writing, you must cite and acknowledge the source of your ideas and quotes in sufficient detail to enable readers to follow up what you have written and locate the cited author's work. These also help support your arguments and provide your work with credibility besides showing the scope and breadth of your research. This is to be done as a matter of firm integrity to avoid plagiarism. The derived idea or information may be presented in your own framework rather than as a quotation. Referencing is to be done within the text and fully recorded at the end of the chapter or thesis/dissertation or report etc.

Documentation

Miller and Taylor (1987, 115) suggest that documentation can be in the form of (i) endnotes at the end of each chapter, followed by references relevant to the chapter; (ii) footnotes at the bottom of each page and lists of references at the end of the text;

226 Catching up with the destination: the finale

(iii) the usual practice of citing author's name, publication date and page number in the text, with the full reference at the end of each chapter; and (iv) author's name, date and page numbers in the text, with the full reference at the end of all the chapters.

These four forms of documentation can be clubbed broadly into two broad arrangements: (i) a system of Notes and Bibliography. The notes, whether footnotes or endnotes or both, are numbered. The numbers correspond to superscripted numbers in the text. It may be supplemented by a bibliography and (ii) a system of Author-Date that uses parenthetical author-date in-text citations and a corresponding reference list — usually titled 'References' or 'Works Cited'. The latter approach is simpler and permits the insertion or deletion of references at will. In case of the former, any reference included or deleted at later stage will necessitate change in all the subsequent numbers.

Among the several well-known systems of source citation in geography, we generally follow Chicago or Harvard systems. Author-date is usually the preferred approach. However, many writers in literature, arts and the history follow numerical approach (notes and bibliography system) for its flexibility in use of commentary on the sources cited. The other popular systems are those of the Modern Language Association and the American Psychological Association, both of which use variations of the author–date system.

Which ever system you use, it is important that you are consistent in its application. Referencing includes in-text references given in brackets and reference list entries at the end of the main text. In Chicago style the parenthetical in-text referencing always includes the author's last (family) name(s), the publication date of the work cited and a page number, if needed. For example: Indicators help us in understanding the social reality and formulation of policies (Smith 1973); or Smith (1973) observed that indicators help us in understanding the social reality and formulation of policies. If the reference has a second name, include it for example (Jackson and Smith 1984). In case three or more names, write as follows: (Booth *et al.* 2013). If the same idea or point has been made in multiple references, write as follows: (Paul 1982; Randinelli 1983). If the reference is taken from an indirect source, it must be recorded. For instance, one study reports that outside donors contribute more than 60 per cent of the programme's funding (Moore as cited in Maxwell 1999, 25). But then it is always preferable to cite the original source.

There are two main ways to use in-text references: 'information prominent' with focus on the information from your source; and 'author prominent' with focus on the author. When it is 'information prominent' the author's name is within bracket. For example: The conclusion reached in a recent study was that . . . (Cochrane 2007) and when 'author prominent', the author's name is outside the bracket: Cochrane (2007) concluded that . . . If the same author has to be referred to more than once in the same year, suffix alphabets in small along with surname (Johnston 1986a), (Johnston 1986b). In case of several works by same author, same year arrange them alphabetically in the Reference List by using lower case letters (a, b, c etc.) and if these belong to different years, place them chronologically. When the date of publication is approximate use circa or c. (Smythe c. 2007) and in case the date of publication is not available use n.d. (Browne n.d.). Here n.d. denotes no date.

Quoting, which is a reproduction of a statement from another person's writing, has to be done with necessary care. Under most circumstances, a large direct quotation should be avoided. While small quotes can appear in the text, reproduction of large passages calls for indenting and use of appropriate font size in the form of a separate paragraph. In particular when 30 or more words are quoted begin quoting the material on a new line, indent it 5 spaces. Use double spacing for your text and single spacing for the indented quote. Make sure the quote is exactly as it was published. For small quotations of a sentence or a part of it, use quotation marks to represent the exact words.

Referencing and bibliography systems

At the end of the research writing, you list all sources in a reference list. It normally includes every source you cited in a parenthetical form in the text. At time you may have consulted some writings but did not cite. These, along with references, become a part of the bibliography.

All reference list entries are to carry the same general form. These are to be consistent in their presentation. Following *The Chicago Manual of Style*, some common situations of referencing are illustrated below:

A. Single-author or edited book

A. SINGLE-AUTHOR BOOK

Author's Last Name, Author's First Name. Year of Publication. Title of Book: Subtitle of Book. Place of Publication: Publisher's Name.
Bala, Raj. 1986. *Trends of Urbanisation in India: 1901–1981.* Jaipur: Rawat Publication.

B. TWO-AUTHOR BOOK

First Author's Last Name, First Author's First Name, and Second Author's First and Last Name. Year of Publication. Title of Book: Subtitle of Book. Place of Publication: Publisher's Name.
Dikshit, K.R., and Jutta K. Dikshit. 2014. *North-East India: Land, People and Economy.* Heidelberg: Springer.

C. THREE-AUTHOR BOOK

First Author's Last Name, First Author's First Name, Second Author's First and Last Name, and Third Author's First and Last Name. Year of Publication. . .
Misra, R.P., K.V. Sundaram, and V.L.S. Prakasa Rao. 1974. *Regional Development Planning in India: A New Strategy.* Delhi: Vikas Publishing House.

228 Catching up with the destination: the finale

D. EDITED BOOK

Editor's Last Name, First Name, Second Editor's First and Last Name, ed. Year of Publication. . .
Misra, H.N., and Vijay P. Singh, eds. 1998. *Research Methodology in Geography: Social, Spatial and Policy Dimensions.* Jaipur: Rawat Publications.

E. SINGLE CHAPTER IN AN EDITED BOOK

Chapter Author's Last Name, Author's First Name. Year of Publication. "Title of Chapter: Subtitle of Chapter." In Title of Book: Subtitle of Book, edited by Editor's First and Last Names. Place of Publication: Publisher's Name.
Mohan, Krishna 2004. "Backward Area Development Programmes in India" In *Reinventing Regional Development,* edited by Surya Kant, Nina Singh, Jagdish Singh, and A.B. Mukerji, 129–138. Jaipur: Rawat Publications.

B. Research journal

F. PAPER IN A JOURNAL

Author's Last Name, Author's First Name. Year of Publication. "Title of Article: Subtitle of Article." Title of Journal Volume Number, Issue Number (Additional Date Information): Page Numbers.
Kant, Surya. 1999. "Spatial Implications of India's New Economic Policy." *Tijdschrift voor Economische en Sociale Geografie* 90 (1): 80–96.

C. Online papers

For a paper consulted online, include an access date and a URL. For articles that include a DOI (digital object identifier), append the DOI rather than using the URL.
The pattern to be followed is as follows:
Author's Last Name, Author's First Name. Year of Publication. "Title of Paper: Subtitle of Paper." Title of Journal Volume Number, Issue Number (Additional Date Information): Page Numbers. Date of Access. URL (uniform resource locator).
Leszczynski, Agnieszka. 2014. "On the Neo in Neogeography." *Annals of the Association of American Geographers* 104 (1): 60–79. Accessed October13, 2014. doi:10.1080/00045608 .2013.846159

A note on the arrangement of entries would be in order here. Though there are many different systems for presenting a reference list, all of them contain the same information (the author, date of publication, paper title, publication title) and, in the case of a book, the place of publication, or for a journal, article, the volume number and page numbers. There are several different situations in referencing. One may choose any standard system and then follow it consistently. Use all the correct syntax (full stops, commas, colons, abbreviations etc.) and font style (e.g. italics or bold), as required by the system.

References/bibliography should preferably be classified by the nature of outlet (books, journals, government publications, internet retrievals and so on) in place of making them run alphabetically. Another commonly used practice is to classify references/bibliography by chapters. This facilitates inclusion of endnotes as a part of the listing of the entries. A geographer may classify the entries by the spatial scale of international, national, regional and local. Still another way of presenting the references/bibliography is to add one line summary of each entry, as Sunil Khilnani (2004) does in his book *The Idea of India*.

In the light of the above, it is essential that one introductory para should be devoted to description of the way the references/bibliography have been listed, with justification.

Finally, for citing specific types of sources such as magazine or newspaper articles, unpublished sources, websites, blogs, social networks, public documents, consult *The Chicago Manual of Style*, 16th edition (2010).

Technical report

A technical report is prepared in response to a sponsored assignment. Sponsorship can emerge from a variety of sources, such as Government of India, National Institution for Transformation of India, World Health Organization and so on. Though a technical report is also research based, it differs in its objectives, style and presentation. First, its task is defined by the sponsoring authority which spells out the terms of reference. Second, it is written strictly in alignment with what has been set out for it, without any scope for deviation or ideological bias. Finally, it is expected to provide an Executive Summary which lists the line of action recommended for sponsoring authority to consider. Therefore, it is always meant to be a handiwork of the professionals in the relevant field. A comparative chart of various points of difference between a thesis/dissertation and a technical report is given in Table 11.2.

Evidently while a dissertation/thesis is expected to contribute something new to the existing pool of knowledge, the technical report is meant to serve as an input to policy formulation.

Research paper

A research paper is a piece of work on a seminal point of inquiry or question. This is the most frequent mode of publication in the world of research. This accounts for publication of a variety of research journals the world over.

Usually research students cull out a number of research papers out of their doctoral or MPhil thesis. The words *article* and *paper* are used often interchangeably. One may distinguish between the two. Article is the one published in a newspaper or magazine for popular reading, and a paper is the one published in a scientific or professional journal addressed to an academic audience.

230 Catching up with the destination: the finale

TABLE 11.2 Salient features of thesis/dissertation and technical report

Thesis/dissertation	*Technical report*
Based on data analysis in the light of research question and hypothesis	Based on data analysis in the light of the terms of reference
A statement of hypothesis is generally provided	No need for a hypothesis
Directed to discovery of new facts, formulation of ideas and construction of theory	Directed to policy formulation
No value judgement	Takes issue-based positioning
Written in a scholarly manner using disciplinary and technical terms	Free of jargon
Bias free	Attuned to the need of the sponsoring authority
Identifies the gaps in research and sets agenda for future research	Spells out need for action by providing options
Places the work in the context of existing research work and provides summary and conclusions	Provides an executive summary
Research student more important; supervisor secondary	Technical experts more important; research analysts secondary

While aiming at a research paper, decide what single message you want to leave for the reader, the one provocative thought you would like to register. It will give you an idea of what route you should follow, what destination you hope to reach and your decision about tone and attitude (Zinsser 2006, 52). Each research paper makes an argument; it states a case and presents evidence to support. For this reason, a researcher must keep the following questions in mind while doing a research paper: What message do I wish to communicate? Why should anyone be interested in my message? How can I communicate my message most effectively (Hart 1976, 225)?

The ultimate destination of a research paper is publication in a journal to report its findings. The manuscript must be prepared in accordance to the style and other requirements of the targeted journal. The writer of the paper, therefore, should carefully read 'suggestions to authors' or look at the latest issue of the journal for guidance. It is desired that a research paper should be submitted to a high-quality journal. Most of these are circulated both in print form and online.

Broadly speaking, there are two types of geographical journals:

i General geographical journals, covering all branches of the discipline and publishing a wide range of research papers, such as *Transactions of the Institute of British Geographers* in the United Kingdom; *Annals of the Associations of American Geographers* in the United States of America; *Transactions, Institute of Indian Geographers* and *Annals of the National Association of Geographers*, India.

ii Theme-specific journals, which focus on a single dimension of the discipline. These are confined to a particular branch of geography. Some such journals may be mentioned as *Economic Geography, Urban Geography, Population Geography, Journal of Biogeography* etc.

In its conceptualisation, structure and style, a research paper is a micro-prototype of a dissertation/thesis. It has to carry an introductory section describing its objective, research question and methodology. A review of previous research carried out on the theme is also its necessary obligation. The content part of the research paper will be in the form of a number of requisite sections. Each section will deal with a specific element of the theme under study. A research paper must have a concluding section, highlighting the main findings and message of the paper. An *abstract* is also required, which in publication will top the main body of the paper.

A research paper in geography often leans heavily on the patterns emerging on the maps and results emanating from quantitative analysis often presented in a tabular form. Maps should be designed in a manner that these conform to the requirements and page dimensions of the targeted/intended journal. Tables should also be so prepared that these acquire a geographical tone, with prominence to areas and their segments and fit into a single print page of the journal selected for its publication. Research papers in geography tend to make special demands on space on account of inclusion of maps, in particular.

Writing of a research paper requires a special skill. Adherence to some basic rules is of great help. Incidentally several of them begin with the letter 'C'. Here is their listing: concision, clarity, correctness, coherence and creativity.

The writing style should follow the tenet of maximum material in the form of evidence, statistics and facts and figures in minimum space and be comprehensive too. Avoid verbosity.

The communication should be clear, intelligible even to an amateur while using disciplinary phraseology (Hart 1976). The non-technical axioms and sentences should be simple and short as they are easier to read and understand. Think of the tragedies that are rooted in ambiguity. If the sentence becomes too involved, break it and replace by two or more sentences.

Be correct. Do not fabricate data or invent results. Report only your results, and represent and interpret them. The writing should be free of personal opinions or biases.

The text should be coherent and tight. All sentences should flow into the next sentence in some relationship. Wherever necessary, use transition words and phrases, such as 'consequently', 'in contrast', 'subsequently', 'in addition' (Sorenson 1995). Likewise, the 'flow' of paragraphs from one to the subsequent should make use of transitional sentences when necessary.

Last but not the least, the piece of writing should be high on the element of creativity. The entire paper should bear the stamp of your ingenuity. This could be in the way you organise your material in the research paper or literary expression you use or the manner in which you conclude.

232 Catching up with the destination: the finale

Special attention needs to be paid in the use of words and phrases. In particular:

- Sentences may not begin with phrases like 'there is', 'there are' and 'there were', as these make a sentence wordy. Instead of saying 'There were many wind-mills found along the coast of Gujarat', say 'Many wind-mills exist along the coast of Gujarat'.
- Words like 'firstly', 'secondly' and 'thirdly' may be avoided while adopting phrasing in a sequence. Instead, simply say 'first, second and third'.
- Qualifiers like 'highly', 'strongly' and 'extremely' may be skipped because these indicate opinion and are unnecessary.

There are many other niggling expressions of the kind. Strunk and White (1979) provide an exhaustive list of such cases. Any curious and learning mind can benefit from this book. Writers on style such as Cooper (1990, 127–136) stress the importance of analogy, metaphorical language, repetition for emphasis, rhythm and the avoidance of cacophony and 'phoney' style to increase the impact of writing.

Use active rather than passive voice in writing. Active voice is usually more direct, concise and vigorous than the passive (Mcmillan 1988; Sublett 1993). Consider this: 'Dead leaves covered the ground', to substitute 'There were a great number of dead leaves lying on the ground'. The use of active voice often needs the use of personal pronouns (Hart 1976). This fixes the responsibility of the writer. Many a time sentence of description or exposition can be made lively and emphatic by inducting an active voice.

This rule does not, of course, mean that the writer should entirely discard the passive voice, which is sometimes necessary. A twist in a sentence may make it lucid. It may inject a nuance.

A research paper must carry an abstract on its cover head. An abstract is neither an introduction, which places the paper in a larger context of knowledge, nor is it a summary which is a more detailed statement of procedures, findings and conclusions. Abstract should be concise, usually no longer than 250–300 words (check the journal's guidelines). It is expected to carry the holistic essence of the paper and normally be in a single unified paragraph.

Abstracts are usually tagged with a few keywords selected by the author. Keywords may indicate the theme, specificity, context and area of study. These may be from 4 to 6 in number. Keywords should generally be nouns instead of adjectives or adverbs. Keywords are important as well-chosen keywords enable your manuscript to be more easily indexed and hence identified and cited.

A research paper may be prepared in two stages. The first one refers to construction of a rough draft. This may be done with the help of a computer or laptop. One can type a rough draft rapidly, knowing that one can, with the utmost ease, make corrections, deletions and additions. One can also move whole paragraphs or sections around to improve the flow of the argument. There is no greater incentive to the improvement of formal structure and argument than the speed and ease with which this can be done.

The second stage refers to finalisation of the draft. Preferably, one should leave the rough draft for a while – to grow 'cold' – enabling to make fresh insight. A few days are better than nothing. It is always better to share it with others for their reactions and suggestions. Verify footnotes, quotations and illustrations for their accuracy. The final draft must be comprehensive, coherent and strong on evidence. The proof reading of the manuscript must be done with utmost care and sincerity.

In its final form, the research paper should be presented as a typescript. A rigorous checking of the manuscript of the paper, before sending it for publication by mail or online, is necessary. Ensure the conformity of the text to the guidelines listed as per requirements of the journal, or publisher. Check for the syntax of every sentence and spelling of every word. Be consistent in every respect, spellings of the proper nouns, details of the maps, titling of tables, interpretation of facts etc. Use word processing as the tool.

An assignment

This is the work allotted to a student on a specific topic to be completed within a stipulated time. It is in the nature of a follow-up of teaching to consolidate what has been taught. At times, it is geared to a specific research goal. Review of literature on a theme can be given as an assignment to finally help in writing of a research proposal. In a way, it is a part of training of a research student in literature survey and writing skill.

An assignment, in its written form, should include an introduction, stating its purpose and defining various concepts; have a main body which systematically covers main features of the topic under study; and provide a concluding statement convincingly reflecting the student's academic maturity and potential for pursuing further research.

The difference between a research paper and an assignment is self-evident. An assignment is defined by the supervisor and a research topic is discovered by the student. While assignment is based on general reading on a theme, a research paper is based on rigorous analysis of data and is expected to come out with something original. Any temptation to copy paste any material from the internet should be deemed as a sin.

Finally, the necessary attributes of a written assignment are legibility, absence of grammatical and spelling mistakes, simple structure of sentences, fixed length of paragraphs with necessary headings and coherence in the presentation of material.

Similarity check

It is most essential that any research writing, be it a paper, thesis, dissertation, grant proposal, report or else, is subjected to an originality check before submitting for publication, or evaluation as the case may be.

Moreover, now it has become mandatory for the students submitting their PhD thesis in universities in India to get their work evaluated for originality before

234 Catching up with the destination: the finale

submission. The universities have set up their limits for the permissible per cent similarity and only those who fulfil the requirements are allowed to submit their work for evaluation. The institutions' academic integrity has come to be linked with an individual's integrity in academic matters.

In the academic world, this is a potential plagiarism check. Plagiarism has now extended its vocabulary much beyond the 'literary theft' to include several types that have been evaluated for the severity of frequency of occurrence. Some of these are: Clone (researchers' work matches with the source, word to word); CTRL-C (substantial text of a single source matches with the researchers' text); Mashup (material copied from different sources and mixed up); Recycle (using your own work without citation); Find-Replace (retaining the basic content of the work with changes in words and phrases) and so on.

Originality is computed by way of 'similarity index' which unfolds the location and percentage of a written piece bearing a similarity with some already existing text. The specific sources are listed under three categories: internet, publications and student papers, with which your writing may bear similarity. The author is cautioned to repair the damage which could arise from accusation of plagiarism. At times, the similarity could have crept in by identical thinking and usage of words, at other times it could arise from an unintended reproduction of some personal notes, or at some other times it could be a case of the usage of a quotation without citing. The author has to be careful about all such situations. Mercifully some leverage in similarity, say up to 10 per cent or 20 per cent, is allowed to the author. One should, however, use this margin of freedom with utmost caution.

There are several originality check and similarity grading software to help the researcher see how they may have inappropriately used or referenced the source material. For instance, turnitin or ithenticate are originality checking and plagiarism prevention web-based services of 'iparadigm assessment solutions' where manuscripts can be submitted and tracked electronically. Others like Plagtrekker, Free-plagiarism checker for students-online are almost meant to lay bare any material lifted from elsewhere. Researchers can also access www.seesources.com.

References

Abler, R., J. Adams, and P. Gould. 1971. *Spatial Organisation: The Geographer's View of the World*. Englewood Cliffs, NJ: Prentice Hall.

Barnes, T., and J. Duncan. 1992. *Writing Worlds: Discourse, Text and Metaphor in the Representation of the Landscape*. London: Routledge.

The Chicago Manual of Style. 2010. 16th ed. Chicago: The University of Chicago Press.

Cooper, B.M. 1990. *Writing Technical Reports*. 2nd ed. Harmondsworth: Penguin.

Day, A. 1996. *How to Get Work Published in Journals*. Aldershot: Gower.

DeLyser, Dydia. 2010. "Writing Qualitative Geography." In *The Sage Handbook of Qualitative Geography*, edited by Dydia DeLyser, Steve Herbert, Stuart C. Aitken, Mike Crang, and Linda McDowell, 341–358. London: Sage.

Gunning, R. 1952. *The Technique of Clear Writing*. New York: McGraw-Hill.

Hart, John Fraser. 1976. "Ruminations of a Dyspeptic Ex-Editor." *The Professional Geographer* 28 (3): 225–232.

Henn, Matt, Mark Weinstein, and Nick Foard. 2009. *A Critical Introduction to Social Research.* 2nd ed. London: Sage.

Khilnani, Sunil. 2004. *The Idea of India.* New Delhi: Penguin Books.

Mcmillan, V.E. 1988. *Writing Papers in the Biological Sciences.* New York: St. Martin's Press.

Miller, J.I., and B.J. Taylor. 1987. *The Thesis Writers Handbook: A Complete One-Source Guide for Writers of Research Papers.* West Linn, OR: Alcove Publishing Company.

Monroe, J., C. Meredith, and K. Fisher. 1977. *The Science of Scientific Writing.* Dubuque, IA: Kendall Hurst.

Shurter, R.L., J.P. Williamson, and W.G. Broehl. 1965. *Business Research and Report Writing.* New York: McGraw-Hill.

Sorenson, S. 1995. *How to Write Research Papers.* New York: Macmillan.

Strunk, William, Jr., and E.B. White. 1979. *The Elements of Style.* New York: Macmillan.

Sublett, M.D. 1993. "The Active Voice: One Key to More Effective Geographic Writing." *The Geographical Bulletin* 35: 23–32.

Wolcott, Harry F. 1990. *Writing Up Qualitative Research.* Newbury Park, CA: Sage.

Zinsser, William. 2006. *On Writing Well: The Classic Guide to Writing Nonfiction.* 7th ed. New York: Harper Collins.

12

THE VIVA VOCE

Preparing and appearing for viva voce

In the course of preparing for viva voce, take it that you never get a second chance to make the first impression. In a small fraction of the total time that you took to complete the thesis/dissertation, you have to represent its totality most effectively. Therefore, viva voce should be taken with all earnestness and not be treated as a mere formality. In all, you should be in a position to defend, explain and elaborate the points made in the thesis. If an unacceptable error is discovered, a typed correction may be handed over by the candidate to the examiner before the viva voce. And if such an occasion arises during the viva voce, an apology is the only way out.

Make an attempt to place yourself in the position of an examiner. Prepare a mental oral summary of your entire work to be presented in about ten minutes. Anticipate the kind of questions which may be asked and mentally frame answers to these questions.

Often questions may start with the title, selection of the study area and type of data used. There could be pointed questions relating to the methodology adopted and main conclusion arrived at. The examiner may also ask to suggest some questions for future research which have arisen out of the work accomplished. Another question may relate to policy implications of the research findings. The candidate is expected to be ready with precise answers to such queries.

The research work of a student may be judged on number of criteria. Hansen and Waterman (1966 cited in Sharp and Howard 1996, 218–220) have proposed a detailed checklist which the doctoral student should seek to satisfy. The most defining criteria include the following:

i   *Indication of a creative investigation, topic researched or the testing of ideas:*

The originality of investigation is to be evinced through novelty of idea; questions raised; a clear, unambiguous statement on the aim of the research; hypotheses (if

The viva voce **237**

any) to be tested; establishing the connect and highlighting the similarities and differences between the present and the already existing research in related topic areas; and identification of gaps in research.

ii   Competence in independent work and originality of the methodology employed:

Establish your competence in independent work with the choice of appropriate and innovative research methodology. Data collection should have been done through valid and reliable instruments or tapping of appropriate data sources, and with due recognition of limitations inherent in the study. The selection of suitable variables properly measured is expected. The conclusions reached have to be justifiable in the light of the chosen methodology.

iii   A comprehension of appropriate techniques:

Full justification of the techniques used to gather and analyse data in the backdrop of the stated aims of research. The techniques should have been adequately described.

iv   Skill to make use of source materials:

The literature cited should be pertinent to the research. Acknowledge the borrowed ideas and techniques of previous workers. Compare, contrast and critically review the literature.

v   Recognising the association of the selected theme with the wide canvass of knowledge:

Establish the connection of your research theme to the broader field of knowledge. For this, review the literature in related disciplines and place in a systematic way your work within an overall conceptual framework.

vi   Distinct contribution to knowledge:

By the close of the work the researcher is to assess it in terms of whether it makes valuable addition to the field of knowledge; the conclusions overturn or challenge previous beliefs, as also clearly defining any new contribution comparing your findings with the findings of any similar studies.

vii   Raising of questions for further work in new areas identified:

The researcher is expected to raise questions for future research based on the accomplished work.

viii   Worthy of publication:

A logically structured thesis could form a basis of several articles or a book.

238   Catching up with the destination: the finale

A volley of questions is raised in the viva voce. These will cover a wide spectrum of topics of the research. The main concerns of the examiner in the oral examination are to ensure that the candidate suitably justifies the selection of the topic and research design to arrive at his findings and conclusions. Students, therefore, should rehearse their answers to an appropriate selection from the above list of questions. Make all effort to remain calm and in a right frame of mind for the oral examination to defend your thesis from a position of strength. Partly, the examiners are lending credibility to the research thesis by approving it.

The entire process has been rendered somewhat easy by the facility of PowerPoint presentation. The challenge now is to make this script as innovative and effective as possible.

PowerPoint presentation

PowerPoint created in 1984 is a competent slide manager and projector. It can be suitably used to complement your presentation through appropriate choice of words and/or images on a slide. Use this technology effectively to your advantage. It is a good way to display the structure of your presentation with the support of visuals but a bad way to convey textual information. Conduct of a PowerPoint presentation is a three-step process: (a) slide creation; (b) content structuring; and (c) presentation deliverance.

(a) Slide creation: This requires deciding the focus, structure and design of each slide for presentation. The content of your presentation should address three basic questions: Who is the audience? What is the purpose of the event? What is the message of your presentation?

Before crafting PowerPoint slides, think of all aspects of your dissertation/thesis, technical report or research paper, which call for display and discourse. Don't just jump straight to creating slides. Remember that your research belongs to geography. Hence your presentation has to include reasonable number of maps appropriately placed.

Draw a preliminary sketch of your presentation. It will help you imagine the large picture. The slides need to connect with your talk and with each other. You may choose to follow an analog approach (paper or whiteboard) to create a layout of rough draft your ideas. Fine-tune it to suit your objectives. Decide on the number of slides you need, which may be roughly one for every one or two minutes. Plan what matter is to be placed on each slide. Having sketched out your ideas, create a rough storyboard on paper which would make it far smooth to lay out those ideas in PowerPoint.

While planning the form of your slide presentation remember David Belasco, a play producer. The essence of each of his successful play could be written as a simple sentence on the back of his visiting card. Following this in spirit, aim to condense the content of your presentation in the form of some lead points.

The classic PowerPoint mistake is to write sentences on a slide and read them while making presentation. Try to recall when you have seen someone doing this. The whole exercise becomes unexciting and lifeless. Never do this. Never read a slide verbatim. Williams (1994) explains the basic slide design principles to make simple and effective slides. These comprise 'The Big Four' – contrast, alignment, repetition and proximity, abbreviated as CARP. An adherence to CARP principles can help in creating a purposeful visual material.

- Contrast in literal sense means difference. It is visually most effective as we are all wired to notice difference. A slide should display clear contrast among elements to make visible the dominant things; otherwise the slide would appear as another assortment of sorts with nothing to excite or of interest. Contrast can be created through various elements of design such as colour, font, size, shape, line, texture, space, type and so on. It can be achieved for example through font size selection for text (serif and sans serif, bold and narrow, big and small), positioning of elements (top and bottom, clustered and dispersed), colour contrast (dark and light, warm and cool). Cool colours seem to recede into the background while warm colours appear to be coming at us.
- Alignment takes care of arrangement or configuration of elements within a slide. All the elements in a slide should be visually aligned. A properly aligned slide looks cleaner, is easier to understand and creates the desired visual impression. Studies have shown that aesthetically organised slides make a real great impression. Work on these lines.
- Repetition refers to an ingenious use of various elements of slide design, such as headings, subheadings font face, bullet markings, background colour, format etc, to ensure that these appear as an integrated whole. Once finalised in their respective disposition and placement, the same are replicated in all the slides. The purpose of this repetition in successive slides is to bring in a sense of connect, coherence and consistency. Such a visual display facilitates an ease of understanding and retention on the part of viewer.
- Proximity simply means to group related items together and to arrange specific slides in sequence to each other to give a more organised appearance. Maintain consistency in presentation of material on each slide such as title with the graphic and coherence in arranging the slides one after another. Nothing should appear disjointed. Robin Williams in her book *The Non-Designer's Design Book* (2014) voices that when we step back to look at our design we must be aware where our eyes rest first, second and so on. Drawing an analogy, in case of slides too when you look at the slide be conscious of the path your eye takes.

Simplicity has to be ensured to win the appreciation of the audience. What material is to be in and what is to be left out is the bottom line question you need to ask yourself while preparing your presentation. It demands meticulous foresight, planning and consideration. Above all, it has to be in sync with the purpose of your presentation and spirit of your message.

240 Catching up with the destination: the finale

Researchers in communication effectiveness have arrived at certain scientifically proven conclusions which would be pertinent to list here:

- The brain has separate channels for processing the visual and the verbal materials. Consequently there is a higher level of understanding in the case of visuals (Mayer 2009). Learning activity is thus enhanced with the use of visuals and narrative than from words alone. Maps and diagrams certainly add to the value of a presentation.
- It sounds strange but is true that listening and reading at the same time do not fall in nature's design (Paivio 2007). So, the same words spoken and shown on the screen at the same time inhibit the communication. Hence slides should not carry material in the form of sentences and paragraphs.
- Keep in mind that our short-term memory can hold only a small bit of information at a time. Therefore, the presentation should not be overloaded by slides.

These three concepts should serve as directive principles for the presenter.

Images, maps, diagrams, graphs, pictures and tables should be used to illustrate. These are an essential part of a geographer's kitty. Ensure that the images can be easily read or seen by the audience. Use animation sparingly. A movement on the screen, by distracting their attention, will not allow the audience to concentrate on the content of your presentation. Every visual must carry a descriptive note conveying its totality.

(b) Content structuring: A powerful presentation structure builds up into a winning story. Begin your presentation with opening slide illustrating your agenda or unveiling a roadmap of your talk. It is of utmost importance without which your brilliant style, delivery and great supporting visuals will not make a difference.

Provide a logical flow to your presentation, supported by all necessary maps and other graphics. Chances are you will have a lot of information to cover in your presentation. Organise all of this in a manner that your presentation communicates a clear, crisp, thoughtful message to your audience.

In deciding the number of slides you should prepare, the optimal is one slide for every one to two minutes. For a thesis/dissertation, you may prepare 20 slides to be covered in half-an-hour; for a technical report, 15 slides will do for a 20-minute presentation; and presentation of a research paper should be confined to 10 slides. This allows time for interaction and dialogue with the audience. Focus on the key ideas you want your audience to remember.

Every slide should have a title, bold enough to capture the attention of the audience. It is important that the titles are self-descriptive and engaging. In fact these should be conversational; for example, cities call for decongestion, countryside needs connectivity and regions demand planning.

The concluding slide is to carry a note of thanks grafted on an icon representing the theme of your presentation.

(c) Presentation deliverance: Determine what is the logical order of presenting the totality of your thesis/dissertation in brevity. The most important message or

key point must be the first, the general in the middle and the special at the final. Remember that the audience's attention span is limited to about 20 minutes, and that should define the duration span of your presentation. Which slides will serve this purpose? At the beginning of the presentation, the main agenda is to be spelt out; in the middle, the main body of your research work is to be delineated, and in the final, the ramifications of the work are to be shared. Rehearse before making the presentation.

You can begin your presentation with a story that helps to introduce your topic. Use a quote or raise a question. Put up a surprise. Speak loudly and clearly with fluctuation. Don't read the slides word by word, use them for reference. Be particular about the time allocated for the presentation.

Be passionate and spirited about what you have to say on your topic. Connect with the audience in a candid, confident and stirring way. Don't hold back. This is as essential as great content, well-designed visuals and slides.

Make a powerful impression in the initial moments of your presentation. The first two to three minutes are the most effective in deliverance. Do not miss the opportunity. Avoid rambling on too long about background information unrelated to the theme of your talk. If you are given 20 minutes for presentation, finish before the scheduled time, say in 15 minutes. Let the audience want more (of you) than to feel that they have had more than enough.

Tailpiece

PowerPoint presentation is a great idea, but also be mentally prepared for any eventuality such as a power or technical failure. Always have a back-up plan in the form of overhead transparencies (if a projector is available) or slide handouts, to avoid any glitch.

The main thing is that you leave every one with an impression of having represented a quality thesis/dissertation in geography. All this should be represented in the structure of your presentation, the value of maps you harness and the phraseology of the messages you intended to convey. A hard task but its rewards are assured.

References

Mayer, R. 2009. *Multimedia Learning.* New York: Cambridge University Press.

Paivio, A. 2007. *Mind and Its Evolution: A Dual Coding Theoretical Approach.* Mahwah, NJ: Lawrence Erlbaum Associates, Inc.

Sharp, John A., and Keith Howard. 1996. *The Management of a Student Research Project.* 2nd ed. Aldershot, UK: Gower Publishing Limited.

Williams, R. 1994. *The Non-Designer's Design Book: Design and Typographic Principles for the Visual Novice.* Berkeley, CA: Peachpit Press.

———. 2014. *The Non-Designer's Design Book.* 4th ed. San Francisco, CA: Peachpit Press.

ANNEXURE 1

For instance: Article 3 of The Constitution of India is listed as follows:

Part I: The Union and Its Territory

Article 3 empowers Parliament to form new states and also to alter the areas, boundaries or names of the existing states. According to Article 3 Parliament may by law:

a) form a new state by separation of territory from any state or by uniting two or more states or parts of states or by uniting any territory to a part of any state;
b) increase the area of any state;
c) diminish the area of any state;
d) alter the boundaries of any state;
e) alter the name of any state.

Provided that no bill for this purpose can be introduced in either house of Parliament except on the recommendation of the President, and the President shall before giving his recommendation, refer the Bill to the legislature of the state so affected for expressing its views within the period specified by the President. It is to be noted that the President is not bound by the opinion of the legislature of such state. The Union Government, thus, has the power to alter the areas or boundaries of existing state or form new states by separation of territory from any state or by uniting two or more states.

For the purpose of aforesaid clauses (a) to (e) 'state' includes a Union territory but in the *proviso*, 'state' does not include a Union territory. The power conferred on Parliament by the above said clause (a) includes the power to form a new state or Union territory by uniting a part of any state or Union territory to any other state or Union territory.

Clause (c) of Article 3 which empowers Parliament to diminish the area of any state does not enable Parliament to cede the Indian Territory to any foreign state. It deals with internal adjustment of territories of constituent states of India. Any agreement between Indian government and a foreign state which involves a cession of part of the territory of India to the foreign state cannot be implemented simply by passing a law under Article 3. Such agreement can be implemented only by amendment of the Constitution in accordance with Article 368.

ANNEXURE 2

Some important pointers from the London School of Economics and Political Science calendar Regulations for Research Degrees; the PhD thesis will:

i   form a distinct contribution to the knowledge of the subject and afford evidence of originality by the discovery of new facts and/or by the exercise of independent critical power;

ii give a critical assessment of the relevant literature, describe the method of research and its findings, include a discussion on those findings and indicate in what respects they appear to the candidate to advance the study of the subject; and so demonstrate a deep and synoptic understanding of the field of study;

iii demonstrate research skills;

iv be of a standard to merit publication in whole or in part or in a revised form (e.g. as a monograph or as a number of articles in learned journals); and

v   not exceed 100,000 words (including footnotes but excluding bibliography and appendices).

Likewise an MPhil thesis will:

i   be either a record of original work or of an ordered and critical exposition of existing knowledge and will provide evidence that the field has been surveyed thoroughly;

ii give a critical assessment of the relevant literature, describe the method of research and its findings and include a discussion on those findings; and

iii not exceed 60,000 words (including footnotes but excluding bibliography and appendices).

(See http://www.lse.ac.uk/intranet/LSEServices/TQARO/Calendar/Regulations ForResearchDegrees.pdf for details.)

INDEX

Abler, Ronald, F. 3, 221
Aboufadel, Edward 124
abstract(s): literature sources 50–51, 67;
   see also research paper; thesis/dissertation
accessibility: data 114; facility 102, 125;
   index 131
Acemoglu, Daron 208
Ackerman, E.A. 3
Adams, P. 116
Adams, W.M. 66
adjacency pair 116–117
Ahmad, A. ix
Albert, K. 203
Alderson, P. 40
Alexander, John, W. 144
altimetric frequency curve 140
Amadeo, D. 3
analytic induction 115
Annals of the American Association of
   Geographers 12, 52
annexure(s) vi, 42, 89, 94–95, 219, 223, 225,
   242, 244
anomalies: distributions 208–209, 211;
   locate 16, 30–31
Anselin, L. 128
Anthamatten, Peter 14
archival: research 60, 67; visit 69; sources 96
area distributions 63, 76, 114
areal association 21; index of 143, 146–147
areal differentiation 3, 6, 12, 21–23, 113
Arunachalam, B. ix
Aspinall, Richard 52
Assad, A.A. 135

assignment 217–218, 229, 233
Atkinson, J.M. 116
Atkinson, P. 113, 117
Austin, David 124

Bachi, R. 123
Bailey, T.C. 119, 127
Balchin, W.G.V. 181
Bamford, C.G. 131
Barber, Gerald, M. 119, 169
Barnes, J.A. 138
Barnes, T. 217
Barnsley, Michael, J. 170
Barrett, H. 68
Bartholomew, D. 157
Batty, M. 142
behavioural geography 7, 12
Bell, M. 131
Bender, B. 210
Berelson, B. 116
Berry, B.J.L. 12
Bhatia, Shyam, S. 144, 151, 153
bibliography 35, 42, 51–52, 218–219,
   226–227, 229, 244
Bird, James, H. 6, 62, 99
Blache, Paul Vidal de la 210
Blaxter, Loraine 211
Blomley, Nicholas 8
Bonnett, Alastair 3, 24
Booth, Wayne, C. 36, 55, 226
box plot *see* exploratory data
   analysis (EDA)
Boyce, R.B. 136

246 Index

Boyzatis, R. 116
Braithwaite, R.B. 98
Braun, V. 116
broad area of research: selection of 29–31
Brotton, Jerry 209
Brunsdon, Chris 119
Buckland, W.R. 74
Bullock, A. 7
Bunge, W. 66, 136
Burgess, J. 69
Burgess, R.G. 85
Burnett, K.P. 9
Burrough, P.A. 63
Burt, James, E. 119, 169
Butt, Graham 181
Buttimer, A. 62

Camagni, R. 138
cartography: methodological tool 24, 40, 92, 121, 139, 182, 185, 195, 202, 204, 209; *see also* maps; network data models
Carvalho, R. 142
Castells, M. 138
Castner, H.W. 137
Castree, N. 8
Cattell, R.B. 157
Census of India 16, 65, 70, 74, 87, 90–91, 97, 120, 166, 182
Central Statistical Organisation (CSO) 93
central tendency: measures of 122–124, 126
Centre for Monitoring Indian Economy (CMIE) 65, 88, 95
Challenge for Geography, The – A Changing World: A Changing Discipline 3
Chandna, M.M. 37, 145
chaos 115, 142
Chapman, J.D. 13
chapter scheme 35, 41, 46, 50
Charlton, Martin 119
charts 181, 202–203, 221, 223
Chatfield, C. 81
Chattopadhyay, Mahamaya 141
Chattopadhyay, S. 141–142
Chicago Manual of Style, The 227, 229
Chilvers, Ian 190
chi-square test 148
Christaller, Walter 6, 22, 31, 37, 99, 127, 212
Christian, C.S. 140
Chrush, J. 9
Chuan, G.K. 66
Clark, P. 127
Clark, W.A.V. 136
Clarke, K.C. 169
Clarke, Victoria 116

class intervals 186–187, 194–197; methods of determining 198–201; selection of 196–197
Cliff, Andrew, D. 145
Clifford, J. Nicholas 39, 62
clinographic curve 196–197, 200
Cloke, Paul 85
coding 61, 114–115, 118
Coffey, A. 113
Cole, J.P. 13
Coleman, A.M. 181
Collins, J. 116
Colomb, Gregory, G. 36, 55
Comtois, Claude 129
conceptual problem 36
condense analysis 115
content analysis 72, 86, 115–117
context, classification and connection 118
conversation analysis 116
Cook, Ian 86
Cooper, B.M. 232
Cosgrove, Dennis 69
Couclelis, H. 169
Coulson, M.R. 195–196
Crampton, J.W. 5, 121, 209
Crang, Mike 60, 86
Crang, P. 68
Cressey, Donald Ray 115
Creswell, J.W. 37
Cresswell, T. 11
critical appraisal *see* literature review
critical geography 7, 8, 12, 68
Crotty, M. 39
Culler, D. Jonathan xi
Curtiss, J. 127
curves 202
Cybriwsky, R. 210

Dadson, Simon 170
Daniels, Stephen 69
dasymetric map 167, 194
data analysis 59, 61, 112; fundamentals 112–113
data collection 39–41, 59, 61–62, 65, 69, 76, 81–82, 98, 112, 118, 208, 237; *see also* hypothesis; indicators
data interpretation 59, 206–212
data reduction techniques 143, 156
data representation 59, 181–204; with areal/spatial symbols 193–194; with line symbols 192–193; with point symbols 191–192
Dauphine, Andre 142
Davies, Andrew, D. 67, 86
Davies, M.C.R. 69

Index 247

Davies, Norman 23
Davis, J.C. 202
Day, A. 220
Dayal, Edison 151, 153
Dayal, P. ix
De Cola, Lee 142
deductive 38, 49, 61, 98–99
Del Casino, V., Jr. 116
DeLyser, Dydia 217
Denzin, N.K. 60
derived maps 186
De Vaus, D.A. 73
diagrams 201
Diamond, Jared 208–209
Dilthey, Wilhelm 62
discourse analysis 11, 117
discursive practice 117
disparity index 149–150
dispersion: measures of 122–123, 125–127
dissimilarity index 148
Dittmer, Jason 117
documentation 118, 171, 225–226;
    endnotes 219, 225–226; footnotes
    184–185, 218–219, 221, 226, 233, 244;
    notes and bibliography 226
Dodge, Martin 66
Doornkamp, J.C. 166
Dorling, D. 62
dot map 191–192
Draus, Franciszek 23
Driver, F. 4
Duncan, J. 217
Dunkerley, D.L. 69
Dury, G.H. 140

Ebdon, D. 123, 135
ecological fallacy 97
Eells, W.C. 124
effective reading *see* literature reading
Ehrenberg, A.S.C. 119
Eisner, Elliot, W. 38
Elwood, S. 204
empiricism 5–6, 67
environment: forms of 21–22; GIS and 67,
    170–172, 203, 209
Enyedi, Gy. 151
epistemology: definition 38
Environmental Systems Research Institute
    (ESRI) 23
Estes, J.E. 63
ethical issues 40
ethnographic accounts 117
ethnography 39, 60, 210
Evans, F.C. 127
Evans, Ian S. 196

exploratory data analysis (EDA) 118–121
Eyles, J. 60

factor analysis 118, 143, 156–165
Fairbairn, D. 62
Fairclough, N. 117
Food and Agriculture Organization (FAO) 89
Farr, Dennis 190
Faust, Katherine 138
Fellmann, Jerome, D. 15, 39, 185
fellowship in a foreign university 46
feminist geography 9
Fidell, L.S. 161
fieldwork 23–24, 32; approaches to 67;
    methods of conducting 40, 66–71, 79
Fisher, K. 222
Flick, U. 113
Foard, Nick 220
focus group discussions 60, 114, 210
Fog Index 220
Foreign Affairs 53
Fotheringham, A.S. 119, 128
Fowler, F. 74
fractal analysis 141–142; fractals 141–142;
    'ht-index' 142
Fractal Geometry of Nature, The 142
Freeman, Linton 138
Freeman, T.W. 4
frequency curves 140, 197
Frey, Allan 145

Gallant, J.C. 140
Gao, Jay 141
Garrison, W.L. 134
Gatrell, A.C. 119, 127
Gee, J.P. 117
Gehlsen, B. 142
generalisation 6, 13, 15–16, 22, 52, 66,
    75, 103, 115, 137, 144, 185, 190;
    generalisability 211
Geographer's Art, The 3
geographic: knowledge 12, 14, 16, 22, 69;
    parameters 21–22; perspective 12–14, 16,
    36–37; phraseology 20; questions 15–16;
    study 15, 24, 42, 77; thinking xii, 14–15;
    thrust x, 21
geographic/al inquiry i, x, 21; basic
    concepts and topics 13
geographical journals 230
geographical population 74
geographic flavour 20, 74, 220
Geographic Information Systems (GIS) xiii,
    7, 169, 202
geography: multidisciplinary 4, 30; space 5;
    style of x, 8, 20–21

248 Index

Geography's Inner Worlds 3
Gersmehl, C. 14
Gersmehl, P. 14
Getis, Arthur 15, 185
Getis, Judith 15, 185
Gilbert, Melissa, R. 72
Gillingwater, D. 135
Gilpatrick, E. 37
Glaser, B.G. 118
Gleick, James 142
Global Positioning System (GPS) 66, 70, 170
Godlewska, A.M.C. 4
Gold, J.R. 67
Golden, B.L. 135
Golledge, R.G. 3, 22
Goodchild, M.F. 136, 142
Goodenough, D.G. 96
Goodwin, C. 185
Gosal, G.S. ix, 9
Government of India x, 42, 86, 88, 90–93, 105, 141, 229
graduated symbol map 192, 194
graphics 181, 201, 203, 240
graphs 130–134, 201–203
Gregory, Derek 11, 50, 129
Groat, L. 118
grounded theory 60, 118
Grounded Theory Institute 118
Gruzd, Anatoliy 138
Gunawardena, K.A. 146
Gunning, R. 220
Gupta, S.C. 124, 168

Haggett, P. 3–4, 24, 145
Haines-Young, R.H. 99
Haining, R. 79
Hall, R. 157
Hammersley, M. 117
Hammond, Michael 40, 70
Hammond, R. 133
Hanna, S.P. 116
Harding, Sandra 39
Harley, J.B. 209
Harris, Chauncy, D. 125
Harris, Cole 66, 69
Hart, C. 48, 123
Hart, John Fraser 230–232
Hartshorne, R. 3, 6, 23, 210
Harvey, D. 6, 8, 24, 63, 98, 168
Harvey, M.E. 7
Hawking, S. 6
Hayford, A.M. 9
Hay, I. 60, 86
Headlam, Nicola 117
Helbing, D. 142

Henn, Matt 220
Herbert, D.T. 12
hermeneutics 62
Heron, J. 68
hierarchical order: determination of 145–146
Hilgard, J.E. 124
Hoggart, K. 86
Holly, B.P. 7
Holt-Jensen, Arild 15, 38
Hope, M. 66
Horton, R.E. 136–137
Howard, Keith 236
Hsieh, H.F. 115
Hubbard, Phil 3, 8, 38
Hughes, Christina 211
Human Development Report 89–90, 155
humanistic approach 9, 62
humanistic geography 8–9, 12
Hussain, M. 151
hypothesis xi, 37–38, 40, 45, 53, 65, 100, 205–206, 219; formulation 35, 99, 115, 128; meaning and purpose 98–99; statement of 99–100
hypsometric frequency curve 140

idiographic 3
Iida, Y. 131
Indian Geography: Voice of Concern x
indicators 36, 37, 50; classification 102–108; definition 101; some illustrations 88–89, 93–95
inductive 49, 61, 99, 118
inferential statistics 168, 182
inset maps 188
interpretivist analysis 116
interviews 70–71, 114, 138; conducting 85, 209–210; method 39, 60
in-text references 226
introductory statement 35; salient components 37
isarithms 193
isohyet map 186
iterative process 118, 166

Jackson, P. 15, 69, 226
Jameson, Frederic 62
Jenks, G.F. 195–196
Jennings, J.N. 140
Jiang, B. 142
Joffe, H. 116
Johns, Jennifer 67
Johnston, R.J. 3, 6, 62, 98, 169, 226
Jolliffe, I.T. 157
J-shaped distributions 198

Kane, E. 36
Kansky, K.J. 132, 134
Kant, Surya 136
Kaplan, Robert, D. 23
Kapur, Anu x
Katz, Jack 115
Kaufmann, Daniel 200
Kendall, M.G. 74, 151
Kesby, M. 68
keywords 50, 52, 232
Khilnani, Sunil 229
Khusro, A.M. 151
Kindon, S. 68
King, C.A.M. 13
Kitchin, Rob 66, 72
Klaasen, L.H. 145
Kneale, P.E. 52
Knos, Duane, S. 195
Knott, M. 157
Kobayashi, Audrey 52
Kraay, Aart 200
Krathwohl, D.R. 44
Krishan, Gopal ix, 10, 12, 16, 33, 79, 101,
    106, 116, 124, 145, 149, 168
Krueger, Rob 118
Krygier, John 190
Kuhn, T.S. 5
Kumar, S. Suresh 142
Kundu, A. 101, 150
Kwan, T. 66

laboratory work 65–67, 69
Lam, Nina Siu-Ngan 142
Lämmer, S. 142
Land, K.C. 101
landscape x, 8, 13, 15, 21, 24, 66–67, 116,
    140; approach 140–141; concept 210;
    interpretation of 237–238; reading
    67, 69
landscape reading see primary data
Laurier, Erich 68
Leedy, Paul, D. 38
Lees, B. 140
Lees, L. 86
Lewis, Pierce, F. 210
Ley, D. 210
life history analysis 117
Lim, K. 96
Lindsay, J.B. 140
line distributions 114
line graph see graphs
line symbols see data representation
literature 20, 36, 37, 45, 223; managing
    54–55; reading 36, 51–53, 217; review
    21–22, 35, 38, 48–49, 52–53, 55, 207,

233; scan 49; search 50; sources 50–51;
    structuring 55
Liu, X. 142
Livingstone, D.N. 4
Lo, C.P. 121, 203
localisation coefficient 143–144
location(al) 13–16, 20–24, 39, 63, 71,
    76–79, 120, 123–126, 128–129, 135,
    139, 143–144, 168–169, 172, 185–186,
    191–192, 201, 234
location quotient 143–144
Locke, L.F. 37, 44
Lofland, J. 117
logarithmic series see class intervals:
    methods of determining
Longley, Paul, A. 7, 87, 142, 170, 209
Lorenz curve 202
Lukermann, F. 14–15
Luo, Wei 137
Lutz, C. 116

Mabbutt, J.A. 140
MacDonald, Stuart 117
MacEachren, A.M. 87
MacKian, Sara 211
Mackay, J. Ross 195–196
Malterud, K. 115
Mandelbrot, B. 141
mappable data and symbolisation 189–190;
    areal/spatial symbols 193–194; line
    symbols 192–193; point symbols
    191–192; visual symbols 190–191
mapping and fieldwork 23–24
maps 53, 63, 71, 87, 91–92, 115, 135,
    140–141, 146, 156, 163, 167, 171–172,
    181, 185–202, 204, 209, 219, 231, 233,
    238, 240, 241; map elements 187–189;
    special features 186–187; types 185–186;
    see also class intervals
Marble, D.F. 134
Marcus, Melvin, G. 3
Mark, David, M. 142
Martin, G. 4
Marxist geography 7–8
Martin, Kevin St. 97
Massam, B.H. 135–136
Mastruzzi, Massimo 200
Masuoka, P. 121
Mather, P.M. 166
Matthews, J.A. 12
Mayer, R. 240
McAdams, Michael, A. 141
McCullagh, P.S. 133
McDowell, L. 8
McDowell, R.A. 63

250 Index

McGuire, W.J. 30
McIntosh, R. 127
McLafferty, Sara, L. 71
Mcmillan, V.E. 232
mean centre 113–114, 123–126
mean distance 108, 126–128
median point 114, 123–126, 168
Meijerink, A.M.J. 140
Meredith, C. 222
Mesev, V. 170
Metoyer, Sandra 14
method: definition 39
Miller, C. 96
Miller, Delbert, C. 38
Miller, J.I. 225
Mitchell, D. 210
mixing-in methodology 68
Mlodinow, Leonard 6
Modifiable Areal Unit Problem 97
Monkhouse, F.J. 201
Monmonier, Mark, S. 200, 209
monochromatic 195
Monroe, J. 222
Montello, Daniel, R. 5, 72, 76, 80, 171
morphometric analysis 139–140
Moustaki, I. 157
Muehrcke, P. 185
Mukerji, A.B. ix
Mukherjee, R. 101
multiple methods 62

narrative analysis 86, 117–118
National Atlas and Thematic Mapping
  Organisation 91–92
National Council for Geographic
  Education 13
National Family Health Survey (NFHS) 80,
  82–83, 94
National Sample Survey Organisation
  (NSSO) 70, 74, 82, 84, 87, 92
nature of geography 4
nearest neighbour analysis 86, 117–118
Neft, David, S. 125
network analysis 23, 114, 129–130,
  137–142; boundary networks 135–136;
  channel (fluvial) networks 136–137;
  socio-spatial network 137–138; transport
  network 131–135
network data models: applications 139–142
Neuendorf, K.A. 116
new quantitative geography 112, 168–169
Niemann, K.O. 96
NITI Aayog 46, 93
Nkwi, P. 114
Nyamongo, I. 114

observation method 67–69; participant
  observation 68, 86, 138, 210;
  participatory action 60, 68
O'Leary, Zina 39
Olson, Judy, M. 3
online access 55, 84, 86
ontology 6, 8; definition 38
Openshaw, S. 128
Oppenheim, A.N. 73
O'Reilly, K. 117
Ormrod, Jeanne, E. 38
Osborne, Harold 190
Ostuni, J. 66

Pain, R. 68
Paivio, A. 240
Paradigm 5, 34, 138
Patton, Michael Quinn 63
Pavlovskaya, Marianna 97
Payne, Stanley, L. 72, 73
Pearce, Sean 158
Penn, A. 142
Perspectives: geographic research 5–14
Peshkin, Alan 38
Petch, James, R. 99
Phillips, E.M. 31
Phillips, Richard 67
plagiarise 221; *see also* similarity check
places 5, 7, 9, 10, 13, 31, 62, 66–68, 144,
  212; detour index 132–133; nature of
  15–16; portrayal of landscapes 210
Poh, W.P. 66
point distributions 114
point of minimum aggregate travel distance
  114, 123–125
Population and Development Review xii, 53
population potential 114, 125
positivism 6–8, 12, 99
post-colonial geographic research 9–10
post-modernism 11, 122
post-structuralism 11–12, 112
PowerPoint presentation: content
  structuring 240; presentation deliverance
  240–241; slide creation 239–240
Pownall, L.L. 144
Pratt, G. 68
primary data xii, 46, 65–66, 69–70, 84,
  87–88, 98, 188, 203
productivity index 150–154
Progress in Human Geography 10, 51, 60
protocol analysis 84, 86
Pugh, D. 31
Pulsipher, A. 185
Pulsipher, L. 185
Punch, Keith, F. 44

quadrat analysis 126
qualitative: data 59–62, 66, 85–86, 97, 113–115, 173, 182, 191, 208; methodologies 61; methods 40, 60–63, 210; techniques 114–118
Qualitative Methods in Human Geography 60
Qualitative Research Specialty Group 60
quantitative: data 37, 59, 60–62, 66–67, 99, 118, 182, 190, 193; methodologies 61; methods x, 4, 62, 113, 128
quartilide dispersion 126
questionnaire 39, 62, 65–67, 70–71, 73–74, 81; administering of 74; content and sequence 73; question wording 73; response format 72–73; *see also* surveys

radical geography 7, 8, 12
Rao, J.M. 150
Raza, Moonis ix
Rea, B.R. 69
Reader's Digest and Oxford, The 100
Reason, P. 68
references 42, 51–54, 219, 225–229
regional synthesis 13, 22
regression: residuals from 147–148
relative concentration: measures of 143–144
relative distance 126
reliability 52, 63, 67, 73, 211
representative 71, 74–80, 85, 121, 129, 182, 185, 211, 225
research design 38–41, 67, 223, 238
research ideas: some approaches 30–31
research paper 229; abstract in 232; writing style 231–233
research problem 35–39, 63, 99–100, 113, 115
research proposal 34–47, 50, 222, 233; definitions 44–45; types of 45–46
research questions: formulation 32–34, 67; framing of 37, 39; illustrations 16–17, 33; *see also* literature review; research design
research topic 33, 65, 233
research writing 38, 56, 116, 207, 217, 225; basic parameters 220–222; writing technique 222–223; similarity check 233–234
Revenge of Geography, The 23
Rhoads, Bruce, L. 67
Richardson, D.E. 137
Riessman, C. 117
Ritchie, Jane 115
River Continuum Concept 137
Robbins, Paul 118
Robinson, A.H. 131, 191, 196, 201, 209
Robinson, James A. 208

Robson, C. 116
Rodrigue, Jean-Paul 129
Rogerson, Peter, A. 128, 158, 163
Rose, C. 62
Rummel, R.J. 161
Rusak, Mazur, E. 137
Ryan, G. 114

Sacks, H. 117
Said, E. 117
Sale, R.D. 201
Salkind, Neil, J. 38
sampling 71, 74; design 75; frame 76–77; method/technique 77–81; pilot survey 81; size 81
Sauer, Carl O. 24, 66, 210
scatter diagram technique 128
Scharl, A. 121
schedule 70–71, 85, 90
Schegloff, E.A. 117
Schreier, M. 115
Schultz, G.M. 195
scientific method 39, 61
Scott, J. 96
secondary data 65–66, 86–87; issues 97; qualitative 96–97; quantitative sources 87–96
Secor, Anna, J. 117
selection of indicators: measures of development levels 154–156
Shafi, M. 151–152
Shannon, S.E. 115
Sharp, John, A. 8, 236
Shen, G. 142
Sheppard, E. 12
Shurter, R.L. 221
Shyam, Madhav 149
Sidaway, J.D. 62
Silk, J. 123
Silverman, D. 85, 116
Silverman, S.J. 44
similarity check 233–234
Singh, Jasbir 151–152
Singh, Nina 17, 32, 37, 106, 118
Sinha, B.N. 151
Slack, Brian 129
slide design: CARP principles 239
Smith, David, M. 60, 102, 163
Smith, N. 4
Soja, E.W. 11
Sopher, David, E. 149–150
Sorenson, S. 231
sources of data 46, 53, 87–88, 95, 98, 222; *see also* secondary data
spatial analysis of areal distributions 142

252 Index

spatial contiguity and geographical clustering 187, 200
spatial data 63, 96, 112–113, 123, 154, 194, 169–173
spatial data analysis 168–169; *see also* exploratory data analysis (EDA)
spatial distributions 146, 156, 182, 185, 187, 195, 197, 201; measures of centrality 123–125; measures of dispersion 125–129
spatial entities: data primitives 63
spatial interaction 6, 12–13, 21, 22, 30
spatial language 63; parameters of 23
spatial organisation 3, 7–8, 12, 16, 21–22, 33, 35
spatial sampling techniques 78–81
spatial thinking 12, 14–15; modes of 14
spatial units 87, 97, 142–144, 167, 171, 184, 192–195, 200; collective treatment 146–154
spatial variation 3, 7, 169
specialisation: index of 144–145
Spirduso, W.W. 44
Stamp, L. D. 151
standard distance 126–127
Star, E. 63
statement of the topic 29, 34
Statistical Abstracts 88, 95
statistical population 74
status of research in India: concerns ix, x
stem-and-leaf plot 119
Stevens, J. 159
Stoddart, D.R. 66
Strahler, A.N. 136, 140
Strauss, A.L. 118
Strunk, William, Jr. 232
style of geography 20–21
Sublett, M.D. 232
supervisor 29–30, 41–42, 45, 230, 233; choice of 31–32; *see also* assignment
Survey of India 90–91, 188
surveys 70–71, 74, 77–78, 80, 82–86, 92
Sutton, J. 135
Sutton, Paul, C. 5, 72, 76, 80, 171
Sviatlovsky, E.E. 124

Taaffe, E.J. 3
Tabachnick, B.G. 161
tables 89–94, 181, 203, 219, 221, 223, 231; basic components 182–185; types of 182
Tainter, Joseph, A. 208–209
Takhteyev, Yuri 138
Tang, G. 140
Tashakkori, Abbas 63
Tate, Nicholas, J. 72

Taylor, B.J. 225
Taylor, P. 138
Taylor, P.J. 128–129, 133, 164
technical report 229–230
terrain analysis 140–141
tertiary data 65, 98
Tesch, R. 86
textual analysis *see* content analysis
thematic analysis *see* content analysis
thesis/dissertation 59, 182, 201, 217–218; abstract in 219, 225; basic parameters of style 220–221; definition and distinction 229–230; elements of 218–220; text of 223–225
Thinking Geographically 3
Thomas, David, S.G. 50
Thomas, Edwin, N. 63
Thompson, D. 157
Thompson, P. 117
Thurstone, L.L. 157
Thyer, Bruce, A. 40
Tierney, W.G. 209
Tight, Malcolm 211
Tobler, W. 209
Tochtermann, K. 121
tools: definition 39
Topophilia 60
Transactions, Institute of Indian Geographers x, 230
transcripts 96, 114–116, 210
trend surface analysis 143, 154
triangulation 62–63, 70
Tuan, Y.-F. 9, 211
Tukey, John, W. 118
Turner, A. 121, 203
turn taking 116
Twidale, C.R. 140
Tyner, Judith 188
typologies 115, 220

Ullman, E.L. 6, 145, 185
United Nations Development Programme 89, 103
Unwin, A. 119
Unwin, David, J. 119
Unwin, T. 4

Valentine, G. 39, 40, 62, 78, 85
validity 37, 66–67, 73, 98, 166, 211–212
Van Belle 61, 201
Vannote, R.L. 137
Van Zuidam, R.A. 140
Viles, Heather, A. 69
Vimal, Bindia 16
virtual space 66

Index   253

visual symbols: for attributes 190–191
visualisation 12, 14, 87, 118, 121, 169, 182,
   201–202
viva voce: preparing for 236–238

Wadhera, Bharti 166
Walrath, A. 170
Wang, D. 118
Wasserman, Stanley 138
Webb, John, W. 144
Weiner, Myron 37
Weinstein, Mark 220
welfare geography 7
Wellington, Jerry 40, 70
Wellman, Barry 138
What Is Geography? 3
White, E.B. 232
Wilkinson, H.R. 201
Williams, Robin 239
Williams, Joseph, M. 36, 55
Williamson, J.G. 123, 206
Wilson, David 67
Wilson, J.P. 140
Winchester, H. 210
Withers, C.W.J. 4

Wolcott, Harry, F. 56, 206, 217
Wong, D.W.S. 97
Wong, Wucius 190
Wood, Denis 190
Wood, H.A. 108
World Development Report 23, 148, 200–201
Wright, John, K. 196
writing technique: possible modes
   222–223
Wulder, M. 96

Xia, Zong-guo 141

Yates, R. 138
Yeates, M.H. 3, 136
Yeung, W. 203
Yin, Junjun 142
Yong, An Gie 158
Young, L. 68

Zhan, F. 128
Zhou, Q. 140
Zinsser, William 230
Zipf, G.K. 142
Znaniecki, F. 115

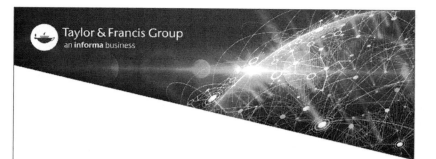